Voices from Vietnam

Interviews, Letters, Vignettes, and Reflections, 1964-1982

Conducted, Compiled & Edited by

Major Bruce H. "Doc" Norton,
United States Marine Corps (USMC) (ret.)

With

Dr. Harry J. Kantrovich
CNO Directed Command Master Chief (CNOCM),
United States Navy (Ret)

Voices from Vietnam

Interviews, Letters, Vignettes, and Reflections,
1964-1982

Conducted, Compiled & Edited by

Major Bruce H. "Doc" Norton,
United States Marine Corps (USMC) (ret.)

With
Dr. Harry J. Kantrovich
CNO Directed Command Master Chief (CNOCM),
United States Navy (Ret)

Academica Press
Washington~London

Library of Congress Cataloging-in-Publication Data
Names: Norton, Bruce H. (editor) | Kantrovich, Harry (editor)
Title: Voices from vietnam : interviews, letters, vignettes, and reflections, 1964-1982 | Bruce H. Norton | Harry Kantrovich
Description: Washington : Academica Press, 2025. | Includes references.
Identifiers: LCCN 2024944035 | ISBN 9781680534344 (hardcover) | 9781680534351 (paperback) | 9781680534368 (e-book)

Copyright 2025 Bruce H. Norton

Dedication

This work, and the play, Voices From Vietnam,
is dedicated to the men and women who served our Country
honorably during the Vietnam War.

Your history will not be forgotten.

"God does not give the hardest battles to his toughest soldiers; he creates the toughest soldiers through life's hardest battles."

- Major Bruce H. "Doc" Norton USMC (Ret)

Contents

Prologue xiii

"These Good Men" xv

Acknowledgments xvii

1. With 3rd Force Reconnaissance Company – 1969-1970 1
2. Vietnam - July 1965 – July 1966 9
3. A Bullet Through the Helmet: A Vietnam Dustoff Pilot's Memoir 21
4. "A Short History of Chow in Vietnam" 27
5. Base Camp Danang 31
6. At the Helm 33
7. My Vietnam Service 37
8. One Tough Marine 49
9. My Tour in Vietnam as an Army Medic 59
10. 1st Force Reconnaissance Company; RVN 1967-1968 and 1970-1971 79
11. Scout Dogs in the Vietnam War 85
12. An Encounter in Pleiku 95
13. The Kindergarten Marines 101
14. "Friendly Fire - 1968" 105
15. Bravo Relay - I Corps, Vietnam 21 March-11 June 1968 109
16. "A Marine CH-34 Helicopter Pilot Remembers..." 121
17. "He sat on my boot..." 131

18. Marine Tactical Data System (MTDS) 135

19. A Soldier's Reflections 139

20. As I Remember It - 1968 143

21. Operation Pegasus – Hill 881 153

22. Wartime Notes 159

23. The Start of the Tet Offensive 163

24. Hue City - January – March 1968 171

25. The Big Fight 177

26. Sergeant Joe 183

27. The Queen of Spades 187

28. *USS Frank E. Evans* (DD-754) – The lost 74 191

29. Goin' to the Nam - 1969 195

30. Tet of 1969 - Attack on the Chu Chi Base Camp 199

31. 1970s Random reflections on service in South Vietnam 1970-1971 203

32. Delta Troop 2nd/17th Operations - June 1969 - November 1970 207

33. A Day in a Year …. A Year in a Life 213

34. Delta Troop 2nd/17th Air Cavalry - 1969 215

35. "Choppers" 219

36. Freedom Bird 223

37. "Days to Come" 227

38. With 3rd Force Recon Company – 1970 231

39. Long Binh 235

40. United States Air Force Security Service 239

41. "Short" 245

42. Melody in the Dark Vietnamese Night 249

43. His name is Ben 251

44. In My Viewfinder: The Epilogue 257

45. The 85th Evacuation Hospital, Phu Bai - 1971-1972 275

46. Letters HMM 362 "Ugly Angels" Ky Ha, Republic of South Vietnam 287

47. A Letter to the Editor 289

48. Letter from a U.S. Army Infantryman 291

49. My Letter Home 295

50. An Australian Infantryman's Letter Long Khanh Province - 1970 299

51. Stateside The Stamp 309

52. The Lottery 311

53. The Women "Dealing with Misery…" 317

54. Eddie Lee Evenson 323

55. "Goodbye, Vietnam" 331

56. My Military Journey 337

57. Nobody had Ever Welcomed Me Home 341

58. A Vietnamese Refugee's Story 345

59. POW/MIA/KIA The Longest Enlisted POW 351

60. Triumph over Captors 355

61. Colonel Donald Cook, USMC, Medal of Honor 361

62. The First A-7 Pilot Prisoner of War 365

63. Missing in Action An MIA Daughter's Story 367

64. My Journey Home 373
65. Finding Answers 381
66. Killed in Action The Long Goodbye 387
67. The Wall 393

Prologue

In December 2022, I was assigned to the United States Marine Corps History Division, found within the Marine Corps University, at Quantico, Virginia. Then, (Acting) Director Lt. Colonel Rob Peterson, USMC (ret.), asked if I would be interested in assisting a nationally known playwright with his latest play, *The Greatest Generation Speaks*, based on the distinguished network journalist and author Tom Brokaw's book of the same title.

Playwright, Dr. Harry Kantrovich was looking for a military historian to conduct a "Question and Answer" session, following the play's premier, to address the Marine Corps' campaigns in the Pacific Theater during World War II. I agreed to help, was given Harry's contact information, and arranged to meet with him to discuss the details of my role in support of the play. *The Greatest Generation Speaks* premiered in Warrenton, Virginia, in February 2023, and as of September 2023, is being presented in more than 140 community theaters around the country, as well as in Canada and Puerto Rico. With that great success, Dr. Kantrovich saw the possibility of creating a new work, similar in style to "TGGS," and asked me to collaborate with him in the creation of a new play, and drafting an accompanying book, which would be an extension of the letters, vignettes and reflections used on stage for this new production.

To create both the play and the book, Vietnam veterans were solicited and the responses have been, in a word, *overwhelming*. *Voices From Vietnam* is now scheduled to premiere in November 2024, at the Journey Theater in Vint Hill, Virginia, located just outside the town of Warrenton.

In compiling these interviews, letters, vignettes, and reflections we have tried to include every branch of service, and multiple Military Occupational Specialties (MOSs): infantrymen, pilots, nurses, corpsmen, doctors, MIA families, generals, admirals, reconnaissance Marines,

Prisoners of War, Medal of Honor recipients, military technicians, and Vietnamese civilians, all represented within these pages.

Chronologically, we have covered the period from 1965 to 1982, to educate you, the reader, as to events which occurred during more than a decade of fighting in Vietnam. Many Vietnam veterans were asked to submit their stories. And, while a number of veterans declined, not wanting to revisit old wounds, lost friends, and bad memories, others stepped up and were eager to have their stories told. And for that we give them our sincere thanks.

I encourage you to find a comfortable place, open this book, and learn from these primary sources; those who were there, on the ground, in the air, and on the water, and discover what their life was for these extraordinary men and women, as they raise their "Voices From Vietnam."

– Major Bruce H. "Doc" Norton, USMC (ret.)

"These Good Men"
by Michael Norman

    I now know why men who have been to war yearn to reunite. Not to tell stories or look at old pictures. Not to laugh or weep. Comrades gather because they long to be with the men who once acted their best, men who suffered and sacrificed, who were stripped raw, right down to their humanity.

    I did not pick these men. They were delivered by fate. But I know them in a way I know no other men. I have never given anyone such trust. They were willing to guard something more precious than my life. They would have carried my reputation, the memory of me. It was part of the bargain we all made, the reason we were so willing to die for one another.

I cannot say where we are headed. Ours are not perfect friendships; those are the province of legend and myth. A few of my comrades drift far from me now, sending back only occasional word. I know that one day even these could fall to silence. Some of the men will stay close, a couple, perhaps, always at hand.

As long as I have memory, I will think of them all, every day. I am sure that when I leave this world, my last thought will be of my family and my comrades ... Such Good Men.

Michael Norman has been a professional writer and journalist for more than 35 years. These Good Men: Friendships Forged in War *was his first book and was followed by* Tears in the Darkness: The Story of the Bataan Death March and its Aftermath. *Michael and co-author Elizabeth Norman spent ten years researching and interviewing for this book. They live in Montclair, New Jersey.*

Acknowledgments

I would like to express my sincere appreciation to these Vietnam veterans and family members; the men and women who contributed their stories to the creation of this work. This book would not have been possible without them, as no one who achieves success does so without the help of others.
– Major Bruce H. "Doc" Norton, United States Marine Corps (Ret)

1. RADM Jon Kreitz, United States Navy (Ret)
2. Brigadier General Mike Downs, United States Marine Corps (Ret)
3. Mr. Michael Archer
4. Command Master Chief Octavia Harris, United States Navy (Ret)
5. Michael Dhunjishah
6. Fleet Master Chief Susan Whitman, United States Navy (Ret)
7. Freedom Museum Manassas, VA
8. Colonel Michael Stankosky, United States Marine Corps (Ret)
9. Master Chief Petty Officer Christi Lee, United States Navy (Ret)
10. Louann Sage Withers
11. CNOCM/Rev. Susan Sanson Fritz, United States Navy (Ret)
12. Ms. Tammy Barboza
13. Colonel Douglas E. Moore, USA (Ret)
14. LtCol Dale Carlsen, United States Army (Ret)
15. Master Chief Thomas J. Snee, United States Navy (Ret)
16. Mr. George Firehammer
17. Mr. Wayne Karlin

18. Captain Bob Quinn, United States Navy (Ret)

19. Mr. John Wentworth

20. Mr. Francis J. "Bing" West

21. Colonel Billy R. Duncan, United States Marine Corps (Ret)

22. LtCol. Clyde Woods, United States Marine Corps (Ret)

23. Brooke T. Stevenson

24. Mike Humason

25. Gilbert "Butch" Hill

26. 1st Sergeant Donald N. Hamblen, United States Marine Corps (Ret)

27. LtCol. D. Blair Craig, United States Army (Ret)

28. Mr. Rick Jenkins

29. Mr. Charles Jameson

30. Mr. Harvey Goldstein

31. Mr. Dell Pendergrast

32. Mr. William Vander Ven

33. Mr. James Slack

34. Mr. T.R. Addis

35. Mr. Richard Lester Houghton Jr.

36. Annette Langlois Grunseth

37. Mr. Paul Keaveney

38. Mr. Thom Stoddert

39. Mr. Garry Adams

40. Mr. Steve Smith

41. Mr. Steven Cramer

42. Diane Carlson Evans

43. Connie Chance

44. Karen Offutt

45. Brittanie Ngo

46. Captain Bill Robinson, United States Air Force (Ret)

47. J. Christopher Cook

48. Captain James Hickerson, United States Navy (Ret)

49. Pam Cain

50. Cindy Stonebraker Reed

51. Colleen Shine

52. Mr. Chase Cooley

53. Mr. Bob Welch

54. Mr. Paul Scott

55. Mr. David Draper

56. Mr. Rick "Rabbi" Rabenold

57. Mr. Lou Kern

58. Mr. Jim Sandoz

59. Mr. George Alexander

60. Mr. Bob Thomas

61. Mrs. Kathryn Willis (editing/proofreading)

62. Ms. Victoria McPhee (editing/proofreading)

63. Mrs. Maria Jackman (proofreading)

64. Mrs. Helen K. Norton (editing/proofreading)

1.

With 3rd Force Reconnaissance Company – 1969-1970

by Major Bruce H. Norton,
United States Marine Corps (Ret)

The mission of a Marine Force Reconnaissance Company was to be the "eyes and ears" of the Force Commander, and at the time that was Lieutenant General Herman Nickerson. The 120 Marines and four Hospital Corpsman, who made up the company were all volunteers and many were both "jump and scuba qualified," adding more lethality to the company's capabilities.

L-R: 1st Lt. C. C. "Bucky" Coffman, Major Alex Lee, and Captain Norman Hisler.

Our commanding officer of 3rd Force Reconnaissance Company was Major Alex Lee, a California native, who was on his second tour in Vietnam. Captain Norman Hisler, the Company Executive Officer, and 1st Lieutenant Clovis C. "Bucky" Coffman, our Operations Officer, were also seasoned combat veterans and incredibly knowledgeable in the art of jungle warfare tactics.

In the spring of 1968, I enlisted in the United States Navy. I attended basic training at Great Lakes Naval Training Center, in Illinois, followed by "A" School there where all Hospital Corpsmen were given their initial hospital training lasting about 12 weeks. Upon graduation, I was sent to Field Medical Service School, at Camp Lejeune, North Carolina, to learn how to function as a Corpsman within a Marine rifle platoon. After graduating from FMSS, I received orders to the Naval Hospital, Newport, Rhode Island, where I was assigned to a "dirty surgery" ward, caring for those patients who had infections following a surgical procedure. Most of these patients were Marines who had been wounded in Vietnam.

In July 1969, I was a twenty-one-year-old U.S. Navy Corpsman, when I volunteered for duty with 3rd Force Reconnaissance Company in Vietnam. Corpsmen had to volunteer for this duty, which was considered as being extremely hazardous.

1. With 3rd Force Reconnaissance Company – 1969-1970

I arrived in the company area on a Monday morning and three days later I was a member of a seven-man Force Reconnaissance team leaving the barbed wire safety of Con Thien, as we headed out across the DMZ (Demilitarized Zone), for a seven-day reconnaissance mission.

Led by a sergeant named Chapman, we encountered an enemy bunker complex, made contact on four separate occasions with the NVA (North Vietnamese Army), and were chased for three days by the enemy before we could be extracted by a CH-46 helicopter, out and away from the DMZ. It was an amazing experience and after surviving it, I thought to myself, "My God, I still have fifty more weeks of this excitement ahead of myself!"

HM-3 Bruce H. "Doc" Norton, USN - 1969.

In early November 1969, with nine long-range patrols under my belt, I had become a well-conditioned member of Team Snaky and had earned the title Doc. Our team was led by Corporal Ted Bishop, from Lufkin, Texas. Rounding out our team was LCpl. Donnel Kegler, our "Point Man," from Nacogdoches, Texas; LCpl. Paul Keaveny, our M-79 40mm grenadier, from New Smyrna Beach, Florida; LCpl. James Furhman, an automatic rifleman, from York, Pennsylvania; LCpl. Guillermo Silva, carrying our secondary radio, from Saginaw, Michigan, and me.

Our mission was to observe and report on an enemy activity in an area south of Phu Bai, and west of the Hai Van Pass, which was north of the port city of Danang. On that mission we noticed four NVA soldiers headed in our direction and the decision was made to capture one of them, hopefully the leader, eliminate the rest of them, and be extracted by helicopter with our prize possession. But plans do not always go accordingly.

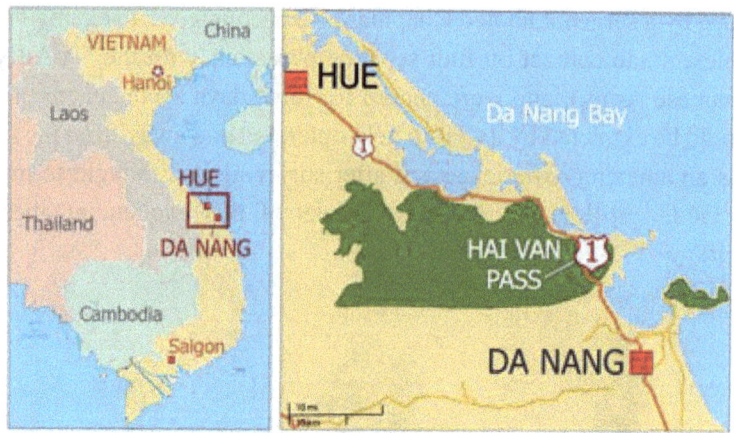

For weeks, we had practiced a "Gurkha-style" prisoner snatch, but it required several events in order to be completely successful. First, we had to identify exactly who our target would be, secondly, who would make the "snatch" and tackle the individual; the last, once grabbed, how he would be evacuated from our area of operation.

Our well-rehearsed plan was for our recon team leader to dive across the trail and tackle the unsuspecting enemy soldier and then, once clear, we would dispatch the rest of them. When everyone was in position, the "thumbs up" was given and the execution phase began with everyone hidden in place.

At the very last moment, Lance Corporal Fuhrman gave the "freeze" signal, and every one of us remained motionless, but at the ready. The four-man NVA fireteam that was approaching happened to be the point element of an NVA infantry company on the move. We froze, face down in the pouring rain, as sixty-four NVA soldiers passed between us and Corporal Bishop, still hidden not but ten feet away. No contact was made, and the NVA company passed by without incident, but the experience caused an adrenaline rush that had us all shaking. After regaining our lost composure, we were able to call in a well-executed airstrike that decimated that NVA company.

1. With 3rd Force Reconnaissance Company – 1969-1970

Team Isthmus – 1969.

By early February 1970, we had been conducting many reconnaissance missions inside the infamous A Shau Valley, a staging area for the NVA, south and west of Khe Sanh. One team from our 4th platoon had been ambushed on the 5th of February, and only two Marines survived that ordeal; the other five were killed. On the 7th of February, my team, Snaky, was flown out to the A Shau Valley and had been on the ground for less than an hour when the team walked into an NVA company which was in a defensive position. Sergeant Arthur M. Garcia, Corporal Ted Jason Bishop, and Lance Corporal James M. Furhman were killed in the first moments of the ambush.

(Left) LCpl. Paul Keaveney, USMC - 1969

Twenty-six-year-old Lance Corporal Paul Keaveney was wounded four separate times during the next three hours of fighting, sustaining wounds to his right leg, both right and left arms, his right side, and with one round striking his .45 Colt pistol and setting off two rounds inside the magazine well of that pistol. Paul received the Silver Star Medal and Purple Heart for his extraordinarily courageous actions continuing the fight.

It was a stroke of pure luck that I was not there with them that morning. I had been selected to go to Scuba School in the Philippines and had been taken out of the platoon a few days earlier for "pre-scuba school" training. Lance Corporal Fuhrman had been carrying my Unit-1 medical bag when he was killed.

A month later, I returned to Vietnam from my training in the Philippines and learned that 3rd Force Reconnaissance Company had been put into a cadre (reserve) status, waiting to be formally disbanded. I chl32ose to remain in Vietnam and requested orders to 1st Force Reconnaissance Company to be with those Marines from 3rd Force who had also gone over to 1st Force to finish their respective tours of combat duty.

On Hill 510 – June 1970.

It was on the 1st of July 1970, while I was on Hill 510, as part of an observation post and radio-relay site, that I was wounded during an NVA mortar attack on our small hilltop position. I was medically evacuated to Yokosuka, Japan, and returned home in September of 1970. I had taken part in twenty-four long range reconnaissance missions during my time in Vietnam and consider myself to be incredibly fortunate to have come home. The leadership by the Marine officers and SNCOs in the 3rd Force

Reconnaissance Company saved our collective lives. It was a teacher/student and father/son relationship with these men, and they taught us how to survive in a jungle environment dominated by the North Vietnamese Army and the occasional man-eating Bengal tiger.

Bruce H. "Doc" Norton served in Vietnam from July 1969 until July of 1970, as a U.S. Navy Corpsman. Both jump and scuba qualified, he was awarded the Bronze Star Medal with the "Combat "V,"" the Purple Heart, the Navy Achievement Medal, and the Vietnamese Cross of Gallantry for his service in Vietnam.

2.

Vietnam - July 1965 – July 1966
by Mr. Michael Dhunjishah

Ft. Benning – July 1965

I arrived at Ft. Benning and reported to Repo Depot. I was assigned to Headquarters and Headquarters Company, 1st 0Brigade (ABN), 1st Cavalry Division (Airmobile). The entire first brigade was airborne. Most of the lower ranks had gone through jump school as a group and, as I understand it, had an easier time than other classes. The senior enlisted paratroopers were from the 101st Airborne as the 82nd was still deployed in the Dominican Republic. The airborne brigade still did not have enough jump qualified troopers, so they levied troopers from the 82nd. More troopers, such as me, filled in the rest of the ranks.

Our first sergeant was Theron V. Gergen who had been reassigned from the 101st. He was known as "Bull Gergen." He was one tough soldier. He served in Korea spending most of his time behind enemy lines. During a later tour in Vietnam, he was awarded the Silver Star. Many years later, he was inducted into the Ranger Hall of Fame. When I reported to him, he assigned me to duty as the company clerk. I had not read my orders in detail, but years later I noticed that my MOS (military occupation specialty) had been changed from infantryman to administrative clerk. In retrospect, I think Sgt. Whitby did this so that I could be assigned to the 1st Cavalry. The Cav needed to fill positions for jump-qualified soldiers with certain MOSs.

Our commanding officer was Captain Groth, a West Point Graduate. He was not unusually impressive and was probably using this assignment to advance his young career. Fortunately, Sgt. Gergen was around and kept things in order and kept our unit from making stupid mistakes. Our brigade commander was Col. Elvey B. Roberts, who had fought in WWII with the

101st Airborne as well as in Korea. He eventually rose to the rank of lieutenant general. Our brigade sergeant major was SGM Herbert P. McCullah, who had served with the 11th Airborne (known as Hell's Angels), in the Pacific theatre during WWII.

We spent time preparing for our deployment. We bought green dye to dye our white underwear. We did PT and I had trouble with this. We tried to get out of this at Ft. Bragg.

(Left) USNS Geiger.

On August 20, we were bussed early in the morning to Savannah, Georgia and boarded a troop carrier, a United States Navy Ship (USNS) *Geiger* which was manned by civilians. We had Red Cross ladies handing us donuts and coffee as we embarked. Each of us carried a duffle bag, an M-16 rifle, and our helmets. We sailed down the Savannah River to the Atlantic Ocean then through the Panama Canal with stops in Hawaii and Guam, finally debarking in Qui Nhon, thirty-one days later.

The ship carried most of the 1st Airborne Brigade which consisted of over 2,700 troopers -- HHQ Company, the 1st and 2nd Battalions, 8th Cavalry Regiment (ABN) and the 1st Battalion, 12th Cavalry Regiment (ABN). Conditions on the ship were crowded. We slept in bunks stacked four high. It took about four hours to feed all hands. I had chosen a bottom bunk near the door. When the guys would go to breakfast, they would inadvertently step on my arm if it was extended. It did not take me long to learn to sleep with my arms tucked in. We did PT on the ship daily. I worked with the 1st Sgt. in what was the waiting room for the medical clinic, when the ship was used for transporting military families. We had manifest (roll) call every day to check that no one had fallen overboard.

2. Vietnam - July 1965 – July 1966

I missed manifest call one time. As punishment, I was not allowed to exit the ship when we arrived in Hawaii. I had to pull guard duty. When we arrived in Guam, we got off the ship and we ran in formation in our fatigues to a beautiful beach. Shortly after we got there, the Navy Shore Patrol arrived and told us that this beach was reserved for Navy personnel, and we would have to go to another beach. We ran over to a beach which was rock strewn and did not have much shade. Some Base Exchange trucks finally showed up with warm beer. We purchased the beer by the case and reported back to the ship well lubricated.

Camp Radcliff, Vietnam.

On arrival in Qui Nhon, we climbed down rope cargo netting hung over the side of the ship into landing craft which put us on the beach. From Qui Nhon we helicoptered via C-47 Chinooks to Camp Radcliff which was near An Khe--about 60 kilometers (clicks) west along Highway 19, which ran east to west all the way to the Cambodian border. Qui Nhon was situated on Highway 1 which ran north to south. An Khe was where the French Mobile Group 100 was ambushed when the French were fighting the Viet Minh under Ho Chi Minh. I used to read a lot of military history and had read about this in a book by Bernard Fall titled "*Street Without Joy*" about the French Indochina war. Indochina was the name for the French colony of Cambodia, Laos, and Vietnam.

We arrived at base camp which was being established. Our helicopters there were located on the "Golf Course" – a level cleared area of jungle with a lot of potholes. Paratroopers from the 1st Brigade, 101st Airborne had initially pulled security for the base. I found out later that some of the guys I had gone through basic, AIT and started Jump School had been there.

As soon as we established our area, we set up camp and pitched our shelter halves (tents). We had mail call and Linda (my future wife) wrote me a letter every day while I was gone. Sgt. Gergen told me I could take time to read the letters. We slept with our rifles locked and loaded as the perimeter was not yet completely established. I swiped a couple of pillows from the ship and gave one to Sgt. Gergen.

We had rain, mud, and heat. About two weeks after we arrived, the monsoons came. We had our first shower since disembarking. We just stripped off and washed ourselves with soap and rainwater. It felt good to feel clean even though it was not for long. We went about building the camp. We typically worked long days, sometimes up to 16 hours. We put in concrete slabs for our large tents, built the mess hall which became the officers' and enlisted men's clubs, the colonel's hooch (living quarters) as well as other improvements. This was an on-going process the entire time I spent in An Khe. I spent several days with another trooper (Frink) digging an 8x8x8-foot bunker—it was tough digging. Linda had given me her high school class ring. I had a Tissot watch given to me by my sisters. I had put both into the pocket of my fatigue jacket which I took off to work. Frink left before me, and my fatigue shirt was gone. I later found it on my sleeping blanket with both items missing. I confronted him about this, and he denied taking them. I could never prove that he had taken them, and warned him that if I had the opportunity, I would take care of him. Fortunately, the opportunity never presented itself.

(Left) Michael Dhunjishah.

I also spent a lot of time working for the first sergeant--typing rosters, reports, after action reports and other items. I also got to make runs to fill up our water trailers. We eventually set up large tents and received cots. We were fortunate that we were in the Central Highlands, as the nights were typically cooler than elsewhere in Vietnam, which allowed for better sleep. We also pulled guard duty along the perimeters. We were allowed to go into the village of An Khe as that's where we could get our laundry done, get haircuts, and fill sandbags at the river. We paid some of the kids to fill the sandbags while we got beer and sat around, went to the bars that sprang up quickly, and bought stuff at the local shops.

Sometime in November, I was promoted to Specialist Fourth Class (Spec. 4). This brought my base pay up from $117 to $163.50 a month. In addition, I continued to receive combat pay of $110, jump pay of $55 and overseas pay of $13 instead of $9. When I had served over two years in April, my base pay jumped up to $204.90 per month. All this pay was tax free! I was sending most of it to Linda so that we could have some savings to start out our life together.

I was enormously proud to be a paratrooper and had an attitude toward "Legs" (those soldiers who were not airborne). One of our helicopter mechanics (I think his last name was Burns) and I did not get along (surprise!). One evening when we were in the chow line, I kept giving him a hard time. We decided to fight it out in a tent after chow. He got the better of me and had me on the ground, pounding away at me. He kept asking if I gave up and I kept saying, "Hell no." Eventually the fight ended with me not giving in. The next day when 1st Sgt. Gergen saw me, he said "What happened to the other guy?" My answer to him was "not much." I did not know that Burns was the boxing champion of the 8th Infantry

Division when he was stationed in Germany. Had I known that to begin with, I would still have done the same.

Operations: I went out on most of the operations that our brigade was involved in. Our first operation, dubbed "Shiny Bayonet" was toward Ben Khe, east of Camp Radcliff in mid-October. It was short--just a few days. The purpose of the operation was 'search and clear'—looking for Viet Cong and their camps and stores. Our brigade had quite a few casualties—over 45 wounded (many the result of stepping on punji stakes; sharpened bamboo slivers that were hidden in the ground and usually covered with human excrement). Several were killed. It was hot and rainy. The operation was short, just a few days long. One day I choppered over to Camp Radcliff to pick up the mail and some dry clothes for Sgt. Gergen, myself, and several others. We flew over An Khe Pass (I had always thought this was Mang Yang Pass until I checked the map) and we were fired upon, but not hit. It was late in the day. Once I got back to base camp, I hitched up with a Captain and a couple of other guys and we decided to go back out to the field. We sandbagged a ¾-ton truck, loaded up the mail and our gear and then flipped a coin to see who would ride in the back of the truck. I lost. The three guys rode in the cab and I set up my M16 on the bipod with several spare 20-round magazines of ammo beside me. It must have been around midnight. It was pitch dark. As we drove through An Khe Pass, my imagination went into full gear, and I kept seeing VC all around me.

Amazingly, we got through without getting fired on. When we got back, Sgt. Gergen thought we were crazy for trying this. But the guys had mail call in the morning, and some of us had dry clothes. This operation was my first experience with lines of choppers (UH-1Ds - Hueys) dropping off troopers into action. I will never forget the sound or sight of this. It was awesome!

I went back out on operations around October 21. We initially went to an established base camp, Camp Holloway, near Pleiku, where we were able to take real showers and then went out into the countryside for a couple of days. Our job was to relieve the Special Forces (5th Group at Plei Me). This was the beginning of the Pleiku Campaign. We were not too far from the Ia Drang River (I think) as I sneaked down to a river to take a quick swim and look at the Montagnard's, (the indigenous people in this area). We were in a tea plantation run by a Frenchman. We visited with him and had tea. He told us that he paid the VC around $10,000 a year to keep them from attacking his plantation. He also told us that they used to hunt tigers in the surrounding jungles.

Our brigade went up against an NVA (North Vietnamese Army) division and VC. I was able to get in some courier missions going back and forth on the Hueys. We captured NVA and VC prisoners. They would be interrogated by a couple of Chinese American guys who did not have any rank insignia--just name tags on their fatigues. Our medic, Doc Shottell, would delouse the prisoners before they would be interrogated. Ron Righton and I along with a couple of MPs escorted some high-ranking prisoners to Camp Holloway. This was super. When we got to Camp Holloway this time, Ron knew someone there so after we dropped the prisoners and MPs off, we got a hot meal. The real treat was when I went to the bathroom. There were a lot of porcelain commodes lined up and a shower area with Vietnamese women doing laundry. The first thing I did was drop all my loadbearing gear and use the flush commode.

We moved our brigade command post to another location and were there for the duration of our time in the area. Our brigade was rotated back to Camp Radcliff around November 10th, as we had about 80 KIAs and 120 wounded. We had killed about 300 of the enemy and captured around 60.

We were replaced by the 3rd Brigade. Their actions were documented in the book and movie "*We Were Soldiers Once and Young.*" We had been at the last area where we set up the brigade command post (CP) for several days. I kept thinking that we would get hit badly, and fortunately we did not get hit. The 3rd Brigade HQ set up in the same location and got hit a few days later, losing seven KIA's and seventeen men wounded. Talk about luck! The 3rd Brigade suffered very heavy casualties: some 200 KIA's and many more wounded. The campaign proved that we could defeat the NVA as they had a couple of thousand killed. The 1st Cav was awarded the Presidential Unit Citation (PUC) for our actions in the Pleiku Campaign. This is the highest award a unit can be given for combat. All of us who took part in that campaign got to wear a blue ribbon on our dress uniforms.

We finally got to make a parachute jump on November 15th. This was great. It was a "Hollywood jump," meaning no combat equipment was worn. We climbed aboard a Huey for the jump, and when we landed little Vietnamese kids bundled up our parachutes and carried them back to the truck for us. All this was done for 50 Piasters, which was about around 50 cents.

We celebrated Thanksgiving on November 25th in base camp. We had a real Thanksgiving dinner. It was nice, warm weather and dry. On December 6th, I went into town and got a puppy, and I named her Tiger.

Christmas came and went, and I continued to work my butt off. On December 28 we had the Bob Hope Show. Boy was this a big deal. It was Top Secret until an hour before, when he and his whole troupe arrived by chopper. Their choppers were shot at near An Khe. The only person in the troupe I remember was Jack Jones, a singer. He taped a short message from some of us and he sent a cut piece of recording tape with our message to our families.

I found this piece of tape recording at my home many years later—my parents had no clue as to what it was. Thirty-five years later, when we lived in Orange, California, my wife and I went to a show featuring the singer Jack Jones. I sent him a note backstage telling him who I was and thanking him for sending the tape. He recognized me at the beginning of his performance and asked me to stand up. He sent me his telephone number, but I never contacted him again as we left California a couple of years later. Besides, I had lost my cell phone which had his telephone number on it.

Early in January, I went back out on operations up to the Plei Me area on Operation Matador. We were operating near the Cambodian border. I was in the field and doing courier flights between the field and base camp. The operation did not result in a lot of action, but I was only out for several weeks. I became company armorer at the end of January and was responsible for all the weapons in the company, obtaining much needed ammo, as well as having some other duties. I went on R&R (Rest and Recreation) on January 30th to Hong Kong for a week. I celebrated my 21st birthday there with friends. I went back out on operations on February 17th.

The Bong Son Campaign, known as Operation Masher/White Wing started in late January by other brigades of the 1st Cav. We operated south of Bong Son along Highway 1, which ran south to north paralleling the coast. This was great fun as Ron Righton and I took a ¾-ton truck, which we loaded up with ammo, and took a drive on Highway 1 for a laundry run.

Since becoming our company armorer, I carried a .45 Colt pistol in addition to my M-16. We heard that there were bars at the river about 20 miles up the road where we had set up a Command Post (CP). Somehow the first sergeant agreed. Along the road we ran into a ROK (Republic of South Korea) Tiger division soldier guarding a bridge. We stopped and saw that he was armed with an M-1 rifle. Never having fired one, we agreed to let him fire one of our M16s in exchange for me firing his M-1. We picked up a reporter hitchhiking up to the river area. We saw several burned-out hulks of tanks left by the French, and I got back to our base camp on March 1.

I went back out on operations around March 10 and was out in the field until March 22. We were back in the Bong Son area on Operation Jim Bowie. At the base camp I did a lot of guard duty at night as the brigade was out in the field. Sometime around the first week of April, I went out on Operation Lincoln. We were back operating in the Plei Me area in the vicinity of the Duc Co Special Forces Camp. I returned to base camp on April 15.

(Left) Michael Dhunjishah.

On May 25th I went out on Operation Crazy Horse at Vinh Thang about 15 to 20 miles from our base camp. This was a Special Forces Camp. I was able to get some radio parts for the SF guys that they needed. The SF communications sergeant offered me a bottle of whiskey for the radio parts, but I chose not to take it. It was the least I could do for these guys. We returned to base camp on June 3. I went back out on some operation in mid- June, but I did not write about it, and I don't recall anything about it at this time.

On July 1st, I went out on Operation Nathan Hale to Tuy Hoa located on the coast midway between Nha Trang and Qui Nhon. The Air Force base was being constructed. The airstrip was on beach sand with Marston Mats and overlaid with some type of rubber membrane.

Then we moved to Cung Son on Operation Henry Clay. I was flying between Ty Hoa and Cung Son or Bohn Blick to get ammo and other items to the field. On one mission, I flew in the co-pilot's seat in a Bell observation chopper, which was great. This area, called Bohn Blick, was located on top of a plateau where we had quite a few Montagnard civilians living there, along with a lot of captured weapons in storage. I returned from operations on July 20 and did not go out in the field after that.

2. Vietnam - July 1965 – July 1966

I received orders for the 101st Airborne Division at Ft. Campbell. I talked with 1st Sgt. Gergen about this and told him I was getting married, and that Linda had a job teaching in Aberdeen, North Carolina. Shortly after that, I received orders which directed me back to the 82nd Airborne Division. When he gave these orders to me, he said, "Here you go alphabet, (he always called me that as he could not pronounce my last name), go be with your schoolteacher," or words to that effect. Linda had graduated from college with a Bachelor of Science in Secretarial Administration and was going to be teaching in Aberdeen, North Carolina.

I'm not certain as to the exact date when I left Camp Radcliff, around July 27. I had always wanted a tattoo. So, the night before I left, Ron Righton agreed to tattoo my arm with a pair of jump wings with U.S. PARATROOPER printed below. He had been with the Hell's Angels motorcycle gang and had done this before. He used a needle with thread around it and India ink. Ron had a little more to drink that night than I did and was not able to finish the tattoo—so my tattoo is one of a kind. We boarded a military plane, a C-130, and we flew to Saigon, Ton Son Nhut Air Base and spent two nights at Camp Alpha (a part of the air base) and then boarded a Braniff International Airways jet for home. We boarded through the back door as the replacements were getting off through the

front door. We flew to Okinawa, got off the plane and bought something to eat in the lounge, then we re-boarded and flew to Elmendorf Air Force Base, near Anchorage, Alaska. Here many of us kissed the ground as we deplaned and then got a real hamburger in the lounge. We then re-boarded and flew to Travis AirForce Base in California. When we arrived, we were checked for weapons. Our duffel bags were checked for anything that might be illegal. I think I took a bus into San Francisco and finally got home. I arrived on July 30 and called Linda on Saturday to tell her that I was back and that we should get married on the following Sunday.

3.

A Bullet Through the Helmet: A Vietnam Dustoff Pilot's Memoir

by Colonel Douglas E. Moore, United States Army (Ret)

Dustoff Medevac Chopper – Vietnam.

Under most circumstances we considered it a cardinal sin to take off over the same route we had used to come in on, but artillery was falling behind us and the "bad guys" were shooting from our left, right and rear, so our only alternative was to take off to the west. The sky above us was filled with flares, so it was a "daylight" take-off due to the illumination.

Just before we reached heavy jungle on the opposite side of the clearing, we began transitioning out of the light of the flares into semi-darkness. At that moment, sheets of enemy tracers came up and began striking the bottom of the helicopter. I saw a bright flash as a tracer came up by my left knee and struck the collective pitch lever before exiting the top of the aircraft. A piece of shrapnel hit my left thumb.

Several more bullets hit us and then I heard a blood-curdling scream right behind me. The medic told me one of the patients had been hit in the back. I started to press the intercom button to ask how he was doing when I felt something hit me and hit me hard. Later we found an AK-47 round had come through the lower right corner of the windshield where it fits into the frame and hit my flight helmet right between my eyes. The bullet penetrated the hard, outer shell of the helmet and followed its curvature around to the side before exiting behind my left ear. The bullet lodged in one of the cross-members supporting the roof of the helicopter and our aircraft maintenance unit dug it out and mounted it on a plaque that's hanging in my "Man Cave" today.

That whole experience was so strange because I remember seeing a bright flash in front of my eyes and felt my head snap back like someone had hit me with a baseball bat. Fortunately, we had a policy in our unit that both pilots would be on controls during all take-offs or landings in tactical areas. My co-pilot, Warrant Officer Steve Peth, told me later that when I was hit, I jammed the right pedal to the floor, pulled up the collective lever, and threw the stick out of both of our hands. I remember looking back down at the artificial horizon and saw we were in a descending right turn about 150 feet off the ground, so I grabbed the stick and centered it before pulling in power to start climbing again. Somewhere in all that confusion, I told Steve I'd been hit. His response showed the worth of all that hard training at Fort Rucker because he replied very calmly, "Roger, sir. I have the aircraft." Steve Peth saved our lives that night.

3. A Bullet Through the Helmet: A Vietnam Dustoff Pilot's Memoir

After I told Steve I'd been hit, I sensed movement behind me just before Tom Roberts, the crew chief, threw his arm around my neck and pinned me against the back of the seat. He was concerned I might fall into the controls, and I knew he was reaching for the lever on my seat to tip me backwards into the patient compartment. After yelling at him to "Turn Me Loose" twice, he did.

By that time, I had recovered most of my senses, so I called the battalion commander and told him we had taken heavy fire about two hundred meters to the west of where we had been on the ground. Barracuda acknowledged my call sign by saying he had seen the tracers and planned to place artillery there as soon as we were clear. Just then, our fire warning light came on, so I called again and told him we had taken several hits while on the ground and during takeoff and had a fire warning light. I asked him to follow us back to Chu Chi in case we needed to put down somewhere along the way. Barracuda said he couldn't do it because his units were under heavy attack, so we were left on our own to get back with a badly shot-up Huey. Later, we found out a bullet had gone through the fire warning system control and set it off without any fire present.

At that point, I still didn't know what was wrong with me. All I knew was that my left thumb hurt and that I had been hit somewhere else but didn't know where. I began feeling pain above my left eye and along my nose and felt something warm on my left cheek. For some reason, I closed my left eye, and I could see the instrument panel clearly, but when I closed my right eye, I could only see a dull glow of light with my left eye, so I surmised something serious had happened. I may have been a little woozy too, because Steve told me later that I kept saying, "Watch out for those wires at the west end of the hospital helipad." I don't remember saying that, but I do remember him emphatically telling me, "Sir, I know where those damned wires are!"

When we got to the hospital, I took off my helmet, laid it on the center console, and sat there. After the casualties were unloaded, one of the crewman and a hospital corpsman came around to my side and said, "Okay sir, let's get you out of there." I remember climbing out and walking to the receiving room. When we got there, it was a beehive of activity, so the corpsman told me to take a seat along the wall.

One of the nurses stopped by to check on me and said, "Hey Major Moore, I didn't know that was you!" A doctor came by later and said, "You brought us some bad ones tonight, so we're really busy right now, but we'll get to you shortly."

Several minutes later, I was helped to an examination table and a perky nurse second lieutenant appeared down by my feet and said, "Hey, Major, these look like new boot laces you've got on. Are they new?" I remember wondering what kind of stupid question she was asking until I saw her whip out a pair of scissors and begin cutting my boot laces. After pulling my boots and socks off, she said, "And these look like new fatigue trousers too" as she began cutting up my pants leg. Very soon, I was lying completely naked on the exam table and surrounded by people, some who I knew.

About that time, George Hurtado, my executive officer, walked in and asked, "Have you seen your helmet?" I answered, "no, why?" He continued, "Well it's got a hole in the front and one in the back. When I saw it, I thought the bullet had gone straight into your head." I didn't have the foggiest idea what he meant until several days later, when I saw my helmet. After examinations and x-rays were done, both eyes were patched, and I was flown to 24th Evacuation Hospital at Long Binh to have metal and Plexiglass fragments removed from my eye and to be evaluated by a neurologist. There was concern that I may have been knocked unconscious after being hit in the head, and, if so, that would have meant an end to my flying career. One of the doctors asked whether I wanted to go to Japan for 30 days to recover. I told him no because that would mean giving up my command and going to a different unit when I returned to Vietnam.

I completed my second tour without incident, but Steve Peth was not so lucky. Steve was an incredibly good pilot and one of the bravest men I'd ever seen. Unfortunately, he was seriously wounded when his helicopter took thirty-nine hits during a patient evacuation mission the following May. One of those AK-47 rounds went through the arch of his boot and another through his arm near the elbow, sending a piece of his ulna into his co-pilot's right shoulder. Steve spent several months recovering before returning to flight status. He was later commissioned and went back to Vietnam for a second tour. Steve went on to complete a very successful military career and retired as a Lieutenant Colonel.

This vignette is taken by permission from Colonel Douglas Moore's book, A Bullet Through the Helmet: A Vietnam Dustoff Pilot's Memoir. *Colonel Doug Moore served in the U. S. Army for thirty years with overseas tours in Germany, Japan and two tours in Vietnam. Other than his several years as a Dust-Off medical evacuation helicopter pilot, he commanded a battalion in the 82nd Airborne Division and a brigade at Fort Lewis, WA, where he served as Mission Commander for the search & rescue effort following the eruption of Mt. St. Helens in May 1980.*

4.

"A Short History of Chow in Vietnam"
by Lieutenant Colonel Dale Carlsen, United States Army (Ret)

In the Vietnam U.S. military base camps, food was the same as back in the States. When troops were out in the "boonies" on an operation, if the tactical situation allowed, cooks would prepare hot or cold meals at base-camp mess halls and would use insulated food containers to transport hot and cold meals to the troops operating in the field via trucks or helicopters. The containers were called Mermite Cans and measured about two feet long, one foot wide and about 15" high.

Normally, however, we weren't that lucky and had to resort to eating cold rations called Meal, Combat, Individual (MCI). Despite the new name, the MCI was still popularly referred to within the military as the C-ration. Each packing case held 12 ration cartons (containing one of each meal) packed in two rows of six rations. They were grouped in three menus of four meals each consisting of a meat (M) unit, a bread (B) unit, and a dessert (D) unit organized by their B unit.

The "M" unit came in 12 basic varieties grouped in three menus of four different entrees but 18 entrees were available in different cases: Beefsteak, Chicken or Turkey Loaf, Chopped Ham & Eggs, or Ham Slices, Tuna fish, Meat Chunks w/ Beans in Tomato Sauce, Ham & Lima Beans, Beef Slices w/ Potatoes in Gravy, Beans w/ Frankfurter Chunks in Tomato Sauce, Spaghetti w/ Meatballs in Tomato Sauce, Beef in Spiced Sauce, Boned Chicken or Turkey, Chicken w/ Noodles in Broth, Pork Steak cooked in juices or Meat Loaf.

The beans and weenies would go first, but the ham and lima beans were packed in semi-solid grease and universally disliked, colloquially known throughout the armed forces as "Ham and Mother Fuckers." When I was out on an operation with my platoon and when a new ration case was opened, I would let my troops have first choice, so I often ate Ham and Lima Beans for breakfast, lunch, and supper. Sometimes they could be heated by making a tin can stove and burning a can of peanut butter. If we happened to remain over night at an Artillery Forward Operating Base (FOB), we could sometimes use the heat from the exhaust manifold on a running vehicle to melt the grease around the ham. At the time, our M-16 variant rifles had an open, forked flash suppressor on the end of the muzzle. These were ideal for breaking the steel band around the ration case but would get caught in branches and were later replaced by a closed-end model.

The MCI case also had accessories such as plastic sporks, a package of a couple of cigarettes, a book of moisture resistant matches, and the handy P-38 can opener that is still on the key rings of many Vietnam vets. Sometimes there would be a bar of tropical chocolate, hard and melt resistant. This was sometimes saved to give to Vietnamese kids. The results were sometimes surprising. During one vehicle convoy as we passed through a small village, my troops threw chocolate bars to the kids. The kids threw them back, yelling "Fuck you, GI, we no like John Wayne bars." We had a better response from the kids in an orphanage about five miles from our base camp. We would visit about every three months and bring them chocolate and gifts sent from home, especially before Christmas. I don't know what happened to their parents, but some obviously had GI fathers. Often just a hug would be received with delight by a lonely Vietnamese kid.

5.

Base Camp Danang

by Lieutenant Colonel Dale Carlsen,
United States Army (Ret)

Not all terrifying things in RVN were heroic, some were just crazy.

It was between division operations, so we were back in our base camp south of Danang, RVN. The mountains there were close to the coast so that the base camp was right on the beach. The Army had taken over the camp from the Marines, but there was still a Marine F-4 detachment at the airstrip. The mountains allowed "Charlie" to get close enough to target us with 122-mm and 140-mm rockets, so occasionally we heard and saw the damage from them.

Officers were living in four-person, wood "hooches" that had been well built and furnished by Navy Seabees. The sparse furnishings included a metal bed frame with a decent mattress. Each bed also had an overhead, open wood box frame from head to foot to hold up a mosquito net. Outside, just a few feet away, was an opening to a mortar bunker. This consisted of a deep trench in the ground with an overhead arch of four foot culvert covered by a thick layer of sandbags.

One night, I followed my usual night-time ritual of placing my rifle, helmet, and boots under my bed, laid my clothing on a bench, and naked, crawled onto the bed, carefully tucking the mosquito netting under the mattress. Suddenly, I was awakened by a series of loud explosions. My next realization was that I was standing in the mortar bunker, naked except for my helmet, holding my rifle and boots, and looking at the entrance. I jumped as a voice behind me said "What took you so long?" I turned, and in the darkness, I made out the grey hair of our fully dressed, CW-4 Crypto Warrant Officer whose Date of Expected Rotation Over Seas (DEROS) was in three days. Later that day, we learned that the "explosions" were from the guns of a U. S. Navy destroyer, just offshore, that was firing over the base camp.

Dale Carlsen, Captain, U.S. Army

Dale Carlsen attended what is now Montana State University, enlisting in the Montana National Guard as an E-4. He was commissioned June 1965 through ROTC as a Regular Army Second Lieutenant in the Signal Corps. Completing jump school, he was assigned to an airborne unit at Ft Bragg. Next was the 1st Infantry Division Signal Battalion located north of Saigon, "The Big Red One." From there was 23rd Infantry Division located south of Danang as a company commander. He attended Command and General Staff College at Ft. Leavenworth, then onto battalion operations officer in Germany. His last two assignments were in the Pentagon. He retired in September 1987.

6.

At the Helm

by Force Master Chief Thomas J. Snee, United States Navy (Ret)

On October 28, 1965, I was a skinny kid from Willoughby, Ohio, and raised my right hand, took the oath of enlistment for the United States Navy, and headed off to boot camp at Great Lakes, IL. I would sail to Vietnam, a country I had never heard of, but that realization would bear down on my heart, as with so many others.

One August night, 1966, this *young sailor* was called to the bridge of my ship, the USS *Vogelgesang* (DD-862) to take the helm, wearing 1JV headphones and steering into harm's way off the coast of North Vietnam to provide naval gunfire support. At that point I still had no idea what was to come next.

USS Vogelgesang DD-862.

I steered the ship to less than seventy-five yards offshore in North Vietnam. The ship was parallel to the coast as the ship's guns pelleted the shore. Suddenly, the Captain gave an "all stop" on the engines. We were just sitting in the water. The awe of the night caused me to look outside, until the unforgiving cries of human voices could be heard. At that moment I froze on the helm, crying to myself because I had never heard a death cry or killed anything, but only to realize I steered my ship to a point where enemy fire ashore had to be fired upon. While fearful at what would be next, the Captain gave the order, "*All ahead, full right rudder.*" I was frozen with no movement and I had to be knocked off the helm just to meet the orders of the Commanding Officer. As the ship sailed out into the Tonkin Gulf, the Captain came up to me and told me, "Son, I understand how you feel and I do not hold you at fault for this. You have done well, Sailor."

Many years later while onboard the *USS America* (CV-66), another young sailor, a member of a flight crew, had the same frightening experience of 'being at war' off the coast of Libya. Having the same uneasy sensation twenty years earlier, I talked with the young Airman. He asked, "Master Chief, am I going to die tonight?" At that moment, call it PTSD or reality, I had to assure this young sailor and told him, "No, you are not going to die."

So, what drives young men to this point; love, dedication, service, commitment, or just plain moving forward? Yes, two young sailors, in different conflicts but with the same emotional drawdown of 'death.'

Today, as a middle school teacher, I tactfully tell students this story. That crew-cut, black-rimmed-glasses sailor with rolled-up sleeves, was destined to experience, bravery, out of fright, shared with driven determination. That was 57 years ago. Yes, my vision, four years later, was to come home, attend Bowling Green State University, and become a teacher, but instead, I '*forged*' ahead to a rewarding naval career. I married my high school love, and we have four beautiful children, and seven grandchildren. I have served, coached, mentored, and led many sailors in those years to be that kind of a sailor in the United States Navy. I eventually became that teacher, giving back from my Navy experiences to my country, students, and many more individuals in those fifty-eight years; the 'skinny kid' from Cleveland, Ohio. I would never give it up, was reluctant to talk about it, but deep in my heart, I am thankful to the U. S. NAVY!

**Force Master Chief Tom Snee,
U.S. Navy, (Ret).**

Retired U.S. Navy Force Master Chief Tom Snee is a Vietnam Veteran with over thirty years of service in various leadership roles. Tom has worked as a Middle School Teacher in Northern Virginia and is a Past National Executive Director for the Fleet Reserve Association.

7.

My Vietnam Service
by Robert (Bob) Thomas Sr.

Upon graduating from Southwest Missouri State College in June 1963, I was commissioned a Second Lieutenant in the U.S. Army Infantry as a reserve officer. I reported for training at Fort Benning, Georgia in July. After training, my first assignment was with the 7th Infantry Division in South Korea for 13 months. In 1965 while serving as a company commander at Fort Gordon, Georgia I was accepted into the regular army and was sworn in as a student in ranger school.

My next assignment was Vietnam as an advisor to a Republic of Vietnam ranger battalion. On my first tour, September 1965 – September 1966, I went to ranger school in July/August/September and was well prepared for acclimating to the Vietnamese jungle climate. On arrival I was assigned as a battalion advisor in the 10th Republic of Vietnam (RVN) Infantry Division. Later the division name was changed to the 18th Infantry Division and was station at Xuan Loc in III Corps.

To join my advisory team, I was put on a local train going to the village of Gia Ray. About five hundred yards from Gia Ray the front of the train was blown up. The train consisted of a series of flat cars and as I was in one of the flat cars furthest from the explosion. Fortunately, I was not hurt.

At times, the battalion performed missions in single, double, or triple canopy jungles. Single canopy was the hardest to move through. Ten minutes at a time, soldiers used a machete to cut through the jungle; it was very slow movement. Double canopy jungle was easier to move through but still meant hacking at a lot of vegetation. Triple canopy jungle was the easiest to move through as there was no lower-level vegetation, but you couldn't tell where you were. You had to pop a smoke grenade. About ten minutes after popping the smoke, the C-19 pilot (there to help in providing artillery support if needed) would tell you your location. In the three-canopy jungle you had to protect yourself from 1-inch red ants that fell out of the vegetation. An ant bite was painful. Your bed was a silk parachute hammock slung between two trees and after a few nights you adjusted and got a good rest. A metal disc was put on the hammock's front and rear cords to protect against ants.

In-Country Encounters

Captain Shultz, a West Point graduate, was the battalion adviser. We were walking around a valley for 60 – 90 days, sometimes with U.S. support and sometimes not. We were taking a battalion sweep and I was with the lead company, and I repeatedly told the RVN company commander to get flank support deployed. Finally, he walked up and said, "I got flank security out." Two minutes later, we received enemy rifle fire from every direction. I called on the radio back to Shultz that we were receiving enemy fire. U.S. air support helicopters arrived and started shooting at us. I hunkered down, squatting, in front of a row of small trees with trunks about the size of my forearm and about ten feet tall. A U.S. helicopter came in shooting at us from about twenty feet above us. I leaned forward and gave the chopper the middle finger salute. I think the gunner saw me do that. The tree trunks I was in front of had been cut down to about three inches after the shooting. If I had been standing, I would have been killed by friendly machine gun fire.

The casings from the chopper's machine gun fell onto my helmet and they hurt! Next day, I still had a headache. Over forty RVNs were killed; no Americans were hurt. Captain Shultz got relieved because he had told the helicopter pilots that anything in front of them was fair game; he had totally forgotten about the RVNs and the two Americans out there. The team radio telephone operation (RTO) recounted this to me. After that, I became the senior battalion advisor. I spent nine months with the RVN battalion. My last three months I was assigned to the G-3 Tactical Operations Center (TOC).

When I was with the RVN battalion in three-canopy jungle, I looked up and saw some shots coming in; we were receiving fire. We were single file. The soldier I was following was about three feet ahead of me. The RVN soldier behind me was about 10 yards away. Other rounds were coming down through the trees. The two RVNs then moved out of my sight. I knew I needed to follow them, along the winding path, which I did for about an hour. When we linked up again, I ask them in my pidgin Vietnamese why they "disappeared," and they said, "VC shoot at you." Their way of staying safe was to stay away from me. I was also about a foot taller than them. No one was injured in this incident.

There was a similar situation, down by the seacoast. A Marine RTO artillery unit, three enlisted Marines, was assigned to my advisory team. We're sitting about a mile from the coast. Rounds are coming in high up; we can tell it's a sniper shooting at us. We moved around and cooked C-rations for supper, ate, chatted, and went to sleep. The sniper couldn't hit the broad side of a barn.

Five inch or 16-inch shells fired from the battleship *USS New Jersey* sounded like a freight train going over our heads. We were going down a road and we came to a tree that was lying across the road. It took about five steps to get over it. After I passed through, and six or seven other guys had done so, another guy stepped on a different spot on the tree and triggered a booby trap. He was blown up and killed.

All major medical support was provided by Saigon facilities. I developed an earache and was medevac'd by helicopter to a hospital in Saigon. The worst pain I had in Vietnam was flying at a couple of thousand feet with a bad ear. At the hospital, the doctor treating me chewed me out for having my carbine with me. I ignored him. He gave me some medicine and I had to stay overnight in a local hotel. That night the hospital was bombed.

The worst terrain I had to navigate through was damaged by a B-52 air strike. Everything had changed. There were holes 10 feet deep or more, huge trees had been toppled, and I could scarcely find solid ground to put my feet on. The RVN battalion had to maneuver through it twice. For some reason I was in Saigon, and I was walking by a Military Assistance Command, Vietnam (MACV) living facility and I heard noise coming from it. I stopped and went in and followed the noise to a large room. The room had seating arrangements and the noise was a radio carrying the Army/Navy football game.

Major Glass, the brigade advisor, made a visit to our field location. He came up to my group and we chatted, and he got in the chopper and left. He saw what physical condition I was in. I knew I was sick; at times I would carry a bucket of water with me in the field to try to stay clean. I had the runs but there were no medics out there. I took malaria pills to clog myself up. A day later a helicopter arrived at our field location. A captain got out and ordered me to get in the chopper as he was my replacement. I got into Xuan Loc and asked Major Glass about it. He said, "Thomas, I didn't even recognize you. I thought you were an RVN." I had lost weight and was down to about ninety pounds on my 5'11" frame. After I started eating American food, I gained weight and felt better. I got to go on two R&R's, one to Thailand and one to Hong Kong.

Sometimes Xuan Loc would receive mortar fire while I was in G3. I would work 24 hours on and 48 hours off. On an off day we would play poker and one night while playing, we were hit by a mortar attack. We had steel folding chairs and, on my way running out the door to a bunker, I caught the leg of the chair and broke a toe. The doc wrapped it.

On my return from Vietnam in September, my brother Jerry was serving as the executive officer of the *USS Black*, a destroyer, stationed at Long Beach California. He met me at the LA airport and took me to a topless and bottomless bar. I was in uniform, sitting at the bar enjoying the scenery. An overweight guy sat down next to me and asked if I had just returned from Vietnam. I said yes, I just got back a couple of hours ago. He said did I enjoy being a baby killer, and other negative things. I got up and went to the restroom. He followed me in and kept making unkind comments to me. I got angry and beat the "hell" out of him. My brother immediately took me out of the bar. Welcome back soldier!

My brother asked me to stay for a while with him and I agreed. He took me to an Angels ballgame, Knotts Berry Farm and Disneyland. Jerry asked me if I should see my brother Bill in Texas and my brother Larry in Kansas City before I flew to Springfield, Missouri to see my parents. I did as they suggested. Jerry had called my brothers and told them to fatten me up before my parents saw me.

When I arrived in Springfield, as I was getting off the plane, my parents were crying. This was the only time I saw them crying. I weighed close to 100 pounds. My family gave me a great welcome back.

Second tour, March 1968 to January 1969 – 25th Infantry Division

On March 7, 1968, I flew to McChord Airforce base. It was 7 degrees in Kansas City. Because I was going to Vietnam, the uniform was khakis. From McChord we flew to Alaska. We had to deboard for refueling; it was 40 degrees below. There was a very long walk on the tarmac to and from the airplane. We flew to Hawaii; it was a lot warmer. We flew to Guam; we flew to the Philippines. We flew to Cam Rahn Bay, and even though it was Vietnam I was very glad to get off the airplane. While waiting at Cam Rahn Bay for air travel to Saigon, I was assigned to the 25th Infantry station in III Corps. We had a visitor. General Westmorland came by and shook the soldiers' hands. The only time Cam Rahn Bay was mortared was the night I arrived.

On arrival at Saigon, I was standing on a corner at Tan Son Nhut Air base. An army jeep stopped near me, and the driver said, "Hey Cap, do you remember me?" I looked at him, an E-5, and said "Yes, I do." He was a trainee in the training company that I commanded at Fort Gordon. He asked me what and where I was going, and I said "Chu Chi. I have been trying to get there for a long time." He responded, "No problem; I am a driver for the command general." We chatted and I asked him how he was getting along and why he tried to go AWOL from the training company. (The company had no AWOLs in over two years and the cadre were very proud of it. We caught him before the absence would have been reported and I gave him an article 15 that kept him broke.) He said that it seemed a good thing at the time. We laughed about it, and he drove me to the airport where I flew to Chu Chi. I had been traveling for so long when I got to Chu Chi and when I was going through the assignment line I asked if I could be stationed there. Yes, I was assigned to the 2nd Infantry Brigade, the *Wolfhounds*. The captain behind me, Captain Mitchell, wanted to be assigned to Tay Nin, and he was. As my trip to Chu Chi was long and from the cold Missouri climate, I had a hard time adjusting to the Vietnam climate. I had a cold, was hacking and coughing, with a swollen nose. Before I took command of B Company, I was put through a week of school, to learn to recognize mines, punji sticks, and spend some days with A Company to learn the ropes before I would take over my own company.

During those five days with A Company, we got into a fire fight, with snipers shooting at us. Some people were wounded and enemy rounds came near me, but I was not touched.

Wounded in Battle

Then, I took over B Company. I can't remember every time I was shot at or received fire. We got into a situation moving among rice paddies, along a tree-lined canal. You couldn't go across in the open; you'd be shot. I had people walking along both sides of the canal. We started receiving fire. I sent a patrol out, with just three people. They received fire and came running back. One guy, Nash, jumped into the area where I was, and he got shot. I was in a grass-lined pit. He fell and I caught him, and we both fell. I pulled him up and could tell by looking at him that he was dead. He was an RTO. I took the radio off him. The round had gone through the radio and him. The radio had been on, and we lost communication with the company. We started receiving RPG (rocket-propelled grenade) fire and I got wounded in the legs – most pieces in the left leg, and some small pieces in the right leg.

We were receiving fire all the time and we finally got orders to pull back a couple hundred yards, which we did. They wanted us to go back that night, but by that time the tide had come in and the water in the canals was above head level. I got across the canal and another guy, a short Hispanic, followed me. He jumped in and sank. I went in and pulled him out of the canal and got his machine gun and kept the troop from almost drowning. I called back and said we couldn't get in there; we would need a rope bridge. So, they called it off. We spent the night out there and went in the next morning. We got some more wounded and killed. I was medevaced, had surgery to remove the shrapnel, and was not there for the end of the fight. I was hospitalized for a couple of weeks.

Hospital staff would wake up at 0600 to give you shots. We were mortared and going down the slide to a bunker below the hut, I landed on my left leg. The hospital had an area where you could get drinks and food. I wanted a beer, so I got in my wheelchair and navigated over a wooden sidewalk that consisted of 2x4s with about three-inch gaps between each rung. The wheelchair hitting the gaps made a thud noise. A medic on guard heard the thuds and yelled something at the top of his lungs and stuck an

M-16 in my face. I fell over and the medic fell with me. He said, "Where in the hell are you going?" I told him; he put me in the wheelchair and took me to the food and drink place and said, "How long are you going to be here?" I said for about 20 minutes. He said, "Great, don't you do anything, I will come and escort you back to your hut." He did and we had a good laugh. I was released from the hospital and on crutches and went to the MARS radio station to make a call to my wife. During the call I said that I was okay, and that I only had some small wounds in my legs. She exclaimed, "What wound?" My letters to her, written while in the hospital, had not been delivered to her in the U.S.

Other Close Calls

We had made another air assault. (One time we made as many as seven air assaults in one day.) We started receiving fire and I told the troops, "You get your entire body inside your steel pot because that's the only protection you have out there." I saw tracer rounds coming in and one guy, my artillery liaison officer, a Lebanese from Ohio, was shot. The round went past my back and hit him in the shoulder. We found out later we had been receiving friendly fire because the VC did not have tracer rounds. I could have gotten hit but did not.

One time, I felt the rounds going past the hair on top of my head (which was military short!) If I had been a millimeter taller, the rounds would have hit me. We went into a village. Night came on us. We were told to stay there. We began receiving fire and started filling sandbags up with some dirt lying around to make bunkers for protection. I don't remember anyone getting hurt. The next morning, we emptied the sandbags, and the choppers flew us out. I later got a radio call and they wanted to review the fire fight and a captain asked if we used the stuff to fill the sandbags. He was giving me a hard time because he said the dirt was valuable. I said, "Look, you dumb sumbitch, we were taking fire. If you want to come out here and take my place, you can make the decisions next time. Out!" Getting ready to go on air assault at Chu Chi airfield, I saw Captain Mitchell, whom I knew, and we had some conversation. He got on the Chinook to go back to Tay Nin and it went up about 100 ft. and exploded. Everyone was killed.

Safe Even While Sleeping

We were in the patrolling in the jungle and I was totally worn out; I could not walk straight. I went to battalion and asked to be medevaced to Chu Chi to report in sick. I was flown back to the rear. I got to battalion HQ, and went to the mess hall, and asked them to tell the XO that I was going to sleep and then see the doctor. The XO was sitting at the same table that I was, but I was so tired I didn't even see him. I went to the company area and showered and got onto my cot. During the night, Chu Chi received incoming rounds. I slept through it all. I woke up lying on my right side facing the wall. I moved to get up and hit something. A three-foot piece of shrapnel was lodged just above my head in the wood frame of the building. I looked around the building and the only things that hadn't been hit were my XO's stereo and me. I went to see the doc and I thought he said, "Take a day." We got mortared again, but I was okay. I felt better after two nights of rest.

In returning to the field, I boarded a CH-47 Chinook and was preparing to take 17 troops back out to the field with me. While at the airfield, I saw the doc and the battalion commander talking about me. The battalion commander asked what I was doing. I said I was taking troops back to the field. Apparently, they had thought I was shirking. We went back to the field. Battalion would fly out to us some things called PSPs, perforated steel planks. These were planks 12 inches wide by six feet long with holes in them, to make bunkers out of, although originally meant for airfields. We got mortared that night. Seventeen troops were injured and had to be sent back. So, I had a net gain of zero troops. I was told that when the Tet Offensive began, B Company was air assaulted to Saigon and began their fighting at General Westmoreland's headquarters. When I joined the company, we were making air assaults from Saigon to the Cambodia border. We began our second air assaults to Cambodia from Ton Son Nhut airbase. Our rear perimeter was the metal fence of the airport.

7. My Vietnam Service 45

CH-47 Chinook.

During this time, we had been away from Chu Chi for over 60 days without any stop. One time our flank perimeter was a small stream. I let each platoon go swimming to get clean. Naturally, the battalion commander flew over, and I got my butt chewed out. We did, however, go back to Chu Chi for a two day break and rest. I was serving as S-1, head of personnel for the battalion. The new battalion commander wanted the S-1 Shop to go to the field. Totally new idea. We got in a Chinook and put in battalion clerks, and company clerks, about 10 people, and their file cabinets. We went to the field, and we worked out of tents. Every time the battalion moved, we moved. We were in a rubber tree plantation, maybe Michelin. I very seldom have any headaches, but one morning I woke up with a throbbing headache. The S-1 Shop and medic tents were so close that the tent stake ropes were intertwined. I walked to the medical tent to get aspirin. Mortars came in and hit the S-1 tent. Out of the ten staff members, the only two people who walked away were myself and my legal clerk. Nine clerks were hit. A big guy, John Huston, was hit in the jugular vein. The medics couldn't do anything for him. I was the only officer, so I was on the radio trying to get support from dust-offs (helicopters to medevac troops). We loaded the S-1 Shop back into a Chinook and went back to Chu Chi.

I was not having a good relationship with the new battalion commander Chu Chi. I was over at G-1, and I heard a major say he needed a captain who had previously commanded a company in combat. I got the job and arranged for a helicopter to take the newly arrived Captain Lopez out to division in the field to be my replacement. I became a G-2 duty officer. Long range patrol troops were assigned to aid me in planting seismic devices, so we could figure out where the VC were going along roads or trails.

On one patrol, two long-range patrol American troops were killed. We ran out of seismic devices, and I was then assigned to be the G-2 at the forward division Tactical Operations Center located at the Tay Nin RVN MACV Headquarters. I received a MARS call while in the field from my wife that my son Robert was born and was healthy. I was later told that the ham operator was from Arizona and was (Senator) Barry Goldwater.

My Pencil Falls: the Map Gets a Purple Heart

My office consisted of a steel desk and a big map. For any operations in the area, we would post them on the map. I was there one night, after dark, and I was sitting at the desk and I dropped my pencil. When I leaned down to get it, a grenade was thrown into the room. The only thing that protected me was the steel desk. But my map was torn. I created a Purple Heart and pinned it on the map. General Homer Long came in the next day and he was a stickler for detail. He saw the Purple Heart and asked me what it was, and he chewed my ass over it. But when he was leaving Vietnam, he did say, "Thomas, if there's anything I can do for you, call me. I don't say this to everyone."

I was reassigned to Division Headquarters and in 1968 Bob Hope did a Christmas show in Chu Chi and as the night duty officer I didn't attend the show. While the show was being performed, we received an A-1 intel message, the highest and most reliable message for an impending enemy attack. Our instructions were the following: Lock all doors, allow no one into the operations area, launch an Apache helicopter company, fire 100 rounds of artillery at the suspected enemy location. We did as we were instructed, but I selected to fire only 50 rounds. I received a telephone call from the Division G-3 operations officer asking what was going on. I told him my decisions. He approved them. No enemy attack occurred. I don't know if the show continued or not.

In 1969, I heard about Long Binh a lot. When I was leaving, I was processed out of there. I recognized it – in 1965/66, we had been ambushed there. After Vietnam: While a student in the 1969 Infantry Officers Advanced Course I was talking to another student who in 1966 was stationed with the 173rd Airborne Brigade. He said that one time this tall RVN officer was walking around the brigade area talking to officers and troops and even asked the mess sergeant to make him breakfast and later we drove by the RVN location and gave them a case of C-rations. I laughed and I told him that was me.

In 1966, there were no camouflage uniforms. I was wearing my U.S. Army field uniform that showed my white name tag, white officers rank, and yellow U.S.A. patch, and ranger airborne tabs. For that operation, my battalion was attached to the 173rd Airborne Brigade. I had an assignment with the USAF 86th Tactical Fighter Wing in Germany. I was asked by the O-6 Squadron Operations Officer why army personnel in Vietnam did not take cover when it rained? I said "Sir, that is the only time we got cleaned."

At Ton Son Nhut, the Army had a place named Camp Alpha. It consisted of rocky paths, tents to sleep in, and tents for bathing and mess halls. Various USAF airmen and officers would ask me what I thought of Camp Alpha. I told them it was great. They thought it was a pig pen. This was an interesting sign of the differences between the armed services at that time.

8.

One Tough Marine

by 1st Sergeant Donald N. Hamblen,
United States Marine Corps (Ret)

In July 1966, I was promoted to gunnery sergeant and in November I received orders directing me to leave Vietnam and proceed to the Marine Corps Air Station, El Toro, California, for further assignment. Having twice been able to extend my tour of duty with SOG (Studies and Observations) Team Romulus for a total of seventeen months and not having a family to worry about, there was no place that I would rather have been than exactly where I was. To continue as an independent SOG team advisor I needed to get those Stateside orders canceled, and to do that required some outside help.

As an adviser sent to Danang from MACV headquarters in Saigon, I did not come under the administrative or the operational control of any Marine Corps command in I Corps, but I thought that if I could use the Marine Corps chain of command to let my desire to extend be known, I might stand a fair chance of getting my orders canceled. I had learned early on that when you go to a gunfight, you take along a big gun. Major General Herman Nickerson – who had personally helped me to remain on active duty five years earlier, after losing my left leg in a parachuting accident, was the man that I needed to see. After placing several radio calls to the division's sergeant major, a meeting time was arranged for me to speak to the commanding general.

The jeep ride from the SOG compound at My Khe to the division's newly constructed headquarters took less than half an hour. After a brief meeting to personally thank the division sergeant major for his help, I was led into Major General Nickerson's office. The General was pleased to see me again, and after offering me a cup of coffee, he asked me to sit down and tell him the type of work that I engaged in as a SOG team advisor. The General knew a great deal about what I was doing. His familiarity with our missions, our area of operations, and our successes in obtaining intelligence from the prisoners we had snatched from North Vietnam surprised me. He was very interested in my team so I told him about the South Vietnamese Marines with whom I was working fearless men who were loyal to me and to our mission. I explained to the General that although my SOG team members were well trained and highly disciplined, they remained very superstitious: they had even painted eyes on the bows of each of our inflatable rubber boats so that the "spirit of the boat" would always be able to "see the way" into our beach objectives.

The General had commented that although our weapons and equipment had changed a great deal since his last days of combat in Korea commanding the 7th Marine Regiment, the one thing that had remained the same was the degree of suffering and pain that Marines endured in combat. While talking about this, the General never lost his sense of bearing, but his mood changed and his manner became almost paternal. The Marines who were being injured were *his* Marines, he said, with the compassion of a father describing his own children.

"General, I asked the sergeant major if I could speak to you personally, and that is to ask for your help, sir. I've been in Vietnam for seventeen months, sir, and I don't want to go back to Stateside duty. With the First and Third Marine Divisions both in-country, there aren't any infantry or reconnaissance units back in the States that need me. I'm getting along fine – no problems with my leg – and I feel like I'm contributing to what's going on here. All that I'm asking is to be allowed to remain here and continue doing what I'm doing. The people at MACV headquarters don't know me from Adam, sir, so they can't go to bat for me with this request, but you do know me, sir, and that's why I've come here to see you."

Major General Nickerson gave several moments of thought to my request before he spoke. "Gunny Hamblen, it seems to me that every time you and I get together, I learn something new and you get what you come for. The last time we had a talk like this, all you wanted from me was permission to stay in the Corps. Now you want permission to stay in a combat zone with a SOG team. Well, I understand your request and I agree with you. As long as I'm here in Vietnam, you'll be here too. The intelligence information that teams like yours can provide is invaluable. I'm pleased that you came to see me and explained this situation, but now I want to ask a favor of you."

"With the marked increase in the number of Marines fighting in Vietnam, there's also been an increase in the number of casualties. When I go to our field hospitals or to the Navy's hospital ship to visit our wounded men, I sometimes find myself at a loss for words. I don't think that I will ever get accustomed to seeing wounded Marines. Gunny, I will need your help from time to time, and ask that you come with me when I make these hospital visits. Your presence and your example of having overcome injuries would be powerful medicine for these men. It would mean a great deal to me and to those Marines. I'll get word to you the next time that I go over to the hospital."

I thanked Major General Nickerson for his help and I assured him that he could depend on me to help him. I did not realize how soon it would be before the General would call in his marker, nor that I had just accepted the most difficult assignment I've ever had.

The U.S. Navy handled all medical assistance given to Marines in I Corps, and Navy personnel managed all the Marine Amphibious Force medical facilities all the way down to the individual battalion and squadron aid stations. At the lowest level of medical responsibility are the Navy Corpsmen who go with each Marine rifle platoon into combat. As part of the Division's organization, two medical battalions, the 1st and the 3rd, along with the 1st Hospital Company, handle all the Marines' intermediate medical facilities found at Chu Lai, Dong Ha, Phu Bai, and Danang. Commanded by a Navy doctor, each of these medical battalions consisted of Navy personnel who were reinforced by Marines for administrative and security purposes.

For the most serious and more complex medical cases, the Naval Support Activity (NSA) Danang, as it was called, opened its doors in January 1966 with only fifty beds, but by the end of that year the hospital had expanded to over 450 beds. With X-ray and modern laboratory facilities, the hospital had departments and clinic in neurosurgery; urology; eye, ear and nose and throat ailments; dental; and preventive medicine. NSA Danang had a large helicopter landing pad located within several hundred feet of the triage and emergency operating rooms. After the introduction of the medevac helicopter, on average, a wounded Marine could expect to be at one of the emergency medical facilities within half an hour after the emergency evacuation request had been made. Of the 6,400 Marines and sailors of the III MAF (Marine Amphibious Force), who were wounded during 1966, only 214 died of their wounds, a mortality rate of less than four percent. To help in the treatment of Marine wounded, the Navy's newly refitted hospital ship, the *U.S.S. Repose* (AH-16) arrived off the shores of I Corps in March 1966. With 560 beds, the *Repose* had medical facilities that could rival any modern hospital or trauma center in the States. Marine helicopters routinely evacuated casualties directly from the battlefield to the deck of the *Repose*, as many as 98 casualties a day.

I was at the SOG compound at Black Rock the first time that Major General Nickerson's office called and left instructions for me to meet him

8. One Tough Marine

at the entrance of the Naval Support Activity in Danang. The general had scheduled a visit to the hospital after learning that several Marines involved in a company-size operation against the NVA had lost hands or feet due to traumatic amputation from mortar shrapnel or from hidden booby traps. After being briefed by the hospital's chief surgeon on each Marine's name, age, injury, and prognosis, the general, a colonel from his staff, and I were escorted into the intensive care ward to talk to these men.

The first Marine the general spoke to was a young private first class (Pfc.) from the 2nd Battalion, 4th Marine Regiment, who had been in Vietnam less than two months. His right arm had been severed by a piece of shrapnel, and as he lay in his bed with the stump of his right arm elevated by a cotton sling attached to his stainless-steel IV stand, General Nickerson moved in close to him and held the private's left hand, assuring this boy that he was on his way home and that he would get the best medical care humanly possible. He told the private the date he was scheduled to leave Vietnam, and then told him that he was terribly sorry about his injury, but that he was proud of him because it was Marines like him who would help to end this war.

The next Marine the General spoke to was a black staff sergeant who had lost his right leg when a booby trap exploded behind him. Married and the father of two children, the staff sergeant was on his second tour in Vietnam and had less than three months' time remaining in-country when the patrol that he had been leading was ambushed, causing him and his Marines to take cover in an area that was rigged with booby traps. After talking with the staff sergeant, the general introduced me to him, so that I could offer my own words of encouragement.

"Will I be able to walk as good as you, Gunny? I used to play a lot of football with my two boys, and now I don't know what they'll think. The General told me that you can still scuba-dive and jump out of airplanes. Is that true?"

"The General is telling you the truth. I was walking in less than a month after I lost my leg. If you want, I'll show you what you'll look like soon."

I sat down next to the staff sergeant and rolled up my trouser leg, exposing my flesh-colored fiberglass prosthesis. His curiosity aroused, I tried to add some humor to our discussion. "If you like, they can make your leg the same color as mine, but that might confuse your family for a little while."

The wounded staff sergeant's laughter suddenly filled the ward and I could tell by the way it sounded that it was his first laugh since being wounded.

Major General Nickerson's visit lasted no more than an hour, but he spoke quietly to every patient whose bed he passed. I know that it was as difficult for him to express his sympathy to each of those Marines as it was for them to express their thanks to him. After we had left the intensive care ward and walked over to the General's jeep, he said, "Gunny, I will never get used to doing this, but I know that it goes with the territory. I hate this damned war and to see the suffering it has caused my Marines. I'm glad that you came over here today, as it made my job a damned sight easier. At least these men can see firsthand that there's hope after losing a leg or an arm. You've helped them, and me, more than you might imagine. I don't look forward to the next time that we'll have to do this, Gunny, but I'll be counting on your help."

USS *Repose* (AH-16).

During the next few months, I went with Major General Nickerson to the hospital at Danang on several other occasions. And, as the General had predicted, these bedside visits did not get any easier. However, our second visit to the *U.S.S. Repose* was the most difficult trip of all.

8. One Tough Marine

The pilot of a Marine Huey helicopter that had brought us out to the *Repose* had been instructed to return for the General in one hour. As soon as the helicopter had cleared the landing pad, General Nickerson, his aide, and I were taken below decks so the General could pay his respects to the ship's captain and crew, and to visit with those Marines and Corpsmen most seriously wounded. As in the past, I spoke with several Marines who were waiting to be transported to Danang or to the naval hospitals located in Yokosuka, Japan, on the Island of Guam, or to the State-side facility nearest their homes.

I was talking to several wounded Marines when I was informed by one of the ship's crewmen that General Nickerson had to leave the ship unexpectedly. Transportation to my compound at My Khe was arranged by the ship's air officer. While I waited for the arrival of the next inbound helicopter, I was approached by one of the ship's surgeons.

"Gunny Sergeant Hamblen, my name is Dr. Jaslovac, and I was introduced to you during your last visit to the ship with General Nickerson. I have a patient, a Marine sergeant, who has just been brought to the intensive-care compartment from surgery, and I was hoping that you would speak to him. Before you do, I should tell you that he has lost both of his legs, his right arm, and that he has also lost both of his eyes. He was caught up in a Claymore mine ambush, and when it exploded at waist-high level, it ripped him to pieces."

The M-18A1 antipersonnel Claymore mine was one of the most lethal pieces of military hardware used during the Vietnam war. It was particularly effective in executing ambushes along jungle trails. The Claymore was a rectangular fiberglass box with spikes fitted to the base so that it could be anchored into the ground. An ominous instruction – Front Toward Enemy – was embossed on the convex exterior. It held several hundred steel balls set in an explosive bed and was detonated by remote control. Hidden in the undergrowth, some distance away from the lethal zone, a soldier would complete a simple electrical circuit to set off the mine. The Claymore could also be set off by a tripwire hidden along a track. Once detonated, the Claymore sprayed its deadly contents out in a sixty-degree fan-shaped pattern that was lethal to a range of fifty yards.

Believing that I would go with the good doctor to visit his patient, I entered the small, darkened compartment only to discover that I was very much alone with a man who would probably have been better off dead than alive. Two intravenous bottles dripped whole blood and antibiotics into what remained of his body and a respirator pumped oxygen down his throat. And as I stood there next to him, I suddenly felt completely useless knowing that I was now supposed to say something to this young Marine that would cheer him up a little.

I had been told during my own time in the hospital that the very last of a person's senses to go was hearing. Fearing that this poor bastard would hear me cursing my own stupidity in having promised that I would visit with the seriously wounded, I kept my mouth shut and thought about what I could say to him.

He must have felt my presence in the room, because when I moved, he turned his bandaged head in my direction. When he did that, I spoke to him. I told him who I was and that I had come to let him know that he would be okay. My words came quickly and I realized they were meaningless. He and I both knew that he was in very bad shape, and I decided at that moment not to continue to insult his intelligence by telling him that he would improve. He would not be okay, and I think that if he had been able to ask me to kill him, I would have done it. I would not have wished this Marine's misery on another living person.

The sense of pain and frustration at my inability to help this young man turned into a seething anger when I thought the recent newspaper and magazine articles I had read that applauded the efforts of American men who had opted to desert their country and hide across the border in Canada to avoid the draft. I wondered what the difference was between this young Marine and those men who had run away, knowing that the chances of their being selected for the infantry and going into combat were less than one out of ten. I was sure that the young Sergeant's mother must certainly love her son as much as those mothers who had excused their sons' acts of cowardice; that made me sad.

While I stayed in the compartment with that sergeant, I simply held his hand in mine. It was all that I could do, but I hoped that in his drug-induced state of comfort, he would still understand that someone was with him who cared. When a Navy nurse finally came into the compartment to check on the sergeant's vital signs, I wiped the tears from my face and went out onto the flight deck of the U.S.S. Repose to await my flight back to Danang.

First Sergeant Donald N. Hamblen, USMC (ret.), was a Pathfinder platoon sergeant, in 1962. On September 21, 1962, during a routine parachute jump with 1st Force Reconnaissance Company, strong winds drove his parachute off course and into electrical high-tension wires at Camp Pendleton, California. Though he never lost consciousness, doctors were amazed that he had survived. Five days later Hamblen's leg had to be amputated several inches below the knee.

Through sheer determination, Don Hamblen fought to remain on active duty. He passed all the arduous physical tests, including a timed three-mile run with pack, and within eleven months was going to the field, parachuting, and scuba diving with 1st Force Recon Company.

In 1965, SSgt. Hamblen volunteered with three other Marines for service in Vietnam with the secret Studies and Observations Group (SOG). Working out of Danang, Hamblen trained teams of Vietnamese for clandestine missions in both North and South Vietnam. By the time he returned to the United States after serving thirty consecutive months in Vietnam, Hamblen had been wounded twice.

1st Sergeant Donald "Woody" Hamblen, USMC - 1968.

As far as it is known, Don Hamblen was the first Marine to have gone into combat with a prothesis. He is one of the few Americans who can document having fought in North Vietnam, and by his extraordinary example, he serves as an inspiration on hospital visits to badly wounded servicemen in that conflict. Don Hamblen is a true Marine who would not quit and repeatedly proved he had the personal courage, spirit, and self-determination to overcome all obstacles.
He and his wife, Reiko, live in adventurous retirement in Oceanside, CA. His biography, One Tough Marine, was published by Ballantine Books in 1993.

9.

My Tour in Vietnam as an Army Medic
by Paul Scott

On December 28, 1965, I wrote to my father telling him that the 25th Infantry Division, known as the Wolfhounds, had been ordered to Vietnam. The letter is in my album. Enclosed in that letter was a power of attorney, that was required by the Army JAG (Judge Advocate General Corps). On December 31, 1965, I wrote to my father again, enclosing my will. Many years later my mother told me that when Dad received that letter he went into his study and wept. He knew the hazards of a forward aid station with the U.S. Army infantry, probably more than I did at the time.

The Cruise to Vietnam

On January 2, 1966, my battalion boarded the ship and left the docks of Oahu. This was a two-week voyage. Our battalion was on the *USS Gordon*, a WWII troop ship. There were about 4,500 troops on our ship. After days of slow rolling, everyone was seasick. This nausea lasted for about four days. We had to go down to where the bunks were and get the sick GIs up and take them up onto the deck. There was vomit on every level, including the stairs. GI's were slipping and sliding everywhere. The navy boys were giving us a lot of grief for messing up their ship. We crossed over the international dateline, which entitled everyone to a membership in the Royal Domain of the Golden Dragon. We arrived in Vung Tau, South Vietnam after two weeks. We had our weapons with us, and as we approached shore and when the landing craft gate went down, there was a band with pretty Vietnamese girls dispensing leis and welcoming us to Vietnam.

Our battalion was located in a temporary base camp shortly after arrival in Vietnam. Our medical unit was on the grounds of the University of Saigon, which was empty. The rooms were used as barracks for the Army of the Republic of Vietnam (ARVN). This was our staging area before the unit moved to our permanent base camp at Chu Chi. One of the soldiers was stung by a scorpion when he put on his boots without checking them first.

Being a captain, our battalion surgeon was technically the platoon leader and I, being a lieutenant, was the evacuation section leader. During my time in Vietnam, I had four other battalion surgeons: Dr. David Shaw, Dr. Mitchell Abousi, Dr. Williams, and Doc Quie T. Chew, so, essentially, I became the de facto platoon leader as the docs preferred to involve themselves with medical issues and not the day-to-day running of the platoon.

The Medical Service Corps Lieutenant's Routine

In combat, the wounded would be initially treated by a line medic assigned to an infantry platoon. My duties, as the evacuation section leader in that situation, were to further stabilize the wounded, and if necessary, carry them by litter, poncho or over one's shoulder to the battalion aid station. There we'd further stabilize, or if necessary, give an IV of glucose, saline or albumen and then evacuate them by helicopter if available. IV's were seldom given due to time constraints. My other duties when in base camp were to give shots by the hundreds, treat maladies, rash, prickly heat, ring worm fungus (tenia pedis and tenia rubreum) and venereal disease. Gonorrhea was prevalent – called "the clap," and treated with 5 cc's of procaine penicillin in the upper right quadrant of the hind quarters. All GI's were to report to the aid station before a three-day pass or when going to Saigon or R & R to secure prophylactics. But, after a few drinks, they'd forget about them and come to the aid station for treatment.

For general hygiene, directions to the troops were not to wear underwear as it created a warm moist environment for "jock itch." "We had one GI with tinea pedis growing all the way up his back from his feet. Some men could take griseofulvin pills orally which would control it, but some were allergic to the side effects. They were given an antifungal salve. I was one of these. Further duties in the base camp were to inspect the mess halls for cleanliness and the cooks for personal hygiene. Most of the company mess sergeants took my inspections well as I tried to be very fair and respectful. These were career Army NCOs and I was a mere Reserve Army lieutenant. For instance, when weevils got in the flour – it was not a serious concern as cooking the bread would kill them. They looked like caraway seeds, were harmless and the soldiers were quite used to them.

My additional duties also included inspecting the latrines. The latrine was a small building with a long shelf structure with toilet seats and a 55-gallon oil drum cut in half underneath. Access to the half-drum was in the back at ground level. Gasoline and diesel fuel would be mixed well with the contents and lit with a match and stirred until it all turned to charcoal. This would be taken to a central location and discarded. The aid station medics treated more than one soldier for flash burns after lighting these waste cans.

The Tunnels of Chu Chi

Astonishingly, whoever decided that the 25th Division would be at Chu Chi did not know of the VC/NVA tunnels found there. Apparently, ever since WWII the Viet Minh, in fighting the French, had dug tunnels from Cambodia all the way to Chu Chi, until the French were finally defeated at Dien Bien Phu, in 1954.

After we set up our base camp there, the Viet Cong, using these tunnels, would come out of their spider holes and shoot at us day and night. One of my medics, Spec 4 Stannard, took a bullet through both femurs. That was very unnerving. Sgt. Barker would stay outside with his shot gun waiting for VC to pop up out of the holes, but he could never get a bead on one. It is unbelievable that Army Intelligence did not know of these tunnels before we arrived.

The Vietnamese Chicken Story

2nd Lt. Paul Scott.

After arrival in Vietnam, we had eaten "C" rations (combat rations) for the last month and were very tired of them. Even the rice, steamed in a pot that Sgt. Bernabe Cenal had shipped over with the medical supplies, was old. First Sgt. Cenal was the medical platoon sergeant. One day a fellow medic, Pete Rios, came excitedly back to the unit, telling me that there were chickens running loose in one certain area nearby. So, we got in my jeep and drove over to where several chickens were running around. I had taken Sgt. Barker's shotgun along with a few shells and I shot two chickens as they ran across the field, and my driver, named Rios, ran over to get them. Then, I heard from behind me in a huge, loud voice, "Lieutenant." I thought to myself "Oh, damn, I've done it now." I turned around and I saw a colonel storming up to me, as angry as he could be. He had thought the Viet Cong had attacked. He yelled, "Lieutenant, what are you doing?" After saluting at attention, I responded, "Foraging for my platoon, sir." How could he argue with that? He sputtered a few words and what I remember exactly is "Lieutenant, my advice to you is to clear your weapon, get in your vehicle and return to your unit." I responded, "Yes, sir." When I got back to the platoon, Rios had a great time telling the rest of the platoon how the lieutenant got his butt chewed by the colonel. I plucked the chickens and cleaned them. That night the medics had roast chicken with rice for dinner while the grunts had C's'

About a month and a half later, the officers had a "command performance" (required attendance) at our brigade headquarters. Before the meeting there were a few cocktails. We were in a big tent, and I saw this same colonel over in the corner. I turned around quickly, but unfortunately he had seen me. I thought to myself, "Oh no, he's walking my way." I turned around to face him and he had a stern look on his face. He said, "Lieutenant, did your platoon enjoy the chicken?" I said, "Yes, sir, they did." He turned around as he said, "Carry on." But I could detect a small smile at the corner of his mouth as he walked away. I'm sure he told lots of his cohorts about this stupid second lieutenant shooting up the base camp as he shot chickens for his platoon.

The aid station in our new base camp at Chu Chi was a tent. Next to us was an 8" artillery piece which fired all night long to keep the enemy at bay. The firing was so loud it would slam your ears. I suspect my tinnitus began then: constant loud ringing like a million cicadas buzzing at the same time. Later we had wooden frames with a tent over it for our hooches and the aid station.

Medcap Operations

We went to numerous villages over the many months, often with only the PF (popular forces) black pajamaed and blue arm-banded forces as security. Either Sgt. Muc or Sgt. Hue, ARVN interpreters, would be with us. I can hear Sgt. Muc saying, after talking with a villager, "She says she has a headache," pronouncing "headache" with a "ch" rather than a "k" sound. During Dr. Winningham's tour, we came across a village which had a case of smallpox in it. The villagers had separated her from the rest of the people. The Doc diagnosed it at once and notified the chain of command and to the 12th Evacuation Hospital. The hospital arranged to have the serum shipped out to us. We inoculated every villager against smallpox and it left us with a good feeling.

During these MEDCAP operations, we would dispense the various drugs to treat the illnesses and used lots of aspirin and soap. I recall one particular instance in which a young boy had a festering sore on his leg just below the knee. The village witchdoctor had packed it with water buffalo dung as his method of treatment. We, of course, cleaned it out, scrubbed it with surgical soap, applied bacitracin and a bandage. We also gave him penicillin pills to take. One week later, when we returned to the same village, the same villager was in line to be treated. When we examined him, we discovered that the witchdoctor had removed our bandage and again packed it with dung. It was infected again and festering. We, again, performed our treatment and we did not return to that village for quite a few weeks, and I never saw that young boy again. I often wondered what happened to him. He may have lost his leg or died.

More Medical Service Corps Duties

Our duties in the headquarters medical platoon/aid station were relatively safe compared to those of the squad, platoon, and company soldier. That soldier was always out front in potential contact with the enemy. The platoon medics usually did such a fine job, all we often had to do was load the wounded onto the chopper. The headquarters medics were usually in the middle feeling fairly protected by the infantry from personal contact with the VC or NV (North Vietnamese Army). There was little room in the jungle to set up a tent, as we were highly mobile and took a large pack with medical supplies as well as a small aid bag for each medic. I carried an M-16, a Colt .45 pistol, a hand grenade, a cartridge pouch, and my aid bag. My aid bag came in handy to use as a pillow when sleeping on the ground at night. Some medics were conscientious objectors (CO's') and they did not carry a weapon, but they were very good medics.

Mines and booby traps were always a problem. One day in early spring 1966, we were on a battalion operation and found ourselves in the middle of a mine field. For some reason, the engineers had not checked it. We looked for newly disturbed ground where a mine could be buried. A mine went off about ten feet from me taking a soldier down. I ran over to him and found his foot blown off at the base of his lower leg – boot with it. I bandaged the stump quickly as there was not a lot of blood. I then retrieved his boot with his foot still in it, sock, and all. He was now on a stretcher. So, I handed his boot to him and told him to hang on to it – the docs may be able to reattach it. I doubt if that occurred. But I always wondered whatever happened to him as he boarded a dust off medical helicopter.

We routinely treated bullet wounds and shrapnel wounds from mortars and grenades. The headquarters medics set up the aid station tent only about a third of the time as we were usually on the move. We'd sometimes be walking through a semi-wooded area with the tankers and often they would offer us a ride. I always refused these offers. I had seen guys wounded in the legs if they were near the sides of the tank. I always walked a safe distance from them since they would blow up all the mines and booby traps nearby.

On March 18, 1966, we were in the field and Pfc. James Williams' remains were brought to me. I was told that he'd been hit by a Claymore mine. There were only some pieces of bone, hair, teeth, and his dog tag left of him. I carried him in an empty sand bag tied to my belt for several days. I gave it to a helicopter pilot to take to Graves Registration in Saigon.

During another mortar attack at about 0200 hours, we were in the rice paddies. I was hugging the ground sucking water and a round exploded about four feet from me. It hit just on the other side of the paddy berm, protecting me but hitting my medic, Spec. Clevester Davis, in his gut. I treated him on site with a compression bandage and the next day I dug up the tail fin of that mortar round. I have it as a souvenir today on my office desk. It reminds me that no matter how difficult a day may be, at one time they were much worse.

On April 20, 1966, we suffered another heavy mortar attack. We were in the field and again in rice paddies. It had been raining heavily and Doc Winningham was treating the wounded in an APC (Armored Personnel Carrier) soldier. I was running around tending to the wounded when I heard another man call "medic" and ran over to two wounded soldiers, SSG. Grover Taylor and Sgt. Roy Watts, both in the same foxhole. It was very dark, but I could tell that they'd taken a direct hit and their legs were blown off from their torsos down. They kept begging me to help them. I could only lie and assure them that I would take care of them and that they would be alright. There was so much mud and blood that I could not get the bleeding stopped to bandage them as their life drained away. I'll picture that night in my mind forever as though it were yesterday.

At about this same time the battalion was out on another operation. Our battalion surgeon was not with us for some reason. I was the only medical officer there. Someone yelled "snake" after a soldier had collapsed in the heat. I ran over and asked where the snake was. No one knew or had actually seen one. I examined the collapsed soldier and he had no fang marks to determine if it were a poisonous or a non-poisonous snake. I concluded it was heatstroke, not a snake that got him and I was able to get him hydrated and cooled down. After a while he was okay.

At the aid station in base camp, we had a pet dog we named Charlie, of course. Charlie was the nickname of the VC. We also had a pet Mynah bird and we'd let him out of his bird cage and he'd fly to the ground. We'd walk with him in front of us grabbing insects as we'd kick them up. After each "catch" he'd look up at us to kick some more of them so he could catch more to eat.

One midsummer morning the battalion was preparing to go out on an operation. One by one the men of Headquarters Company (HHC) developed severe gut pain. They were lying all around the grounds between the HHC mess hall and the aid station, writhing in pain – throwing up and with bloody diarrhea. The operation continued by helicopter without these HHC men. But one by one it hit more men who were in the field. After three days in the field, I succumbed and had to have myself evacuated by helicopter. Again, I was admitted to the 12th Evac and placed on IV fluids. We later determined it was the shigella bacteria causing shigellosis from spoiled potato salad in the headquarters mess hall. Tetracycline was the treatment we prescribed.

Crossing the River

Most of the time we were out on operations about 25 out of every 30 days. I recall one during the summer in which I was in a long line of soldiers crossing the Saigon River. I had my aid bag and rifle over my head, while walking through the muddy river about to step over my head and waiting for the VC to open up on us. I thought, looking in front of me and behind me, "This is the real deal, how did I get here? What was I thinking when I turned down a desk job?" About two months before, after having received good OER (Officer Efficiency Reports) that were sent up to the brigade headquarters, I was offered a desk job. This would be to move to brigade headquarters and be the personal assistant to Major Otterstedt. Being comfortable where I was, and not wanting to leave my platoon and knowing that my men did not have the same opportunity, I refused the offer. There were also times thereafter when things got really tough that I asked myself, "What was I thinking?"

1st Lt. Paul Scott.

Tank Rescue

In those days, I could carry a man twice my size over my shoulder. I believe it was in July, and we were on an operation in the field. The aid station received a call over the radio that a tank had been blown up in the middle of a mine field. They asked for medics to go by chopper to retrieve the injured men. Staff Sgt. Bernabe Cenal and I grabbed our aid bags, jumped on the chopper, and we flew out to where the tank was disabled. The pilot set us down about seventy yards away in the adjacent field because he did not want to blow any other mines. We ran across the field and crossed an extremely wet area. Bernie sank up to his hips in it. (I grew up by the water and lived next to a marsh, so I knew how to walk through marshes without sinking). I pulled him out and we went on our way. We ran over to the tank, climbed up on it and with some effort pulled two men up out of it. One was unconscious and the other was conscious. Both had blood coming out of their ears from the explosion. He and I each carried a man over our shoulder to another field where the chopper had moved and was waiting. We put them on the chopper.

While in the air, I took an airway and placed it down the throat of the one who was unconscious and began to breathe for him. From the running, the carrying and breathing for him, I became dizzy and began to fall to my left out of the chopper. Ever alert, Bernie grabbed me and pulled me back in, saving my life. He had been giving life-saving treatment to his patient. He then tried to continue to breathe through the airway for my soldier. About that time, we landed at the MUST unit (Medical Unit Self-Contained Transportable). The medics there took them from the chopper. We often wondered how those two men fared. We never knew, as we headed back to our unit.

On August 29, 1966, we were in an operation in the jungle. B Company took some casualties. Capt. Bob Garrett was hit in the leg by a Chi COMM (Chinese Communist) grenade, Sgt. Alameda the same. Lt. Carter Ashcraft had a gut wound when he came into the aid station. I cleaned it up and put a compression bandage on it and then he climbed on the same helicopter with the others. He was taken to the 7th Surgical Hospital for treatment.

On another occasion in the fall, the battalion surgeon and I were in our aid station with litters on stands. We had a wounded soldier who had blood all over his upper extremities. We cut off his fatigue shirt, and he was fading away fast. He actually had a "sucking chest wound" but we couldn't see it. The bullet had come in through his upper right arm just below his shoulder and out underneath his armpit and pierced his chest. His lungs had collapsed before we could save him. I always felt particularly bad about that one. Maybe he could have been saved had we been able to diagnose it quicker. It was dark, we were on light discipline and we only had small lights in the aid station with the sides down. Another one of life's regrets – what if's . . .

Sniper

I believe it was in October that the battalion was in a blocking position on a larger operation. We had set up an aid station tent about thirty yards from the woods. Nothing much was happening and I was sitting in a camp chair beside the entrance to the tent. A soldier approached me and was about five paces away when he said "Lieutenant Scott . . . " just to get my attention. Just seconds later, he was knocked hard to the ground. The other soldiers nearby knew right away what had happened. They ran into the woods and came back with a dead Viet Cong sniper. He had shot at me, an officer. Just then the soldier who wished to speak with me stepped between me and the bullet. He was struck in the right shoulder from behind. The sniper was likely aiming for my chest. Now is that luck or what? The soldier who took my bullet was treated and survived. I expect it took him out of commission as an infantryman and may have earned him a trip back to the states. Had I been hit or KIA'd, I could see the headline in the newspaper back home: "L. Scott shot while sitting on his butt!"

The Battle of Attleboro

This operation began as part of the 196 Light Infantry Brigade probing for the enemy near Tay Ninh. The operation was named after the town of Attleboro, Mass. The 196th was organized at Fort Devens, Massachusetts and well to the west of Attleboro. Upon making contact, the Wolfhounds joined them. Elements of the 1st Infantry Division, 173rd Airborne Brigade and several ARVN units would also be engaged. It was the largest U.S. operation of the war to that date.

On November 3, Charlie Company of the First Battalion of the 27th Infantry Regiment was ambushed in the jungles near the Village of Dau Tieng. They had run into heavily reinforced Viet Cong and North Vietnamese Army (NVA) regulars. There were concrete bunkers well in place and Charlie Company sustained severe casualties. Its captain, Fred Henderson, a West Point graduate, his First Sergeant, Samuel K. Solomon, whose nickname was Mongoose, and one of his platoon leaders, Lt. Clyde Perkins, were killed along with others. After Fred was killed, another West Pointer, Lt. Norm Gill, took command of the company while still under fire. Sgt. Solomon was pure Hawaiian and said to be descended from royalty. Dick Siebel, Henderson's RTO, was so saddened by Solomon's death that he, years later, had a medallion made with Solomon's image on it. He made a gift of one to me.

On Nov. 4, the rest of the regiment, including the medical platoon and battalion surgeon, Dr. Quie T. Chew, from Chinatown, New York, were air lifted in by helicopter. The medical platoon manned the forward aid station for the regiment. Dr. Chew was always concerned that if he were to be captured he would be tortured because he was Chinese. There were 11 rifle companies in this battle from the units mentioned above. Our medical platoon was the only forward aid station servicing the entire battle. Of the U.S. troops, there were 155 killed and 494 wounded. The enemy sustained 2,130 killed and 44 were taken as POWs.

As we would be on the move, I had chosen not to take an aid tent and to carry as many medical supplies as we could on our backs. I had directed Sgt. Cenal to remain in the base camp at Chu Chi in order to keep us well supplied. He knew people with the Medical Battalion and the 12th Evacuation Hospital and how to beg, borrow or steal whatever we might need. He was not happy that I had asked him to stay behind as he felt his place was with the aid station in the field. However, he knew the supplies needed and how to get them better than anyone else and we went through many supplies in that battle.

As we walked into the jungle, the battalion began taking automatic weapons and small arms fire coming from bunkers and snipers hidden in the trees. The rifle platoons returned fire. I had walked out ahead of the rest of the aid station medics and treated the wounded in place. Although difficult under these circumstances, I was able to give an IV to a soldier who was wounded severely and going into shock. With the bleeding stopped and with the IV flowing, I could see his color coming back. Later that day, I and the other wounded made it back through the jungle to the rest of the aid station medics. The medics there had also stayed in place once the firing started. We set up no tent, just a spot in the jungle next to an open space for eventual helicopter dust-off to evacuate the wounded. Over the next two days, I and several medics went back and forth between what had been set up as the front line and the dust-off. We used litters to carry the wounded, then ponchos, then carried them over our shoulders as we ran out of the litters. We loaded the helicopters with so many wounded that the choppers had difficulty getting off the ground. Several times I had to throw reporters off these medevac helicopters. They had come to get their photographs and stories and then wanted to hop on the choppers to get out of the battle space. They were taking up space for the wounded but they didn't care.

On one of my trips between the front and the dust-off, I passed by the TOC (Tactical Operations Center). The battalion commander, Major Meloy, motioned me to the ground beside him. Since wave after wave of the enemy kept hitting our lines, he was concerned about the possibility of the battalion being overrun. Ammunition was becoming critical. He told me to put the Doc Chew on the next helicopter and get him to safety. I ran back to the aid station and told the Doc that the major said he was to leave. I then put him on a helicopter. After he was on the chopper he asked me if I was going to join him. I responded "No, my place is here. This is about you." He then got off the helicopter and said he was staying. I ran back to the major, and I told him of the Doc's refusal to leave. He muttered something, but I do not recall what it was. He had much on his mind and had to get back to his radio. He had eleven rifle companies under his command at that point and had been wounded by a mortar round. There was also an unexploded 60 mm mortar round lying on the ground about 6 feet from the Major, marked by toilet paper.

The enemy attacked the battalion lines, wave after wave. Under huge stress, our guys held the line over and over. Their stamina was heroic. A distinct recollection of mine is the loudness of the bombs dropped by our jets. Just a split second before the sound of the explosion I'd hear the crack of metal, then the explosion. It was so loud your head felt as though it would explode. And these were "friendlies." The heavy shrapnel would hit the trees around us, but they were again "friendly." I believe that my tinnitus today is related to these close explosions.

Knowing the battalion commander was concerned about the Doc, I radioed him during a lull in the fighting and assured him that the doctor was okay. As it was not the custom for a lieutenant to talk to the battalion commander, he did not recognize my call sign: Mustang 1-6. Usually, the platoon leader goes through the company commander, but the company commander for headquarters company was not present at this battle. The immediate chain of command for the medical platoon was directly with the battalion commander. This was a first as to date, we had not been in this large a battle. So, I had to identify myself. I also assured the Major that the medics had the wounded under control.

By the last day of Attleboro, I had given all of my water and C-rations to the wounded. I spied the olive drab rim of a C-ration can in the mud. Being thirsty and hungry, I looked around to see if anyone else had seen it. I then slowly crawled over to it and picked it up. It was an unopened can of peaches. I took my P-38 on the chain with my dog tags and opened it. I inhaled it – peaches, juice, and all. To this day, peaches have a special place in my heart.

The wounds during Attleboro were horrific. One I recall was of a soldier whose eyeball had been blown out of its socket by an enemy grenade. His eye was hanging by tubular tissue out of his head. All I could do was gently put it back into its socket and put an ace wrap around his entire head. Since he was now completely blind, I assigned a walking wounded to hold him by the arm as we put him on the chopper. He was also to continue to help him until arrival at the hospital. Another GI had taken a bullet into his helmet. His helmet had stopped the bullet but it and the helmet were stuck into his skull. There was little blood. So, I again assigned a "buddy" to watch out for him on the chopper until arrival at the hospital. One of my medics assigned to "C" Company, was Specialist 4 Albert Gosling. He suffered a severe wound to his arm which had to be amputated. He later visited me in Fredericksburg as he adapted to his prosthetics.

There is a tape recording of a crucial segment of the Battle of Attleboro. How did this tape come about? One of the reporters who crawled toward the front lines stopped at the TOC where Major Meloy was located. This was the place in the jungle where the major was in touch with all of his companies by radio. From there he directed the battle. The reporter stuck a tape recorder on the back of his radio, and it recorded several hours of the battle. A week or so later, when the battle was over and the regiment was back in base camp, the reporter came into the major's hooch and retrieved the recorder from the back of the radio. All of this was unknown to Major Meloy until this time. Many years later, Major Meloy, as a retired two-star general, mailed a copy to his former Wolfhound officers who were involved in Attleboro.

To wind down the battle, Major Meloy had the most forward rifle company pull back as artillery rounds pummeled the area, and the next one would pull back, and the next one would pull back. As we loaded helicopters leaving the jungle, I looked back and I could see broken and discarded equipment and gear strewn around, bandages, broken trees. This reminded me of the old photos of the aftermath of the 1860s Civil War battles, being a student of that war.

On or about November 12, General Westmoreland came to Tay Ninh. He gave us a pep talk; then we all took showers and had a steak dinner. He sent us back in to chase the NVA north through the jungles. As usual, we set up no tent. I had gathered soft leaves to sleep on and was using my aid bag as a pillow. At about 1100 hours I was awakened by Sgt. Major Jack Eakins. He had crawled through the jungle from Major Meloy's TOC. He said, "Lieutenant, the Major wants you. Bring your aid bag." So, I crawled back through the jungle following the Sgt. Major and found Major Meloy in pain as his wounds had begun to fester. He said, "Scotty, take this shrapnel out of my arm." He had been wounded in the right elbow, shoulder and behind his left knee. The elbow wound had been bandaged by his RTO (radio telephone operator) shortly after he received it. It was from a 60-mm mortar round fired by the enemy back on the 4th of November. Because of light discipline the sergeant major held a poncho and flashlight over the two of us. I took the probe out of my aid bag and probed into his arm next to his elbow until I heard the clinking sound of metal. I reached in with long forceps and pulled out a small piece of metal. I probed some more and there was nothing else. I am sure it was quite painful for him to endure as it was well inflamed and there was no anesthetic. The Sgt. Major said, "Let me see it." I had it in my hand and I dropped it into his hand. It bounced off his hand and fell to the jungle floor. We looked for it but couldn't find it. The Major was not too happy about that. Anyway, I packed the wound with bacitracin and bandaged it up. Then I crawled back to my spot in the jungle and went back to sleep.

The next few days we were in heavy jungle in the semi-swamp Prek Klok area. We were in very dense jungle with lots of standing water. The jungle floor was crawling with leeches, gazillions of leeches, blood-sucking leeches. The leeches would also fall out of the trees on us, which gave us concern when we slept at night on the ground. Pulling them off was difficult so we used cigarettes. When touched with a lit one, the leach would withdraw and drop off. There was some concern about them crawling into our ears and noses at night, which did not happen.

Worse than Leech City, evidence of the VC clearing booby traps was discovered by Capt. Bob Garrett's "B" Company patrols. Major Meloy obtained Colonel Tarpley's permission for a daytime move 2500 meters northwest. We all griped about it at the time. Ten years later Meloy received confirmation through captured VC documents that a major attack was planned for the night of November 13. It would have been a blood bath. That daytime movie had saved us all.

On November 23, in the jungle after Attleboro we did have an aid tent sent up. That night, there was a heavy mortar attack. The darkness was lit up like daylight from all the explosions. Mortar rounds were even hitting the branches and trunks of the huge jungle trees. The medics had constructed a bunker of sandbags about 10 meters from the aid station. At the beginning of the attack, we all ran toward the bunker. We had earlier treated an injured soldier and he was lying on a litter about five meters from the aid tent. He had a leg wound and could not walk. He was struggling to get up so I stopped and put my left arm around his waist with his right arm around my right shoulder. We were making our way toward the bunker when a mortar round slammed down immediately in front of us. Had it been a few inches closer, it would have physically hit us. Waiting for it to explode, we stood there motionless. Miraculously, no explosion occurred as it was a dud. With my two good legs and his one good leg, we hobbled to our bunker for protection.

That night, one poor soldier, Pvt James N. Cagley of "B" Company, had been too close to the entrance of his platoon bunker. He took a direct shrapnel hit to the back of his head. He was brought to the aid station on a stretcher. The stretcher was placed on "logs" to create an operating table. I placed my helmet underneath the head of the stretcher so that I could work on him. Blood was coming out of his head so much Doc Chew and I had difficulty getting it stopped. He died on the table. There was nothing further we could do. So, I put my helmet back on. It was full of his blood. It drained all down my head and fatigues.

So ended the Battle of Attleboro for the Wolfhound medics.

What always puzzled me was why did he have me, a Lieutenant, remove the shrapnel from his arm deep in the jungle a week after he had received his wound. He had been to Saigon; he had briefed generals and had plenty of opportunity to have the battalion surgeon, Dr. Chew, or any other physician remove the shrapnel from his arm. For years it was a mystery to me. It was not until about 55 years later that I learned the answer. Retired Col. Arno Ponder and I had seen each other at a Wolfhound Reunion and been in touch on other matters. So, I took the occasion to ask Colonel Ponder who had been the XO (executive officer) of the battalion. Why would the Major not have had a physician remove that shrapnel early after the battle? Col. Ponder said, "I know, because he knew any of the medical officers who were captains or above could put him on light duty and remove him temporarily from command. He knew he had to continue the battle chasing the VC and NVA north through the jungles after Attleboro. So, he purposely did not have Dr. Chew, the battalion surgeon, come on the follow-up operation. His intent was to have you as the sole medical officer of the battalion in the field during that time. He had confidence in you and knew you could do the job. That's why he had you do it and no one else. And he knew you as just a lieutenant could not put him on light duty and out of command." The mystery was solved after all these years.

Coming Home, Christmas - 1966

I had been in country with the unit since January and my replacement had been assigned. But on December 15th, Major Guy S. Meloy, III, the Battalion Commander, called me into headquarters and gave me the bad news that my replacement had been directed to another duty station to replace a wounded MSC officer. So, I went to my hooch and wrote to my parents that I would not be home for Christmas again this year.

That, however, changed on December 23rd. I was on an operation in the field with the unit when Major Meloy personally flew out in his helicopter and told me to get my gear and that I was going home. He then flew me back to base camp where I bid the rest of my men goodbye. Apparently, a Lt. Allen Hinman from Brigade Headquarters had volunteered to replace me so that I could go home. Many years later at a Wolfhound Reunion, Allen reminded me of our meeting in my aid station as I bid my platoon goodbye. I have no recollection of it. He was later wounded in the shoulder and evacuated first to Germany then to the States. He later became an Episcopal Priest.

Meloy had also arranged a helicopter flight for me to Ton Son Nhut Air Force Base near Saigon. There I began the military processing to leave country. Soon after, I developed a sudden high fever and felt extremely ill. This risked my being able to leave Vietnam, so I kept it to myself. One of my classmates at the Medical Field Service School, Alex McCauley, had left his .45 pistol at my aid station during a visit. So, with my fever rising, I took a lambretta across town to his office and delivered it to him. After that during the required medical physical before leaving country, I didn't place the thermometer under my tongue. That way it would not register a temperature. After standing in processing lines, I boarded a civilian 747 airplane contracted by the military along with many other soldiers who were also leaving Vietnam. Dorsey Weeks, tunnel rat, was also on that flight. The pilot took off under lights-off discipline to reduce the risk of being hit by enemy fire. As the plane took off and gained altitude, I saw from the window firefights and tracer bullets on the ground below. I felt empathy for the boys on the ground still in the fight, yet I was leaving. When the plane was out of range and over the South China Sea, the pilot announced, "Boys, you're going home," and turned on the cabin lights. All let out tremendous cheers. By this time, my fever was raging and it continued throughout the long flight. As was the custom in those days, smoking was allowed and most lit up. The smoke made my fever almost unbearable. But, I was going home.

We reached Okinawa and had a short layover. During the layover I walked around the tarmac. The sergeant whom I had helped to the bunker when the dud round hit was there also. After recognizing me, he walked over, shook my hand, and thanked me and the medics for all we had done. Then began the next leg of my journey to California. Little did I know there would be more obstacles ahead before being back in Virginia. After processing through Oakland Air Force Base, I caught a cab to the civilian airport. On seeing soldiers hitchhiking as we left Oakland, I paid the $20 fare for the whole cab and had the driver pile in as many soldiers as he could and give them a ride. With my fever pitched, I booked a hotel room before my flight east the next day. I awoke soaking wet the next morning to find my fever had broken sometime in the night. I felt drained but much better. I showered, put on my uniform, had a quick breakfast, and headed to the airport. Having made it this far and having made up a day traveling east, I decided not to call my family and to surprise them upon my arrival.

During the flight to Washington, DC, on December 23rd, the pilot said that the entire east coast was gripped by a blizzard. It was dark when I stepped off the plane around 6:00 pm, into the worst snow storm I'd seen in a long time. I was able to catch a cab to the Greyhound Bus Station and bought the last seat on the last bus going south that night. As I was sitting in the aisle seat on the first row, the driver opened the doors and allowed an elderly woman to get on. She looked down the aisle for a vacant seat but there was none. I offered her my seat and she accepted. The only remaining place to sit on the bus at that point was on the steps next to the doors. My blood was thin from living a year and a half in tropical climates. The only coat I had on was my cotton field jacket, which I wore over my regulation tropical worsted short sleeved shirt. No tee shirt underneath. I had on Army issue low top shoes and thin socks. During the entire slow two- hour ride, the doors continually flapped open letting ice and snow spit through the gaps onto me. I shivered the whole way.

After arriving at the Fredericksburg Greyhound Bus Station, it took me a while to find a cab with chains willing to carry me in the storm. The cab drove me a couple of miles west on Plank Road to Scotswood, my parent's home, where I expected my family would be gathered for the holiday. I finally allowed myself to be excited about actually being home. I learned later that my grandfather, Paul Tucker, had gone into the garage to get an orange when he saw a cab coming up the drive. He told Mom, "They must be lost." After the cab driver dropped me off at the end of the driveway with my duffel bag on my shoulder, I walked through the snow to the back door and rang the doorbell. I then heard my grandmother Tucker say, "There's a stranger at the door, Babe, but don't open it!" But mom turned the light on and looked out. She immediately recognized that it was me and opened the door. I was standing at the door grinning from ear to ear. Mom shrieked "Paul's home!" for all to hear as I walked through the door and she threw her arms around me. The rest of the family rushed from the living room to the family room to see for themselves. Every close member of my family, mom, dad, granddad, grandma, brother, sister-in-law, and my sister, crowded in and we had hugs all around. Mom stayed close to me the whole evening, not letting me out of her sight. There was so much excitement no photographs were taken.

Dad offered to get me anything I wanted. He was surprised when I told him I wanted a vanilla milkshake, assuming they had the ingredients. I had warmed up from all the excitement. Even though they didn't, Dad insisted on driving his car (which had chains) to Earl's Food Market in the snow for the necessary ingredients. That was the grandest reunion and the best Christmas anyone could ever imagine.

Paul Scott returned to Virgina after his service in Vietnam. He attended law school and became a prominent lawyer in Fredericksburg, Virginia. After retiring, he and his wife, Dee, enjoy a comfortable life at their home on the Potomac River.

10.

1st Force Reconnaissance Company; RVN 1967-1968 and 1970-1971

by Rick "Rabbi" Rabenold

Corporal Rick "Rabbi" Rabenold, USMC – 1967.

    The helicopter gunships buzzed the landing zone just west of the top of Hill 405 without taking any fire so our pilot swooped down into the landing zone which turned out to be a swamp. Pistorino and I jumped off of the chopper's tail gate and were promptly up to our waste in mucky swamp water and mud. Pistorino could hardly move as he headed toward the wood line. I couldn't move a lick carrying eighty odd pounds of gear and ordnance upon my skinny frame. Then, as luck would have it, the enemy opened up on us from the high ground to our east. Christ, I was a sitting duck. I then felt a tug on my ranger strap. Finley Johnson had jumped into the swamp, recognized my dilemma, and grabbed a hold of me. He pulled me through the swamp by my ranger strap, until I could move on my own, moving like a road grader all while we were taking fire. Finley was also carrying the twenty plus pound PRC-25 radio. The rest of our team entered the swamp and made it to the wood line without issue.

Amazingly no one was hit. It seemed to be only one or two enemy soldiers and their firing continued at us once we were in the woods. The insert bird was long gone. I was wondering if the enemy was possibly cross-eyed when Finley, whose big body was sticking out on both sides of a three-inch diameter tree, jumped up dancing impervious to the bad guys still firing. He was slapping and brushing himself off. What the hell was his problem? Ants!!! His tree was covered with large black ants that naturally now included Finley in their environment. I looked toward Pistorino, smiled, and waved goodbye to Finley, and signaled to move out as the helicopter gunships deterred the Viet Cong from continuous firing. I was glad that I wasn't that poor Viet Cong who not only could not hit anyone but was now subject to rocket and machine gun fire from the Cobra gunships. Noise discipline was not a concern as we hustled during the gunship's fire power display. I do believe our arrival ruined the bad guys' day.

Two peaceful days later, on Pistorino's nineteenth birthday, we found a heavily traveled trail. We set up a hasty ambush for an hour and then moved into an observation point to see the well-used trail. Over the next three hours we had five sightings totaling nineteen Viet Cong. The artillery fire missions we called in resulted in a secondary explosion but we couldn't see any positive KIA results. We were extracted a day later without incident.

As we were finishing telling our first platoon teammates, Team Countersign, teammates McNemar, Hawk Hauxhurst, and Pee Wee Palmer, about that patrol into the Que Son Mountains, twenty-five miles southwest of us, Sgt Bowser entered our hootch, called 'the Ghetto,' and told us that we, Team Dogma, was going out the next day; the 18th of June.

Man, 1967 was flying by. The patrol briefing was at 1300 hours. Well, that put a crimp on our hanging out with our buddies, we only got to see them a couple days at a time. 2nd Lt Williamson, a "Mustang" officer who had come up through the ranks, informed us that we are going into the Elephant Valley and the Garden of Eden area northwest of Danang looking

10. 1st Force Reconnaissance Company; RVN 1967-1968 and 1970-1971

for enemy staging areas, base camps, and enemy movement along the Song Cu De River and into the mountains.

Our briefing completed, we scrambled around getting cases of C-rations, ordnance, and communications shackle sheets and whiz wheels. We were taking five Dogma team members and a radioman from the communications group with us. Pistorino was carrying the Stoner light machine gun and running point, I was the backup point and taking my M-16 instead of M-14. Our team leader, Lieutenant Williamson was walking third, Finley Johnson is our primary radio operator, and Bob Swatzell was secondary radio, and Sgt Bowser was the assistant team leader and Tail-End-Charlie. We practiced our immediate action drills and hand signals ensuring Swatzell was up to speed, test fired our weapons, then we finished packing for morning insert.

We took off from LZ (Landing Zone) Finch at Camp Reasoner for the short ten-mile flight about five clicks (kilometers), northeast of the Dong Den radio relay site. Our landing zone was a good one. The CH-46 landing spot was up a river valley and a click and a half from the Song Cu De. The recon team up on Dong Den could see our choppers as we headed into the valley led by the two alert Cobra gunships scanning the area. We spiraled into the landing zone, once again touching down in a swamp. This time it was only a foot deep allowing easy movement to the nearest tree line.

We slowly moved northeast, traversing the difficult lower hundred meters of the extremely steep mountain range to our north, as the heat of the day intensified. Pistorino was stepping between thick vegetation and suddenly stopped. I signaled the team to halt as I watched to see what caused Mike to freeze. I couldn't see anything. He didn't move. Slowly I moved the few meters towards him. He was looking down. As I checked our surrounding area, I could see he parted the bush revealing a clean high speed, apparently highly traveled trail.

I looked down and saw he had stepped on a punji stick. Motioning to Lieutenant Williamson to come forward, I bent down to evaluate our situation. The Lieutenant put out security along the trail. I could see the punji stick in Mike's boot laces and reached around the back of his leg a few inches above the ankle. Damn, this was not good. I could feel the tip and worried it went through his lower leg.

Meticulously I untied and loosened the boot laces trying not to disturb the punji stick. I then raised his utility trouser boot blouse. No blood. What luck! The punji stick went right up the laces, between the inner boot material fold, and angled along the outside of his leg without so much as scratching and breaking his skin.

With a sigh of relief, Mike redid his boot and we moved out paralleling the trail. Nerves on edge, we continued about fifty meters before moving away and finding another trail. Slowly approaching, we could see two small one man brush shelters. Empty but recently occupied. The enemy definitely frequented this area. Man, we were beat and stressed when, at late afternoon, we stopped for chow and a head call, before slipping twenty-five meters away into our harbor site for the night.

Morning arrived after a peaceful but miserable moonlit night casting shadows upon us through the canopy. We laid there supported by treed in our sloped harbor site. I got a canteen out to rinse my mouth out but when I raised the canteen I couldn't open my mouth. I got Pistorino's attention and he found a leech attached itself across my lips. He squirted some bug juice on it until it fell off. I squashed that little sucker full of my blood and then stabbed it for good measure.

Shortly after moving out, we came to a clear running stream. There were three stakes in the middle of it. We thought they were there, probably to mark the water level, but we were unsure. We topped off our canteens and crossed the stream. Once on the other side, Pistorino saw a man and a boy who also saw him and they ran away. Feeling compromised, we moved away as briskly as possible. We didn't have any enemy activity.

By mid-afternoon we were slowly moving under a canopy about forty feet high with occasional sparse areas. The secondary growth was moderate so I stayed three to eight meters away from Pistorino. We were headed toward a location we felt would be a good observation point when Pistorino flashed halt then motioned to move out at a ninety-degree angle.

I checked my wrist compass and motioned to go forward toward the observation site. He shook his head "no" and once again motioned for me to detour. Again, I motioned to him to go forward and once more he shook me off. I looked back and the Lt. was getting irritated. I moved up to Pistorino. He had stopped at a dry streambed that had stickers and briars along the edge. I looked down into the streambed and about eight to ten feet away was a freaking Bengal tiger sitting on its haunches calm as could be.

I met Mike's eyes as he continued to keep his Stoner machine gun trained on the tiger. I signaled Lt. Williamson to deviate and as I had done to Pistorino and the Lt. signaled me to go forward. After a couple more signals the Lt came up to me, clearly looking sour, peered into the streambed and upon seeing that big tiger he motioned "detour, detour, detour." No spoken words needed. We hurried tactfully on our way continually looking back over our shoulders. After about a hundred meters we got back on course without incurring any further contact with the large cat. Sergeant Bowser, our Tail-End-Charlie, was still sweating bullets when we reached the observation point.

We had a good field of observation to the tributary flowing into the Song Cu De River. We observed for a few hours without any enemy sightings, however it was eerily quiet. There were no bird or animal noises, only the occasional sound of leaves rustling in a faint breeze. Our vigilance intensified and the hair on the back of my neck was standing up. I wondered if the man and boy by the stream had contacted some Viet Cong or NVA and told them of us being in the area.

Late in the afternoon, after chow, we cautiously moved out looking for a harbor site. We found thick brush and bramble among some trees along a stream. Being by the water to harbor up is not normally a very good idea. Then, again, neither is moving at night. At 2000, not feeling comfortable with our situation and feeling the enemy had silently crept near us, Lt. Williamson had us move the several feet to the stream. Quiet as could be, each team member entered the cold waist deep stream. Each sound amplified in the silent night, the soft swish of the Recon Marine bodies in the water had taken my senses to a new level when SPLASH…Pistorino stumbled and went under. I went quickly to him and was assured he was okay. Fortunately, he held onto his Stoner. We had to proceed a bit more hastily down the stream and away from this area. Still quiet, we didn't hear any response to our noise. Our nighttime adventure took us about one hundred and fifty meters down the stream and we left the stream and huddled in the jungle to listen. After ten minutes or so all was still quiet and we had a little night vision. I was shaking from being cold and wet. We harbored half wet and cold hoping for an early warm sun.

Pistorino was totally soaked and freezing. Finley, Mike, and I tried spooning to stay warm. There was nothing much we could do except wait. Morning arrived and had all survived. There was no sign of any bad guys stalking us. As we took turns eating, Corporal Johnson relayed a message to the Lieutenant that we are to be extracted this morning. Wow, this was great news. A couple hours later we were at the CH-46 helicopter's landing zone. Shortly, the sound of the choppers reached us. The Cobra gunships scouted the area and the CH-46 flew in for us for an uneventful extraction. The flight back to Camp Reasoner was truly a period of thoughtfulness because of the many different scenarios we had encountered. Alas, these days were the subject of thought and contemplation for many years to come.

11.

Scout Dogs in the Vietnam War
by George W. Alexander

Scout Dog Platoon Headquarters, Danang, February 1967.

An Early Warning Alert System

During the Vietnam War, the U.S. Marines used Scout Dogs to detect enemy forces. The tactics and what differentiated Scout Dogs from Sentry Dogs in Vietnam is that Scout Dogs served as an "early warning alert system" for Marine units on patrol. Sentry dogs are often typified as aggressive and even known as attack dogs. However, Scout Dogs were trained to be silent and alert on airborne scent to detect enemy forces and give an advanced notice of their presence. They were taught not to track or sniff the ground as this could lead troops into an ambush. Indeed, the mission of these dogs was to keep our troops from walking into an ambush. They were trained not to bark or make any noise when signaling their handlers while detecting the presence of enemy forces. A Scout Dog would alert his handler by his body language and movement and indicated the presence and proximity of enemy forces. Often a dog would raise his head high in the air and make a sniffing movement. This was his way of signaling his handler. Indeed, some dog handlers and their dogs were so attuned to one another a handler could know how many enemy forces there were and how far away they were by the dog's reaction to the enemy's scent. Indeed, these dogs saved many American lives.

Off to the Nam

After attending a three month-long Army Dog Handler School at Ft. Benning, Georgia, I was off to the "Nam." Once in country and during the period of February 1967 to November 1967, I was assigned to the Scout Dog Platoon in Danang, Vietnam. There were only two platoons [1st & 2nd Platoon] of Scout Dog handlers in Vietnam. Soon after my arrival in country I was assigned to a dog; named Major OB36. He was a large 125 lb. "White" German Shepard. Our platoon of dog handlers went through a month-long orientation and further training with our dogs. We practiced patrolling, booby trap detection, and repeatedly ran our dogs through the obstacle course. During this training I served as a decoy. Basically, this meant I would go down a trail and hide in the bushes. A handler would then come down the trail with his dog and get the dog to alert. As a sort of reward, the handler would walk the dog up to the decoy and praise the dog for his efforts. At this point most dogs became aggressive but the handlers kept them away from the decoy so he was not bitten.

I didn't say Scout Dogs were harmless! During this training exercise, the handler was a guy named Fuentes and as his dog was walking close to me, it became aggressive. I was crouched down in the bushes and when the dog was a few feet from me, it reared up on its hind legs and was in attack position. Suddenly, the leash attached to his harness broke and in a second the dog was on me. This was not one of the more, bad-ass dogs that in we had in Scout Dog Platoon and I was able to fend him off by grabbing his throat with my left hand. Meanwhile, I yelled to the handler, "Fuentes! Get him off of me!" Fuentes froze! All the while I'm fending off the dog and yelling at Fuentes. Eventually the dog bit down hard on my left bicep. Suddenly Fuentes snapped out of his stupor and finally pulled his dog off of me by its harness. It wasn't that big a deal but the injury to my arm could have been avoided if Fuentes would have reacted faster. In any case, I was treated by the corpsman for the bite. I had a laceration and a few punctures and continued with the training.

As an aside, I mentioned that Scout Dogs were trained not to be aggressive but these were military dogs and not household pets. They were weapons of war! Oftentimes, depending on the individual dog, they were aggressive by their very nature. I recall two dogs in particular that were vicious and could only be described as sociopaths. One dog was a beautiful black and tan German Shepard named Shane. The other dog was a silver and black German Shepard named Baron. These dogs were okay with their handlers but with anyone else they were looking to attack! Both of them would look at you with menacing eyes and were hoping you would make a mistake by getting too close, so they could rip you to pieces. One night, Shane did attack a "grunt" sergeant who was drunk and had gone to "pet the nice doggie!" while Shane was tied up. The sergeant wound up with stiches all over his body.

The author (L) and Scout Dog Major Danang, February 1967.
Major running the obstacle course, February 1967.

My Time in the Bush

After our Scout Dog orientation training was complete, I started going out on patrols with the grunts and running point. Prior to arriving in Vietnam, I had been in the Marine Corps for nearly three years and had completed many infantry schools including Scouting and Patrolling, Land Mine Warfare, Explosives & Demolitions, Camouflage School, Amphibious Reconnaissance School, and Counter Guerilla Operations. I had also spent time with 2nd Force Recon Company in Camp Lejeune, North Carolina. In addition, I was also trained as a scuba diver before going into the Marine Corps. Ultimately, because of my recon experience in the States and desire to work with recon "in country" I was chosen to work with the elite 1st & 3rd Force Reconnaissance Companies. These units consisted of the most highly motivated and well-trained men in the Marine Corps. Their specialized mission was long-range reconnaissance patrolling for the Force Commander.

There were approximately five dogs in Vietnam out of fifty-five that were good enough along with their handlers to work with the Force Recon units for stealth was an absolute necessity to the survival of these reconnaissance teams. The five dogs and their handlers were excellent scouts and were extremely quiet even under fire.

With Scout Dog Major, 1st Force Recon Company, Danang, After the Happy Valley Patrol, June 5, 1967.

The mission of Force Recon in Vietnam was to conduct reconnaissance patrols and report the presence of enemy forces while still being undetected. Force Recon was charged with operating behind enemy lines while performing special operations. The unit's methods of insertion and extraction via airborne, heliborne, waterborne and submarine/amphibious methods are similar to those used by the Navy Seals, Army Rangers and Special Forces/Delta Force and Air Force Combat Controllers. But Force Recon's missions are typically in support of Marine ground units consisting of Marine expeditionary and amphibious operations. These highly trained stealth operators are often recruited by the CIA. Indeed, joint CIA and Force Recon operations were used during the Vietnam War and were known as MACV-SOG. These units were mainly employed in Laos and Cambodia.

During the Vietnam era, Force Recon evolved two types of "deep reconnaissance" missions that I was involved in. One type of mission was called *Keyhole* and the other was called *Stingray*. These types of operations and deep reconnaissance missions further became known as Green Operations [Keyhole] and Black Operations [Stingray/Direct Action]. Basically Keyhole missions are operations conducted with stealth to gain enemy intelligence information through surveillance. What we used to call in the bush, "Snoop & Poop!" You spied on the enemy and they never knew you were there! Stingray operations were geared towards small-scale offensive actions conducted as a special operation in enemy territory, unauthorized or denied geographical areas or politically sensitive environments. In this case the enemy was engaged.

In Vietnam, Force Recon literally had millions of dollars' worth of ordinance at their disposal. This included naval gunfire, artillery, Huey gunships and fixed wing aircraft as supporting fire. However, a salient point here is that a Keyhole operation or patrol once compromised [detected by the enemy], could quickly and unexpectedly turn into a direct action where the enemy was engaged. This was often the case in Vietnam. Indeed, Force Recon functioned as a counter-guerilla unit by harassing the enemy and taking the offensive in the enemy's own area of operations.

In essence, we took the fight to them as opposed to them taking the fight to us. We patrolled in areas that had known enemy activity. The definition of guerrilla warfare includes the use of small units to attack larger units using "hit and run" tactics to wear down conventional forces. Force Recon was using these same tactics against the NVA and the Viet Cong via Stingray patrols. Throughout history military leaders and commanders who fought guerrilla forces often used counter guerilla tactics to include the modification of conventional tactics and strategies. Flexibility and speed are key factors that differentiate counterguerrilla tactics from orthodox military doctrine. Stingray patrols were highly successful due to the ability to rapidly call in artillery and air strikes on the enemy.

Force Recon units requested scout dogs [by Lt. Colonel Bill Floyd] to run point for them. In 1966, several recon teams [consisting of only four men] were dropped deep into enemy territory; and they were never heard from again. Initially, the table of organization supported Force Recon teams to consisted of only four to six men. Four men could not put out enough firepower once surrounded by a superior enemy force to stave off an attack. They would simply be overrun. So, the size of the patrols was increased to eight men including a Navy Corpsman. These patrols often ran into superior enemy forces consisting of a platoon-sized force all the way up to an NVA regiment. By using scout dogs, the recon teams were prevented from running into an enemy ambush. With only an eight man patrol if they walked into an enemy ambush there was no question that they would probably all be killed. The scout dogs prevented this from happening by sniffing out the enemy and saving many Marine lives. The only thing the dogs couldn't do was to prevent a chance encounter with superior NVA forces. Oftentimes, after playing a cat-and-mouse game for several days in the jungle, Force recon teams were completely surrounded and outnumbered five or even ten to one.

From personal experience, while I was there, 3rd Force operated primarily along the DMZ. Three patrols were kept in the bush at all times to monitor NVA activity. The Recon teams there including a team I had the honor of being the defacto or temporary patrol leader of was known as Spring Week II. Another team was known as Great Divide I. We were engaged in many heavy firefights with the NVA and encountered on at least one occasion an NVA Recon Killer Team. They didn't fare so well as the hunters became the hunted! This is a testament to the effectiveness of both 3rd Force and 1st Force Recon Company's presence in and around Danang.

Major OB36 The Infamous Camouflage Dog

At some point after going back to Scout Dog headquarters in Danang, perhaps in June or July, I requested to be permanently transferred to 3rd Force Reconnaissance Company and became a member of the company. Now I was billeted in Dong Ha at the 3rd Force Company area. As a result, I was running patrols on a regular basis. So, it finally occurred to me as a recon team member and ultimately a team leader, that I was running point with a 125 lb. pure white dog that could be seen from a mile away. Given the scuttlebutt [rumors] that the NVA offered a $10,000 reward for a Scout Dog and/or his handler I thought I was quite vulnerable. So, I did the logical Marine thing - I camouflaged my dog!

To do this, I smeared camouflage stick all over my dog which broke up the pure white figure that could be seen from a mile away! The next day Major and I went on a patrol on the eastern side of the DMZ near the Gio Linh River. There was no enemy contact on this patrol so all went well except for Major. He had a noticeable personality change once he was camouflaged! He seemed depressed and unhappy.

Inside a bunker at Gio Linh (L). Major Camouflaged but not happy.

After we got back from the patrol, I went down to the showers at the company area and washed all the cami stick and grease paint off of him. He suddenly began jumping around and was a happy dog once again! The other patrol members noticed this as well and commented on it. Since my dog had such a negative reaction I never did it again and soon forgot about the event. Many years later while talking to Lt. Colonel Floyd he mentioned the story to me. He said his daughter was an animal lover and she had told the story many times. He said, "You and your dog are part of the Recon folklore!"

3rd Force Recon Mission. U.S. Marines infamous Camo Dog Major OB36 & the author conducting hydrographic survey of the Gio Linh River, Republic of Vietnam, 1967.

Scout Dog Alert - Welcome to the Nam!

The Author Team Leader & 3rd Force Recon Team "Spring Week II."

One patrol I remember was one that left out of Con Thien right onto the DMZ on July 24, 1967. On this patrol Major alerted on an estimated NVA platoon. He kept us from stumbling into their position. The NVA became aware of our presence as well. This area near the DMZ was defoliated and provided little concealment. We played cat-and-mouse with the NVA force but eventually we were surrounded and used artillery and close air support to keep from getting overrun. We found an old defensive position with foxholes, so we used those for cover. We had Huey gunships for air support and they laid down suppressing fire with rockets and machine gun fire! The patrol leader was Sgt. Jerry G. Owens (Hartford, AK). During the firefight I was next to LCpl Casimer S. Sudol, Jr. as he opened fire with his M-60 Machine gun. He killed three NVA and then his machine gun jammed. I was firing my weapon simultaneously at enemy troops.

In any case, the firefight lasted about four hours but we were eventually extracted in a hail of bullets by a chopper. A skilled pilot flew us to safety while taking fire from the enemy. Instead of flying back to the Dong Ha airstrip we crash-landed inside the wire at Con Thien! The Con Thien base was close to where our recon zone was and where we were extracted. As soon as the chopper landed, I casually walked off the bird thinking, "That was harrowing, but I'm safe now. I survived that!" Another Marine who was getting off the chopper at the same time was running past me and said, "What the hell are you walking for? Run! That chopper took bullets to the gas tank and could explode any minute!" I looked back at the chopper and sure enough there was a lot of gas running down the skin of the bird! I could see it glistening in the sun against the olive drab color of the chopper. I quickly sprinted to a bunker and hunkered down out of harm's way and waited for the blast! The chopper didn't explode but later I was told that it took 18 rounds, many to the gas tank and the hydraulics were shot up and damaged. That is why we landed inside the wire at Con Thien instead flying back to the Dong Ha Air strip. They say, "Ignorance is bliss!" but I have to thank that Marine who told me to run. That bird could have exploded with me next to it! In any case, this was another patrol where we would have to fight our way out of a dangerous situation. I was glad Major alerted on the NVA force and kept us from walking into their position. It was estimated that we killed 18 NVA soldiers during the firefight! "Welcome to the Nam!"

12.

An Encounter in Pleiku
by Mr. Wayne Karlin

Homer R. Steedly, Jr.

On **March 19, 1969**, First Lieutenant Homer Steedly Jr. turned a bend in a trail in Pleiku Province and came face-to-face with a North Vietnamese soldier, his weapon slung over his shoulder. Homer stared in astonishment. "At first it was almost surreal. I mean we're all in green fatigues, muddy and sweaty, and really looking like guys in the field. Here this guy comes around the corner, and he's got a light khaki uniform, a clean light khaki pith helmet. You've seen the red Pleiku mud. You can't stay clean up there. You're tinted red. Your uniforms are red, your fingers are red, it's just – it gets everywhere. And here's this guy that's walking down the trail perfectly clean - not a wrinkle anywhere. I mean not a hair out of place. "I must be hallucinating, the heat's gotten to me."

Hoang Ngoc Dam

The soldier, Homer Steedly, Jr., was confronting a twenty-five year old medic named Hoang Ngoc Dam, from the village of Thai Giang in the Thai Binh Province – a fact the lieutenant would not discover for over three decades. There was no time then for more than a quick glimpse of each other. As soon as Dam saw Homer, he snatched his weapon off his shoulder and began to bring it around. Later, Homer would recall how he shouted, "Chieu Hoi" the phrase he thought meant "surrender." "But he continued to draw down on me." My weapon was already down at my waist, so it was ready to fire. I hollered at him, and he didn't stop. He tried to get that weapon down, and just before he got it level on me, I fired. In my total abject fear of that moment, I just cut loose and killed him instantly. I could look in his eyes, we were so close together. We were thirty feet apart, and then later I looked at him, and he was so young."

For a time, he stared at the body, dazed. He noticed some more details. Not only was the young man's uniform starched, but the SKS rifle clutched in his hands still had the greasy cosmoline used as an antirust agent congealing on the bayonet hinge. "Someone new to the war," Homer concluded, an officer. In a description of the incident in a letter home, he called the dead man a major. He was wrong on both counts. Dam, whose rank was sergeant, had by that time, already been in the war for over five years. He survived the Tet Offensive and many other major battles. Homer bent down and went through the dead man's pockets, drawing out a notebook with a colorful picture on the front cover of a man and woman in what he took to be traditional or ancient Vietnamese dress, and on the back cover, a daily and monthly calendar grid, labeled with the English word "schedule," a smaller black notebook; and a number of loose paper – letters, ID cards, and some sort of certificates. The spine and corners of the first notebook had been neatly reinforced with black tape.

Thirty-six years later, when I first touched that notebook, I was struck by the care Dam had taken in binding it up. He was a soldier in an army where nothing could be thrown away, nothing wasted. I thought of what the appearance of that book must have meant to Homer as he looked through it on that dark trail. Raised on small, hardscrabble farms, Homer knew the preciousness of things that could not be replaced. The way he had shot Dam was unusual: a gunfighter duel in a war in which more often than not the enemy remained faceless to the Americans, only sudden flashes of fire from the jungle, just targets to be annihilated. That invisibility was frustrating to the GIs, but at least it allowed them the

12. An Encounter in Pleiku

comfort of dehumanizing the enemy, making him into a ghost, a demon, a target. Now to see not only the face of the man he'd killed, but also the carefully re-bound covers, the force of will that the meticulous writing and drawings inside the book revealed, confronted Homer with a mirrored and valuable humanity. He tried not to think about it. There had been no time to think, anyway. His enemy had been armed and ready to shoot him. Homer had simply been quicker. It was what could be and was called a good kill.

Homer sent the documents to the rear area, where he knew they'd be assessed and then burned. But later that evening he changed his mind. He contacted a friend in S-2, intelligence, and asked him to bring everything back. Homer couldn't bear to have the documents, the last evidence of the life he had taken, be destroyed.

Years later, Homer, along with Wayne Karlin, travelled with Dam's family to the graveyard in Pleiku where Dam's body was in one of 36 unnamed graves, and they were able to identify his remains and take them to his village, where they were reburied in a ceremony attended by hundreds. Then it was time to bring Dam to his grave.

The young soldiers, their olive green fatigues as clean as the ones Homer saw Dam wearing on the day of their accidental encounter, pith helmets on their heads, were called up as casket bearers, and then Homer was called up also. He took one corner, and the six of them, the American veteran and the five young Vietnamese soldiers, lifted and carried Dam's heavy casket to the funeral wagon. It is wooden, painted red and gold, and decorated with gold dragons, and six pushing stakes sticking out along its sides. Homer placed his hands on the stake at the front left corner of the cart and begins to push. We were out on the main road that went through the village now; a small palanquin holding Dam's altar and photo, then the casket and its cart, and then hundreds of people, the entire village, walking slowly behind, at the pace of the cart. Mr. Dieu, the grim undemonstrative veteran, and a family member, suddenly puts his arm around me, his face strained with emotion. He is the one member of the family who has seemed the most standoffish, sure of himself, sure of his enemies, proud and without regrets for his past. He looked into my eyes now and embraced me, his eyes filling, the marchers breaking around us, and somehow this gesture, from this man, means the most to me. Then he pushed me to the other side of the funeral wagon, the front corner opposite Homer. The soldier there stepped away and Dieu put my hands on the wooden stake.

There was a lag, and then I pushed against the weight of it, and we went forward. "Are these truly Dam's remains I'm pulling?" One way or another, of course they were, I told myself, the weight of this soldier coming home. It is the war we are all burying here. The heat was physical and fleshy again; it pressed like hands at my temples. My eyes burned from sweat trickling into them. Heat waves lifted off the paddles, distorting the air. Someone tilted a water bottle into my mouth. I was grateful that I had thought to wear a hat, but Homer had none. Suddenly, the writer and documentary director who travelled with us, Minh Chuyen, placed a floppy green jungle hat on Homer's head.

What several of my friends feared, a scream of rage at our presence, followed by a shower of stones, did not happen. Instead, I was being cut open by a myriad of acts of kindness. I searched the eyes of the people lining the side of the road and saw only curiosity or compassion or understanding. We were out of the village now. We could see the cemetery, still far up the road. It is in the middle of the rice fields that were all around us now. Tears were filling Homer's eyes. He was looking, he would tell me, at the fields and thinking of the fields of his own boyhood, and he was thinking these are the fields that the man he had killed rose to every morning and walked into in the dawn, and whose earth and water and rice he had felt cupped in his live hands.

We arrived at the gate in the waist-high wall around the graves. The tombs in the first section of the cemetery were all symmetrical; it was only after this enclosed area that the individualized family tombs rise in irregular clusters, like a small village, larger or smaller because of wealth or property, prestige, or anonymity. But here, in the first section, all the graves were of the same height and of the same reddish stone. These were the soldiers graves, those returned out of the 200 lost from the village and that now include Dam. Some were inscribed with names, and the rest were unmarked except for the words War Martyr. I had always found that phrase pretentious or false: martyrs are pure victims; soldiers kill. But it seemed appropriate now, an accurate way to name all the fallen soldiers of the war, and many more who still walk the earth husked and hallowed.

We stood in front of the opening of Dam's family tomb, made in the earth, to take him back, and with a tombstone above it, inscribed now with his name and those words Liet Sy, War Martyr. The altar, Dam's photograph still on it, is placed next to the grave. Two men lower the heavy casket into the hole, using two wires slung underneath. The wire cuts into their palms, and the casket lists and lies tilted in the grave when they finally get it down. The two men holding the wires manage to straighten the casket. We kneel at the graveside, and I shield Luong's match as he lights more incense. He hands the joss sticks to us, and we bury their ends in the ground in front of the altar, the earth resisting and then parting for them.

A moment later Luang hands Homer and I chunks of that earth to throw into the grave. Homer's fingers work the ball of dirt, crumbling it, giving it back, and later he says to me that it is the feel of that earth in his hands, Dam's earth, that he will always take with him on his skin, replacing the red Pleiku mud. I say my farewell to Dam, a final one now, and think of the grace notes of this day. The grace and courage of a soldier who brought back the body and the soul of the man he had killed to that man's family, town, and earth, taking onto himself their own rending grief. The grace and mercy of a family and a village that take this former enemy soldier to their hearts and allow their gratitude to now be shown.

I remember what Phan Thanh Hao had said when we brought Dam's documents to the village, three years before: "In Vietnam, you know, we have a certain spiritual relation that we karma…We think that Dam was a sacred soul. He was so sacred that he could gather us together: the ones who had fought, and the ones who were thirsty for peace. He was so sacred to gather all of us here, to do this thing, to meet today. So, that is what we believe."

I looked at Homer, He is staring again at Dam's photograph in front of the tombstone now, held by Dam's eyes. Dieu's daughter goes over to him, puts a hand on his shoulder, and whispers, "We forgive you." Later, when I ask him how her words affected him, he says, "The only person that can forgive me is Dam. He's the one I took everything from. And I do think he will. He was a good man. I think he was a better man than I am. So, I do think he will forgive me. But I won't feel forgiven until I hear that from his own lips. And I look forward to that. I told my wife that when I die, if I don't die suddenly, if I have lingering death, where I have the time to think about mortality, life, death, and what I have and haven't accomplished, that I'll think about my mom and dad, and my sisters – brothers and sisters, and – my wife, and her family, but I think that my last thoughts as I pass out of this world will be Dam. I don't think it'll be a negative thought. I think it'll be a euphoric feeling. A going forward to meet friends. I think I have a guide on the other side that's going to help me along. I certainly hope so. I would like to know him. I really would like to know him."

I think of the scenario I had fantasized when we first saw Dam's altar. How each soldier must forever carry one of the dead he made back to the family. How he must bear the weight of the body and the weight of their grief. But looking at my friend now, the earth of Dam's grave still on his hands, I know that he is not who should be here, helping to bury the remains of the man he killed. I know who should be here, bearing the weight of this grief all around us, and I know that will never happen.

Wayne Karlin is an author of numerous books of fiction and nonfiction. He served in the U.S. Marine Corps in Vietnam from 1966-1967. In 1998 he was awarded the Patterson Prize in fiction and in 2015 received an Excellence in Arts Award from the Vietnam Veterans of America. He lives in Maryland where he teaches at the College of Southern Maryland. With permission from Wayne Karlin's book: Wandering Souls.

13.

The Kindergarten Marines
by Captain Francis J. "Bing" West,
United States Marine Corps

In early December 1967, I returned from a patrol in the paddies south of Danang, South Vietnam, to see a squad clustered around a radio, glad to hear that Secretary of Defense Robert McNamara had resigned. At that time, Marines were fighting two vastly different wars on two fronts. Up north along the Demilitarized Zone, they defended against never-ending artillery bombardments and ground assaults launched from North Vietnam, four miles to the north.

Every grunt knew that the DMZ was a hornet's nest. A year earlier, my five-man reconnaissance team had been on patrol in the DMZ when we came under intense fire; we escaped only because a bold F-8 pilot, Capt. Orson Swindle, diverted from his assigned mission to drop two 2,000-pound bombs on the NVA who were chasing us. Then, Secretary of Defense Robert S. McNamara had ordered Marines to hold the line, a temporizing strategy that cost thousands of American lives. The only way to secure the top of South Vietnam was to maneuver through Laos and hit the North Vietnamese from their rear. But Washington wouldn't allow it. Instead, American soldiers and Marines were stuck defending along the DMZ, a battle of attrition in miserable places like Khe Sanh that went on until we pulled out of the country in 1972.

Farther to the south, in the higher-populated lowlands, the Marines were fighting a different war. The concept was to drive out the Viet Cong guerrillas by sending small groups of Marine volunteers into the villages to train bands of farmers, called Popular Forces or P.F. My regimental commander sent me (a grunt captain) to a remote village seventy miles south of DaNang to report on the progress. There, a combined action platoon, or CAP, of fifteen Marines and thirty P.F.s was trying to control five hamlets (small villages) containing 5,000 Vietnamese. Their adversaries were a company of about one hundred guerrillas who hid during the day and moved at night. Like the farmers and guerrillas, we fought with rifles and grenades, which we could throw farther than most Vietnamese.

We had no night-vision devices and, to keep down the noise when we moved at night, never wore helmets or flak jackets. In the dark inside the hamlets, we couldn't see five yards. Firefights erupted at close range and the P.F.s often ran away. But they couldn't go far. We Marines and the P.F.s (including the village chief) all slept on cots in a one-room schoolhouse. Due to constant patrolling, the P.F.s improved. But the guerrillas did not back off. Of the 14 Marines and 3 P.F. farmers who fought the Viet Cong, four were wounded and nine were killed.

Most of us didn't make it out. But we never called for artillery or air support inside the village because we lived there. Seeing that we weren't rich or better armed and yet took higher risks than other troops, the villagers gradually welcomed us into their thatched homes. We had been issued ham and lima beans in C-ration cans that had been sealed in 1955. Instead, we ate duck eggs and rice, peanuts, and coconuts.

In early 1967, the CAP commander, Sgt. Jim White, rotated home. The village chief, Trao, wrote to White's parents in broken but legible English: "Sgt. White and his Sq. (squad) every days every night go to empust with P.F. ... They work very hard and never look tired ... My people are very poor and when to see a marine they are very happy ... P.F. and Marine to fight V.C. Maybe die ... Jod bless you all."

Sgt. Vinnie McGowan took over. Like Jim White, Vinnie had fought against the North Vietnamese regulars and was tactically sharp. From the West Side of New York City, he had an outsize personality and within a few months knew hundreds of the villagers. The guerrillas, about one hundred in number, had been losing men night after night. Vinnie encouraged the villagers to point out where the remaining guerrillas were hiding. By the end of 1967, the guerrillas had pulled out and the firefights ended. After 485 days of combat and camaraderie, the Marines moved to another village, leaving behind a competent group of about 30 P.F.s.

This was happening throughout the Marine area, about 160 miles long. The CAP had begun as an experiment in one hamlet in 1966. By 1970, 114 of these platoons had secured more than eight hundred hamlets, protecting more than half a million Vietnamese. Not one village was ever retaken by the Viet Cong. It was the most successful counterinsurgency program in Vietnam. Five years later, North Vietnamese divisions armed with artillery and tanks conquered South Vietnam, whose top levels of government were in disarray. But at the village level in the Marine sector, the Viet Cong guerrillas had lost much of the support of the farmers. When I returned to the village in 2002, I was welcomed back with genuine affection. Because we had lived in the schoolhouse, the villagers referred to us as "the kindergarten Marines."

Here in the United States, the Vietnam War is still divisive. As a culture, however, we share decent values that our soldiers carry into every war. A full 90 percent of Vietnam veterans are proud they served our country. As President Ford's secretary of defense, James Schlesinger, wrote to our troops after Saigon fell, "Your cause was noble; your dedication was determined."

This does not excuse policy blunders, then or now. In Vietnam, Iraq, and Afghanistan, I have been on hundreds of patrols and operations with our grunts. In all three wars, our top leadership failed. In Vietnam, we lacked commitment. The same was true of Iraq and Afghanistan, with the additional insurmountable hurdle of religious culture. But there's one difference: Twenty years from now, it's doubtful our grunts will be welcomed back the way I was in Vietnam.

Lest we become cynical about our own belief in freedom or the appreciation many harbor for our sacrifices, we should remember the words that Ho Chi, a village schoolteacher, wrote in 1967 when Jim White was rotating home:

"To Sgt. White's Family ... I hope in my heart that Sgt. White does come back when my country is at peace. Many of my American friends have died. I'm very sorry this has happened to your people. I hope someday we will all have peace and Charity. Your friend always, Ho Chi."

Francis J. "Bing" West is an American author, Marine combat veteran and former Assistant Secretary of Defense for International Security Affairs during the Reagan Administration. He is the author of The Village, *a narrative of a combined action platoon (CAP) in Vietnam, and eight books about our wars in Iraq and Afghanistan.*

14.

"Friendly Fire - 1968"
by George Firehammer

Lt. George Firehammer. Standing (far left) with his Marines.

My most vivid and memorable vignettes of Nam are when my gracious Lord and His angels sheltered me and my Marines during firefights and most dramatically "friendly fire" incidents. There is no such thing as "friendly fire." I never used the term other than a pejorative. Every friendly-fire incident I participated in was due to the agents not following protocol.

I will give an example. During Operation Allenbrook, in May through August of 1968, we had two such incidents. One involved thirty rounds of 8-inch, 105mm and 155mm rounds quick fused fired as a time on target. The person who authorized it and called it in to the FDC (Fire Direction Center) was a Major using the Commanding General of the 1st Division's authority even though he was told there were friendly troops in the area. He demanded it since he claimed rockets were coming from that grid. They were not. Fortunately, all our troops always dug in, when setting up, and it was after we were set in when the rounds were fired. Several rounds landed within ten feet of my Marines' positions but there were no casualties. That was our first deliverance. The story concocted to cover this asshole's ass was that a Force Recon Team had been overrun and the North Vietnamese Army had called it in. I knew we had extra special protection and I gave my Almighty Maker and Protector all the credit and glory for our deliverance.

The second incident happened later when we had assaulted a village suspected of being under enemy control. There was no resistance, and we were working through checking for any bunkers or tunnels. I had my Marines spread out along a river as we were moving to a new area when I heard what sounded like an F-4 Phantom jet approaching from our left flank. I had not heard any radio traffic on a close air support mission and wondered what it was up to when suddenly, a horrendous ear shattering roar emitted from his Vulcan cannon. It was as though the earth was being rendered apart and approximately one hundred 20mm rounds landed all amongst my platoon. I thought I had lost my entire platoon and was amazed that my radio operator and corpsman and I had survived it. I almost soiled my trousers, but then I was immediately pissed off when I saw him circling for another run. I called in to my M-60s machine guns, (I had four of them) which were on either flank of my platoon, to send up interlocking fire to shoot him down if he started another approach. We dropped smoke to show us as a friendly area and were yelling into the radio handset to get this guy off our ass.

Fortunately, he pulled off at the last second, and it was fortunate for that pilot since I was out for blood. We found out later he was a U.S. Naval Aviator flying off an aircraft carrier, and not on our Tactical Air Control frequency, and had been given the word it was a "free fire zone." That was a term I never used either since there is no such thing.

Again, the Almighty had His angels around us. We checked where the rounds had landed, and they were in small clusters exactly in the middle of each one of my men's interval which was usually 15 to 20 feet. It was very muddy near the river and the angle these rounds hit was absorbed in the mud. There really was no physical explanation as to why I didn't take any casualties unless you give Christ and His angels the credit and glory. I do. I could never deny Him for not only this but many other times I and my Marines were the recipients of unmerited favor which is the definition of grace. "To God be the glory, great things He has done!"

Captain George Firehammer, USMC (Ret).

15.

Bravo Relay - I Corps, Vietnam
21 March-11 June 1968
by Lou Kern

Bits and pieces of that time still blow around in my mind. It was so unusual, so isolated, so beyond the reaches of safety, and so frightening. Those bits and pieces run out of my memory like dry sand out of open hands. Living in a tiny dirt cave for weeks on end without shaving or showering, often without drinking water, eating canned food dating from the late 1940's, sucking the juice out of cans of fruit just to stay hydrated, constantly surrounded by the NVA and for one ten-day period, writing and re-writing last letters home, certain that we would be overrun and slaughtered by the NVA.

The Location

The Annamite Mountains run north and south for 680 miles, paralleling the coast of Vietnam in a gentle curve, embracing both Laos and Cambodia. They are old mountains and looking down from a helicopter the peaks appear as the spine of an ancient giant warrior that had fallen, face down, in battle. Some of these peaks had names: The Rock Pile, Mudder's Ridge, Tiger Tooth, and the Razor Back. Most had numbers for names: Hill 558, Hill 861, Hill 881 North and South, Hill 1371, Hill 1015, and its sister peak Hill 950. Named or numbered, these peaks are famous in Marine Corps history.

These numbered peaks surrounded the plateau of Khe Sanh, often referred to as the Khe Sanh Valley. There had been a small native village in the valley called Khe Sanh. The Battle of Khe Sanh refers not only to the main base, Khe Sanh Combat Base (KSCB), but also to all the hills surrounding KSCB. Nothing was more central and horrific to this area than the Siege of Khe Sanh, January 21st to April 6th, 1968. During the Siege 6,000 Marines held off an estimated 20,000 NVA. Some military historians consider the Siege of Khe Sanh as one of the ten most significant sieges in the history of mankind.

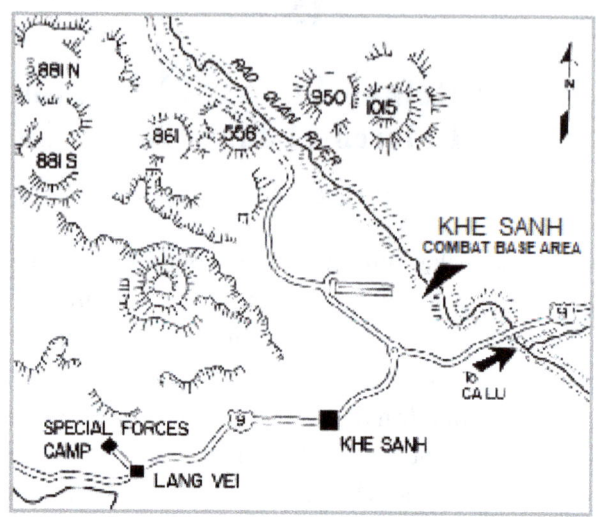

The Annamites were covered with a dense, sub-tropical and ancient forest. Up high the tree coverage was lighter, but down in the draws and valleys the forest was a 100 foot tall triple canopy sheltering a vociferous jungle. Leeches, fire ants, poisonous snakes, rock apes, torrential rains during the monsoons, suffocating heat in the summers…and tigers. The Annamites had been the premier tiger hunting area in the world before the war started. This was significant to our Force Reconnaissance operations. By nature, tigers stayed away from the larger groups of soldiers comprising mainly of the NVA, but a tiny Recon team was prey. The NVA had to hide down under this canopy…they had no choice. Our air power would obliterate them if they exposed themselves. So, they hid in the jungle.

Marine Recon: Stealth

I was in 3rd Force Reconnaissance Company. We worked hand in hand with 3rd Reconnaissance Battalion. Our job in Recon was to go out into enemy territory, into this dense, hungry, and deadly jungle, and to locate and spy upon the NVA. Out there were thousands of enemy soldiers, any of which would be happy to kill us. We went right out into this hostile place and thumbed our noses at them…using a tactic we called stealth. We painted ourselves with camouflage and tied vines and twigs to our rifle barrels. We communicated silently with hand signals, learning to push our way through dense underbrush without making a sound, and we slept on the composting jungle floor that was alive with hungry insects and leeches. We positioned ourselves near enemy trails and observed as they walked right by us, unaware we were there. Stealth.

I also learned later that my small company, 3rd Force Reconnaissance Company, was credited as one of the main factors in defeating the NVA at Khe Sanh. The enemy called us the Green Ghosts. We were always out there in the jungle in four man teams, spying on the NVA right in their back yard. It caused them great grief. If they wanted to move a unit to assault Khe Sanh from a different angle, we knew. If they had a favorite supply route, we knew. We found their caches and destroyed them, we called in artillery or Phantoms or Skyhawks on their base camps, we took prisoners and captured sets of orders from runners we had killed.

Field Radios

Along with stealth there was one other ace in the hole that Recon had…radios. Line of sight field radios. PRC 25's. The radios were our life line, our umbilical cords. Stealth was not fool proof. Things often went wrong out there. When they did go wrong a small recon team usually ended up in a gun fight with the enemy. We called this "contact." A Recon team completely on their own and vastly outnumbered in contact with the enemy may have 10-15 minutes to live. But with a radio the team had huge power at their fingertips. Like Thor's lightning bolts, artillery could be called in within minutes, if not sooner. During daylight hours friendly air support was usually less than ten minutes away: AO's, Phantoms, A-4s, SPOOKY gunships, helicopter gunships and often CH-46 helicopters to pick the team up.... often under enemy gunfire. None of this would have been available without radios...line-of-sight field radios.

Tracer fire from the "Spooky Gunship."

Of all the peaks surrounding Khe Sanh Hill 950 was the best place for a radio relay. There were two reasons for this. One was that Hill 950 provided the best over-all view of the valley...an essential element for line-of-sight radios. Secondly Hill 950 had exceptionally steep sides. Three sides were sheer drops from 100 to 400 feet down. The only way Hill 950 was approachable on foot was by a natural and very narrow saddle over to sister peak Hill 1015. This meant that Hill 950 was much easier to defend. The enemy could only come at Hill 950 from one narrow approach.

The Heart of Darkness

In Vietnam we did not charge in a light brigade nor go up river in a boat. We went about by helicopter. I was sent up, not exactly at my choosing, from our base camp at Dong Ha the last week of March 1968. Every radio operator had to take a three month turn on a relay someplace in our area of operations in I Corps...so I swallowed my luck and went. It was sooner for me, not later in my tour, but I had no real choice except refusing and embarrassing myself. It was a war...fraught with death by design.

I boarded a CH-34 at Dong Ha. I did not realize that CH-34s did not go up to 950. They were old and slow war birds and it took far too much of their fuel to make the climb. Instead of Hill 950, I got dropped off at KSCB, Khe Sanh Combat Base, at the height of the Siege. There was so much incoming that helicopters and airplanes were not landing there. In fact, the CH-34 I was on didn't land. When it was three feet above the tarmac at KSCB I was literally pushed off.

KSCB was about the size of a small town, a very small town. At that point in time, it was receiving 1000 to 1500 enemy artillery and mortar rounds a day. There was essentially no life above ground there save a dead run to the next trench or bunker. Hats off to the 26th Marines and Bravo company, 3rd Recon Battalion, who were there for the entire Siege. The place looked far worse than any city dump. Sanitation? Would you rather be clean and dead or dirty and alive? Home was a whole series of trenches and bunkers dug into the hard red clay. Hell on earth? Well, close enough. Bunkers and trenches did not protect anyone from a direct hit. Direct hits happened and everyone knew that every time they inhaled it could be their last breath. I sat in a dark bunker four days, underneath this constant pounding, before the incoming artillery allowed enough of a break for a CH-46 chopper to scoop me up and deposit me right up on Hill 950, my spirits freshly softened up by all the artillery, my ears still ringing.

HILL 950

Hill 950 was a tiny, steep perch high above KSCB. A sister peak, Hill 1051, was just a few hundred yards away. A gentle, tree covered saddle joined the two hills. Unlike 1051, which was very symmetrical and cone shaped, Hill 950 had a shear drop on three sides and was approachable from only the one side where the saddle was. This geography meant that while 1051 could be attacked from any direction, Hill 950 could only be attacked from one. Hill 950's defensibility, along with the spectacular view to the west it provided over Khe Sahn Valley, made it a prime piece of wartime real estate. In addition, the hill offered an almost unrestricted view to the east of the whole countryside down the piedmont and out to the blue waters of the Gulf of Tonkin. This combination of eastern and western views meant that our radios could be in contact with the teams out in the Valley and at the same time talk to artillery batteries and our base camp at Dong Ha to the east. In the relay bunker we had four PRC 25s…..each tuned into a separate frequency allowing us to be in communication simultaneously with teams, artillery, AOs, and our command. Everything flowed through that relay on 950 and it was a huge responsibility. Our relay meant life or death to our teams in the bush.

Hill 950 had changed hands a few times in the preceding years. American forces had overrun the hill and taken it from the NVA, only to have it taken back again in fierce, close-in fighting. Evidence of the different occupants and battles was all over. The hilltop itself was about 30 yards by 30 yards and any vegetation mother nature had nurtured there had long since been blown off. There was a small helicopter pad right on the top, ringed in part by a trench. Randomly placed, and on either side of this trench, were the small holes which led into handmade dirt caves. The NVA had made some of these caves. Their ceilings were supported with tree branches. The caves we Americas had dug had ceilings supported with slabs of runway steel.

Concertina wire was draped like a necklace outside this ring of caves. The strands were thick and garbled near the saddle and got thinner and thinner as they wrapped around to the shear drop sides of the hill. The wire was rusty and so full of trash that only the top most strands showed. This amounted to the "city dump" on Hill 950. This dump, and the entire hill top, was swarming with plump rats. The Siege at Khe Sanh was very good for rats because organized waste disposal was non-existent.

When I jumped off the CH-46 up on 950 another Marine jumped aboard. I guessed I was his replacement, but I barely saw his face. The CH-46 roared off to a point of no return. I was out of the belly, the womb, of that CH-46. The end of the line. Then I was immediately abandoned by the mother ship to an ugly pile of broken dirt.

Hill 950.

I quickly found the Recon bunker and met Hag; Roy Hagino, a good-natured blue collar kid from Flint, Michigan, and proud of it. He would be my soulmate for the next 8 weeks. A decision had been made to run the relay with two men instead of 3 and to compress the radio relay cave and our "living quarters" into one cave. That cave was six foot deep, eight feet wide and five and a half feet tall. Neither Hag nor I could stand up in it. The door to our "suite" was a small oval hole much like the hatches on ships. Right outside our doorless hatch was the trench. That trench was mostly on the east side which was where Hill 1015 was located. The NVA tunneled into the top of Hill 1015 and were fond of taking sniper shots at us on a random basis. The trench was about 4 feet deep and if you bent over you could duckwalk around the trench without exposing yourself to sniper fire. Likewise, the top of the oval hole into our bunker was below the top of the trench line so that a random enemy bullet going right over the top of the trench would be too high to get into our bunker. We considered this a luxury.

The floor and all four walls of our cave were dirt. The ceiling was metal runway sections. We managed to squeeze two cots, four radios, a lawn chair and everything we had into that space, as well as two very fat rats that became named companions. We spent almost all our time inside that cave. There was absolutely nothing to do outside the cave other than duckwalk over to the west side of the hilltop where the NVA on Hill 1015 could not see you. Over there you could lie down a bit under the sun or under the stars at night. Otherwise, we were in our tiny cave. We worked 6 hours on and six hours off because we lost track of days and nights that way and time seemed to speed up a bit.

The battle that raged below Hill 950 was a non-stop 4th of July fireworks display. The other hills, now famous in Marine Corps lore, were the scenes of almost constant battles, including the Hill Battles of 1967. Imagine the biggest fireworks display you have ever seen. Now imagine it non-stop for weeks and months on end. Artillery, arch-light, Spooky, Basketball Flare ships, napalm, rockets, mortars, 20 MM cannon, Vietnamese anti-aircraft guns, Phantoms, choppers, and AO's (arial observers) in their little Cessnas, and of course the endless stream of tracer rounds; both ours and theirs.

It wasn't just something you saw. It was a big brass band in perpetual motion. Every sound meant something. We all soon learned the distinctions and verbally passed them on to others. "105. Hear it?" "No, man, that was a 155, over at Con Thien. Listen! It's a little slower." "Oh yeah. You're right." "Hush, be quiet." In this way we passed on a knowledge of survival and desperation. We measured out the sounds along with our lives. That's part of how life and death occurred on the battle field; not moment by moment, but sound by sound. The "pooch" of a mortar round leaving its tube. The "vrrrrvh" of a howitzer erupting. When we heard those sounds we knew that we had a split second to react. We might be dead by the time we dropped to the earth. It was a sliver.... just a scrap of time.... but it was all we had. It was different with rifle fire. You never heard the one that got you. Bullets traveled faster than the speed of sound. Dodge your fate, make your peace, save your buddy, clutch that photo in your pocket, freeze. It was all and everything, wrapped up in an instant.

Every sound could well be the last you ever heard. We lived that way. Day in and day out. All of our lives were in that sliver of time between the sound and the impact. It was also something you felt. The ground would tremble and pulse from the daily arch-lights, or the shells and rockets landing nearby. Arch-lights was the name given to the B-52 bombers, which were said to have dropped more bombs on the surrounding hills in the battle of Khe Sanh than was dropped in all of WWII. It seems like I felt and heard most of them. Added to this show below was the fairly constant whistling of our own artillery rounds lobbed right over our heads at Hill 950 and into the valleys beyond. The 105's made a faint, quick whistle. The 155's were louder and with a slower whistle. The 175s from Fire Base Stud sounded something like a spinning freight train, muscled passed us, fracturing the sky.

But then things happened. Just two years before I had been a farm boy in Iowa. Mom and Dad had been nearby if I needed help. First the Marines. Then Force Recon. Then Vietnam. Then one of the most forlorn, vulnerable, and tiny outposts in the world. I was right in the teeth of death, like a tiny morsel of food already chewed and yet to be swallowed, stuck in some crevice. Moment by moment I was rotting in that crevice while the jungle rotted below. Without Hag I surely would have gone mad!

Death Row

And then it got worse. Hope may indeed be sacred but nothing is sacred in war. The Laotian Monsoon, sometimes called the Late Monsoon, hit us in mid-May. Low, thick, dark clouds and heavy rain. Our one ray of continual hope up on 950 was air support. The hilltop was too small an area for artillery to be effective. And it was very steep. If the artillery was off just a few feet it would disappear down the sides of the mountain. So artillery was out. But if the NVA tried to overrun us during the day we could call for all sorts of air support: helicopter gunships, F-4s or A-4s with napalm, Spooky. If the NVA hit us at night we could call in the deadly SPOOKY gunship. But none of this was available if we were socked in by heavy weather.

The NVA had overrun Hill 950 a few months before in the summer of 1967. Nothing was stopping them now…not with the weather this bad. The 26th Marines were in charge of holding the Hill and protecting us up there. They had a platoon of baby faced NICs up there to hold the hill. Twelve to fifteen 0100 MOSs. In military slang a NIC is "new in country" and 01s are trained as clerks, not infantrymen. This was not reassuring to us. Hag was the natural leader of our two man band. He talked about strategy and I listened. He was near the end of his tour and had run many patrols before being sent up to relay. In a war zone seniority is not rank, it is experience. There was no escaping an assault, Hag said. We would stay with the radios at first, but when the NVA got very close we would be better off outside with rifles and hand grenades fighting them off as best we could. There was not a lot of strategy because there were so few options.

The first few days we waited in hope that the weather would blow over. It didn't. The NVA over on 1015 knew they were now safe from our air power so they took advantage by coming out of their caves. They built camp fires. When the winds died down for a few moments we could hear them talking. "They are massing to come at us," Hag said. Under the heavy cloud cover the days were almost as dark as the nights.

One dark moment followed the next, slowly and without pity. We envied our teams out in the bush. How lucky they were. We had nowhere to run except off a shear drop of hundreds of feet. We started writing last letters home, our tears blurring our eyes and falling on our letters. Hag asked me to pledge that I would make sure his parents got his letter…if I lived through the assault and he didn't. He promised the same to me. The next morning, we would re-read our last letters home and tear them up. What had seemed so heart felt the night before seemed terribly insufficient and maudlin the next day. Hours passed without a word between us and then later in the day we would write another last letter home. Again, we cried as we wrote and again the next morning our writing reeked with tearful sentiment. The next day we repeated this process. Wasn't there something…anything to say that was true, timeless, and real? Were we already dead inside? Had war and its thousand mile stare completely occupied our hearts. Or had war and imminent death simple exposed who we really were before we even went to war? On the tenth day the Laotian Monsoon left and the NVA did not assault us, weak and defenseless as we were. Hag and I never talked about our letters again. I am sure all combat veterans have these thoughts. I do not remember what I did with the last letter I wrote.

Hag's service time was getting short. Obviously, we felt very lucky and buoyed in spirit to still be alive. Hag began talking about the new Firebird he was going to buy and some of the girls he remembered from high school. Then he was gone.

I have no memory of who it was that replaced Hag. I would have had to stay with him in that same tiny bunker for over a week. I began calling HQ and telling them that I was seeing little people. Not NVA. Hallucinations. I am sure they thought this was some kind of silly ploy to get down off of Hill 950. They were right. I called in this same request five days in a row and finally they said they would send up my replacement.

I came down from Hill 950 on the 11th of June 1968. I was wearing the same clothes I had worn up there 11 weeks prior. I had not shaved nor bathed or exercised in 11 weeks. I was placed on Jim O'Flynn's team and was his Assistant Team Leader until August when Jim rotated home. I became the Team Leader and ran patrols in the jungle until I rotated in December of 1968.

**Lou Kern on HIll 950, 1968
Photo courtesy of Lou Kern and Bob Fuller.**

Years later when the Internet came around, I tried to find Hag. I did, a year after his death. He died at age 50, leaving a family behind. He had tried to stop an armed robbery of the restaurant he managed and he was shot four times. He never really recovered and he died a year later.

16.

"A Marine CH-34 Helicopter Pilot Remembers..."

by Captain Brooke T. Stevenson,
United States Marine Corps

Captain Brooke T. Stevenson, USMC.

Event 1

Every day that we flew in Vietnam there was an event, yet there were those that are much more traumatic, disturbing or life threatening than others. This is the first of many.

I had been in country for just less than four weeks and had been cleared to fly only two weeks earlier. On October 18, 1968, I was in a flight of two helicopters as copilot of the lead aircraft. We had been assigned, as the second section, to a division of four helicopters dispatched to support the 3rd MARDIV in the Northern I Corps area along and inside the DMZ for resupply and medical evacuation missions. The days seemed routine and when it was time to go home the pilot told me to take us home. It was getting dark and I was leading the flight of two helicopters to return to our home base at the Marble Mountain Marine Air Facility (MMAF) in helicopter YZ-61 (Yankee Zulu), Bureau Number (BuNo) 148120.

The pilot, Captain Engel, was trying to get some sleep and I started to notice his instruments were starting to act in a strange fashion. The needles on the gauges would, one at a time, start to vibrate then fall to a "0" (zero) reading. I could smell what I thought was smoke, so, I asked the crew chief through the intercom if he smelled it and he said not to worry it was only hot hydraulic fluid. Pretty soon all of Captain Engel's instruments were now at "0" and mine started to act in the same manner. I once again asked the crew chief if he did not smell smoke because now it was an acrid burning smoky smell, but he was telling me it wasn't anything to worry about. Just then the wingman, Captain Bennett, in YZ 78, radioed to tell us that we were on fire! It was now dark and with the flames going underneath the helicopter, we didn't see anything until Captain Engel awoke and took full control of the helicopter. He immediately initiated a full autorotation, which instantly caused all of the flames to come up over the nose of the helicopter and engulf us inside this giant ball of fire!

I knew from flying with Captain Engel that he was an excellent pilot but being inside the fireball scared the Hell out of me. Captain Engel completed a perfect autorotation, flared away, and made a positive landing. The flames stayed in front of the windscreen and we all jumped out of the helicopter. Captain Bennett, pilot of the second helicopter, landed to the right of us as we were in enemy controlled country and could not take any chances. We boarded Captain Bennett's helicopter as fast as we could continue getting back to our base. It was determined later that we had taken a bullet in the engine compartment which caused a leak of oil and fuel to drip onto the exhaust manifold of the engine, which eventually caught fire. Being inside that fireball was extremely traumatic and terrifying.

Event 2

On October 22, 1967, I was in the lead helicopter of a flight of four helicopters dispatched from MMAF, where we were assigned, to spend a twelve-hour Emergency Medevac and Resupply Mission in northern I Corps in support of the 3rd MARDIV, in Quang Tri Province and in the Dong Ha area along the DMZ. At approximately 2000 hours (8:00PM) local time, we were called out for an emergency reconnaissance team extraction! When we took off we picked up another helicopter that joined our flight of four and proceeded to the designated coordinates. There was a Huey gunship flying above the area controlling all the air operations and had ordered us in a holding pattern to the east of the zone at about 2000 feet above ground. The Huey gunship finished up with support jet fighters and bombers and then ordered that illumination flares be dropped from a C-130. The Huey pilot contacted us and asked the one of the pilots if he could see the zone. My pilot said that he could not see it and asked the other helicopter aircraft commanders (HACs) if they could. They all responded "negative." I told him I could see the zone. I described it to him as a total eight Marines were in an oval with one of them, in the middle of the team, held up a red flashlight pointing straight up and he still could not see it, so I radioed the gunship pilot and described what I had told him and the gunship pilot acknowledged that was correct.

The pilot, Captain Ratliff, told me to begin an approach. I began a high speed approach that came swooping in and I needed to do a big flare to air brake and to set down in the zone. Once I initiated the flare, Captain Ratliff said, "I've got this," and then he set his helicopter down right where I was going. The wingman had been flying too close to us and as I had initiated the flare. He had to go over the top of us, 'waving off' and not being able to land. As soon as we landed the whole world lit up with automatic weapons fire from all angles and radians. We were like a bicycle hub, and all the bullets and tracers of all sorts of colors, were the spokes. I wasn't sure if we would get out of there. I called out the positions of the most intense firing positions to my gunner and crew-chief and continued to check the gauges and back up controls of the helicopter.

After what seemed like an eternity, finally, the crew chief yelled "Go, Go, Go," in the intercom and we took off. I was without emotions and not sure what to think or feel, but knew it wasn't a pleasant feeling to have all those bullets coming right at us. The firing followed us up as we took off like a "Cone of Fire"! As we climbed out of the range of the cone of fire Captain Ratliff asked the crew chief how many we had picked up, and he said "One." We did not know the state of the other Marines.

We flew back to Dong Ha operations shack with the one Recon Team member and waited for more orders. The location of the Recon extraction was close enough to Dong Ha that we could see the flares and gunship controlling the fixed wing air support as they continued to bomb, strafe, and napalm the area around the Recon team. We were called back out after midnight about 0100 (1:00AM) to try to recover the rest of the Recon team. We discussed that we had made a mistake and had our rotating beacons (lights) on along with our running lights, which didn't help us hide very well. After a discussion of how to approach going back out, I suggested that we split the flight of four into the two sections; (the 5th bird stayed at Dong Ha this time). I also suggested when we began our approach the lead two helicopters would go in with their total lights out, then, once in the landing zone the following section could stay about a quarter mile behind and above us by 500 feet, turn every light they have on their helicopters; (including landing and hover lights [bright white lights]) in hopes that if all the softening up by the bombing, strafing, and napalm did not do much good, it may draw the fire away from us long enough to get in and out of the landing zone.

Once we were out at the area again, the Huey gunship asked if we could see the site and as with the first attempt, I was once again the only one that could see the site. This time Captain Ratliff let me take the helicopter all the way in, and my wingman stayed in a chase position instead of an echelon position and was able to land to the right of us. As we touched down, the second section of helicopters were advised that we were "in the zone." They flew over at 500 feet turning on every external light they had. Immediately the enemy "Cone of Fire" went directly up to the two lit-up helicopters, but just as quickly, it dropped back down on us. I was once again calling out automatic weapons positions to my gunner and crew chief. Much more quickly than the first time, the crew chief yelled into the intercom "Go, Go, Go," and we did.

When we got back to Dong Ha we had been successful in extracting the remaining seven Recon team members. The two parts of the operation were extremely frightening and intense. We did not know if we would make it out or not.

Event 3

On the evening of 25 March 1968, I was HAC (Helicopter Aircraft Commander) for "night med-evac chase." Our mission was to support the night medevac flight leader, another H-34, in case it went down in the zone or could not make it back and had to land. We were there for "back-up/rescue" of it and its mission. The hours of this duty were from 1800 (6:00PM) to 0600 (6:00AM). During the first part of the evening, we had a couple of short easy runs. We came back to settle into the bunker and get some rest. It was the monsoon season, so it was rainy, windy, and pretty chilly for South Vietnam. Sometime after midnight, between 0030 and 0130, the Viet Cong and North Vietnamese Army "walked" rockets across the Phu Bai Air Base. We did not know it at the time, but several of the last few half dozen rockets landed in the officer's tent area. About 0430 (4:30AM), we were called up to go to the other side of the air strip below the control tower to pick up some medevacs.

Once we arrived below the control tower, some wounded people started coming out and getting on the lead helicopter, but none were emergency cases. There was a lieutenant commander in his dress khaki uniform carrying a manila envelope going between helicopters, and then two guys brought a stretcher to my helicopter and got on board. This was not standard procedure for anything on the chase bird! Then two walk-ons came and boarded my helicopter without a scratch or bandage on them. I thought that I recognized the ashen gray colored medevac on the stretcher, but also looked as if he had already expired. I asked my crew chief if it was who I thought it was and he acknowledged that it was our CO

(Commanding Officer). The CO looked like he had the back half of his head blown off. They had bandaged and wrapped his head, making him look like he wore a giant turban. But he appeared to me as if he was not breathing. The crew chief told me the two men who had brought him on board were Navy corpsmen and were trying to keep him alive.

The flight leader requested permission to take off and I wondered what we were doing because this was not our mission. This was a transport mission. It would force us to abandon our real mission for the next two hours. The flight leader was a senior major and that made it difficult for me to question his decision. The tower gave clearance for take-off and advised our flight leader to switch to departure control, but to take off and climb to 4000 feet on the 090 radian of the Phu Bai TACAN to Point A (Alpha) approximately thirty nautical miles out. We would be above the South China Sea and would make a turn back and to a new heading and fly directly over the natural harbor of Danang. Then we would proceed to the Naval Hospital located next to Marble Mountain Air Facility (MMAF). We would be radar controlled to avoid all obstacles and other aircraft.

There were mountains and hills between Phu Bai and DaNang. But as he took off the major told the tower "Negative, Negative!" "I'm going Special Visual Flight Rules (SVFR)." The tower told him he had to contact Departure Control, so we switched to that frequency and he took off, with Departure Control finally agreeing to let him go SVFR. I tried to take off next to him but was slightly delayed as medical team was getting settled in the cabin below. We had put the windows in place so the rain would not enter the cabin and I was immediately trying to play catch-up to close in on the flight leader. With this heavy load, and taking off slightly behind the flight leader, it didn't make it very easy to fly close to him.

Helicopters fly in formation with the chase, or rear bird, flying above the flight leader to one side or the other or directly behind. As I climbed I ran into the clouds for the first time at 700 ft, I had to drop back down to keep the flight leader in sight.

I continued to try to close the distance between us, but he was not doing what he was supposed to, which is to do slow, lazy, "S" turns to help me catch up. Flying at this altitude of about 500 feet left us in a dangerous position. The shore was coming up but it was pitch black and raining. At that time of the morning, we could not see anything but the flight leader when he wasn't going through the clouds, and then he would disappear again. I had to ask the copilot to start reading the altimeters; mine and his along with the radar and the altimeter and asked my crew chief to please see if he could see the flight leader.

The shore line, just south of the 090 radian, has some stubby little hills that are up to and above 500 feet, and we are hoped that we are going to miss them. The copilot read "500 feet, 500 feet, 500 feet" into the intercom. We could not see the flight leader so I called him on the radio and ask him if he saw us. He responded that we are at his 7 o'clock, which means he should be at our one o'clock, but he wasn't there; I can't see him, my copilot can't see him and the crew chief can't see him. I was concerned now that we needed to break off and climb, because we were now over the curvature of the earth and low enough to lose TACAN contact which allowed us to know our position in an attempt to keep the flight leader in view.

The natural thing to do is a subconscious subtle pressure down on the collective and at the same time add throttle and pull the cyclic back, doing three things at once (increase engine and rotor RPM and pulling on the power for the climb). Just as I did that, "DEAD STOP and DEAD SILENCE!!!" I first thought that we have flown into one of the hills along the shore, but something is very wrong. All the instrument panel lights were still glowing the night red, but two things immediately come to mind; the cabin light (white) had been on and it was now pitch black and I could not feel my legs below my knees. I reached down and my hand got icy cold. I immediately told my copilot not to open the window, as we had been trained to wait until the water settles before we exited, but he didn't listen and he panicked, opening the window letting the South China Sea into the helicopter.

The impact ripped my copilot's helmet off. It was on top of the instrument panel. I stayed in my seat until the water stopped swirling around and I had a nice pocket of air to breathe. I slid the window open and climbed/swam out. I could see the instrument panel lights through the cockpit window. I pushed away from the helicopter and tried to see which way the bubbles were going. I started to swim with the bubbles but then I was surrounded by a cloud of glowing plankton. The more I swam the deeper I felt I was.

I had a ceramic bullet bouncer plate on, my Mae-West life preserver, with flares, smoke grenades, my shoulder holster with revolver, flight helmet, kneeboard, emergency radio and standard steel toed flight boots and maps in my pockets. I was not making any headway and I was running out of air. I pulled the cord on the Mae-West, which inflated instantly, but the snaps in the front came apart and it was riding high up under my armpits and up around my ears. I was scared. I didn't want to die.

I started taking in water because I was now out of air, Finally I reached the surface coughing and gagging. My copilot was fifteen to twenty yards away yelling out for anyone. The wind was blowing and we were in white-capped choppy seas. It was spitting rain, which felt like getting pelted by sand. We finally got together, continuing to call out for others, but there were none.

About this time, I was angered to a rage with any beliefs that I had regarding religion and concluded that there is no such thing as God. What I may have ever believed and had been taught to me when growing up went away with the wind, cold and rain. How could God let things like this happen to good men for such a purposeless event? With the problem with my Mae-West, and all the extra gear I wore, my copilot helped me to get rid of the ceramic plate, my shoulder holster and gun, my flight helmet and anything that was not functional, including the emergency radio.

We both were now down to our flight suits, Mae-Wests and had a few smoke flares and pencil flares. We even dumped our flight boots. I was riding so low in the water because of the damaged Mae-West, my copilot had to help keep my head above water. We looked around and it was still pitch black except for one direction. We recognized the outline of the Hi Van Pass from the flares being dropped over and around Danang, so we tried to swim in that direction. After about half hour to 45 minutes, a helicopter was overhead but not down below the clouds. It was still up in the lower layers but flying an "S" pattern appearing to be looking for us. We fired our pencil flares, which worked but with no successful contact. Then a fixed wing aircraft came and dropped illumination flares, but all they did was make the clouds glow and the first helicopter left, but then another one began the "S" pattern again, with no success.

Finally, first light began to appear. We could see we were not that far off shore but we were still about a mile or so away from land. We had been swimming parallel to the beach. At about this time we saw a Jolly Green Giant helicopter flying along the beach to the extreme south of us. We waited until it was closer and ignited our last smoke grenade/flare and that helicopter immediately turned toward us and picked us up. The Jolly Green Giant took us to MMAF. I lost the CO, my crew chief, my gunner, two Navy corpsmen and two other passengers.

This incident, where other orders superseded our original mission, led to miscalculations and errors, which resulted in the deaths of too many good men. It should never have taken place. accident was a flight that should never have taken place. I live with this emotionally, and visually, every day.

Event 4

On 7 June 1968, while flying a support mission for Task Force Hotel transporting personnel, cargo, and POW's, I followed the flight leader to a landing zone approximately two miles south of Khe Sanh to drop off a couple of returning Marines and pick up a couple of men who needed to be pulled out to go home. As I started liftoff into a hover and transitioned into normal flight, the engine went to idle. I had to act at once, leaving me with no choice but to try to do a very risky maneuver by kicking my tail way up into a vertical attitude and by keeping my rotor RPMs as high as possible, since I now had no power. I could at least control the oncoming crash. The slight breeze that had hit the helicopter upon take-off had pushed us off of the tiny area that we had landed on, and the only way down was by rolling and tumbling end over end down the hill or, by try to build up some airspeed and control the descent into the trees.

All on board were not sure what was going on, but as I struggled to try to get power, the engine just stayed at idle RPM. The quick maneuver was to head down the hill, and just a few feet above the ground and trees, until I reached about 45 knots of airspeed and would not run out of real estate.

I flared the helicopter to slow the descent and pulled up on the collective so that we would not have such a hard landing, but we still managed to disintegrate the main rotor blades into pieces and impaling the helicopter on about a dozen small tree trunks about six inches in diameter, causing the fuel cells to be punctured and spilling fuel all over the ground below the bird. We were now outside of the protected area and had to evacuate the helicopter as fast as possible, then trying to get back up to the ridge line to be in a safer area. This was extremely frightening and scary until we were met and surrounded by Marines that came running down the ridge to escort us back up to the hilltop.

Captain Brooke Tracy Stevenson, 76, died Friday, October 8, 2021, at his home near Glenrock, Wyoming of natural causes. He was born Friday, August 17, 1945, in Mendota, Illinois, the son of Tracy Edward and Marjorie Lucille (Flickinger) Stevenson. Brooke served in the United States Marine Corps during the Vietnam War from 1965 to 1970. He was honorably discharged on May 1, 1970, as a Captain. His Helicopter Squadron was HMM-363, the Lucky Red Lions. Two of the helicopters he flew are on static display; one at MCAS Miramar, CA., and the other aboard the USS Hornet CV-8.

Captain Stevenson is survived by his wife, Stacy Stevenson and siblings, Mark (Terry) Stevenson and Judy Stevenson.

17.

"He sat on my boot..."
by Jim Sandoz

L-R Jim Sandoz, D.T. Neary and Kevin Jones.

I enlisted in the Marine Corps in April 1966, but delayed my entry until August of that year. My parents were aghast when I told them, and angry. I pointed out to my father that although he was too old for military service at the beginning of World War II, he joined the fray by signing up in the Merchant Marine. That observation didn't make them any happier, which, today, I now understand.

After boot camp, infantry training, and radio telegraph school, I was assigned to 1st ANGLICO (Air Naval Gunfire Liaison Company), in Hawaii. This small airborne company specializes in combined arms, fire support and communications capabilities in order to partner and enable any assigned unit across the range of military operations.) I requested transfer to Sub Unit One in Vietnam and was sent there in November of 1967, arriving just before Thanksgiving.

In Sub Unit One, I served in Nha Trang (the Atlantic City of the South China Sea). It was a beautiful place and the members of our platoon lived in a big house downtown. During the Tet offensive of 1968, four of us decided to contribute to the war effort and grabbed our M-16s and a few hand grenades and then went out to the streets to shake things up. We did just that.

After Tet and when things calmed down, our officer-in-charge decided to separate us, like a teacher separates unruly kids. I was sent north to Tuy Hoa about 50 miles north of Nha Trang. In Tuy Hoa my job was to fly in the back seat of O-1 Bird Dogs - a single engine two seater Cessna. I spent about three hours of flying in the morning, and again in the afternoon, looking for North Vietnamese Army or Viet Cong. In that region there wasn't a lot of action for us and it was impossible to see through the jungle triple canopy. I felt guilty for having a plush job with little danger and I extended my tour by six months and requested a transfer to 3rd Force Reconnaissance Company located in northern I Corps. I wrote a letter to my folks telling them I was re-joining the Marine Corps.

(Left) 01-Bird Dog Aircraft.

As I left 1st ANGLICO, I was promoted to corporal and after my 30-day leave, I reported to 3rd Force Recon. I'll deny saying this but during the time I was with 3rd Force, the company was at its nadir, training-wise and manpower wise, too. Hell, the only recon training I received was on the job. I was initially assigned to Lance Corporal Kevin Jones's team. He pulled me aside and said, "You outrank me, Jim, but in the bush I'm the one in charge." I agreed enthusiastically; my knowledge of reconnaissance operations was nil, but I was smart enough to follow directions and to be quiet in the bush. I was lucky in that the majority of my two dozen or so patrols were uneventful, but the one I'm about to describe was most eventful!

We were running four-man recon teams at the time. It wasn't unusual for a team leader to get his warning order, but not have three other men to saddle up and go with him. He'd go to a different platoon and ask if anyone wanted to go on his patrol. To my knowledge, no patrol was ever cancelled for the lack of four men. Somebody always volunteered.

On the eventful patrol, Allan Bierlein was our team leader; I was the assistant team leader/radio operator; Mike Mochel was our rifleman; and the team rounded out with a Gunnery Sergeant. The gunny was on the patrol as a rifleman. This old gunny (he must have been thirty years old) had worked with Bierlein in the motor pool. He cornered Bierlein and begged him to go out with us. Allan asked if I was OK with it and I was. The gunny wanted to stay out of sight for a while because he was sure he was going to be transferred out of 3rd Force Recon and he thought that if he wasn't seen, he wouldn't be transferred. Mike Mochel was known as 'Medivac Mochel' because he had been a medivac on three earlier patrols. Never due to enemy fire: he sprained an ankle, had appendicitis, and contracted malaria.

We were scheduled to be inserted and our time was scheduled for four days in our reconnaissance zone. On the fourth day we encountered some animal traps, so we requested a one- day extension of our patrol to keep this area under observation. It was granted.

We were in a cluster of small trees and brush. Near dusk, Mochel and I searched nearby for a harbor site, a secure place where we could hide and sleep. While searching, I happened to glance down the path to where the animal traps were and spotted what looked like the whole damned North Vietnam Army was headed our way. It was actually about fifteen NVA soldiers walking nonchalantly up the path. We ducked down and ran back to our observation area and whispered and signaled to Bierlein that the NVA were coming up the path and would pass by us shortly. Bierlein, a really smart team leader, told everyone to hunker down and let these fuckers walk on by. However, they decided to take a break right next to our position, directly across from a stand of trees. One of the NVA soldiers plopped his ass down right on top of my foot. I'm still amazed that he didn't hear my heart pounding. I kept as still as I have ever been.

Bierlein decided to just wait until they had rested and would take off. We were all on one knee, locked and loaded, and very silent. Bierlein's plan would probably have worked, but one of the NVA soldiers, while taking off his back pack, made eye contact with Bierlein. Bierlein opened fire and the rest of us fired into the field on the other side of the trees, and then we took off running down the path and throwing grenades towards the enemy. When throwing one of my grenades, my hand brushed against a branch. The grenade didn't go quite as far as it should have and the gunny caught a piece of shrapnel in his leg. He was later delighted; to a career Marine the Purple Heart Medal was a prize. We reported the contact while running back down the path hoping to find a suitable LZ. No joy, so we crept back to where we had been.

A O-1 Birddog was in the vicinity and came on site to help us out. He reported a large enemy force was approaching our position from the direction where the original NVA had come from and saw a ton of muzzle flashes. A Huey helicopter was dispatched to pick us up and did just that, landing in the field where the dead NVA were. Those helicopter pilots and crewmen had balls of cast iron.

I found out later that if a helicopter heard of a contact on the radio they would vote on whether or not to assist, and that vote had to be unanimous. Brave men.

That night, back at 3rd Force Recon Company, Bierlein and I were lounging on top of a bunker drinking beer. One of us said "We could have been killed out there!" and we both broke out laughing at the absurdity of just coming to that realization.

Jim Sandoz left Vietnam in July 1969. He was soon employed at a company that made paper cups. He married the love of his life and went back to college and earned a master's degree and taught biology in Maryland. He volunteered for "hospice duty," visiting terminally ill veterans. He later volunteered at the National Museum of the Marine Corps and helped in restoring a World War II Dauntless dive bomber, now on display at the National Museum of the Marine Corps at Quantico.

18.

Marine Tactical Data System (MTDS)
by Colonel Michael Stankosky,
United States Marine Corps (Ret)

Vietnam 1967-68

My time in Vietnam was directly influenced by The Marine Corps' decision to employ the Marine Tactical Data System (MTDS) at that time. MTDS was the most advanced Air Control and Defense system (ACD) in the U.S. arsenal of such systems. It was deployed in the I-Corps area, which was the northern-most combat area in South Vietnam. Marines were taking a more active combat role there, especially in air combat operations. MTDS had unique and critical capabilities that could easily integrate the ACDs of the Navy and Air Force. The outcome was a common-shared picture of the air war amongst the three services. Additionally, because of the preponderance of Marine operations in I-Corps, it made tactical sense to deploy such a system, as the Marines were daily trained to integrate air-ground combat actions. MTDS was deployed on Monkey Mountain, overlooking the Danang airfield, and co-located with the Air Force's ACD. TA Marines Hawk battery was also deployed there.

What started out as a field development testbed ended up as the primary ACD in I-Corps. Over the span of its deployment, from 1967-71, MTDS controlled over 470,000 aircraft in theater. When it redeployed in 1971, part of the system remained to integrate the Navy and Air Force ACDs. MTDS was an integral part of supporting air supremacy in I-Corps, which allowed the ground maneuver forces, attack and support aircraft, and helicopters to operate with a high degree of assurance.

My initial role was as an Air Defense Control Officer, responsible for directing Combat Air Patrols (CAP), ever vigilant against possible MIG incursions; enroute-following; directing attack aircraft to designated points; and overall air deconfliction. Many other functions were performed, in coordination with Navy, Air Force, and Army aircraft, ensuring deconfliction and safety missions. My last 6 months were as a Senior Air Director, responsible for overseeing all the ACD personnel on watch, and making key decisions – by comparison, the Maestro of the air orchestra/air operations in I-Corps.

My rotation was in April 1968, in order to make room for follow-on personnel who would be trained in MTDS. During my time in country, there were a few noteworthy events. First was the Tet Offense [January 31, 1968]. I had a bird's eye view from Monkey Mountain of the whole conflagration happening, from the airfield to Marble Mountain. We were terrified, not knowing if we were also targeted, given the footprint of our radars. There are several reasons postulated why we were spared, but the two I am convinced of are: It was my mother's birthday and it was the Chinese Year of the Monkey; and hence, a sacred place for them. The second event was that I was able to safely detect and direct two Navy F-4Bs to safety, minutes before they were to eject over enemy territory. And last, a Navy F-8 crashed into Monkey Mountain, 100 yards from where I was on watch. The pilot was eventually rescued, and the aircraft's bombs defused.

Marine Corps F-4B.

In summary: In terms of modern warfare, the deployment of MTDS was singular and historical. All the follow-on Marine tactical data systems in ground maneuver, intelligence, artillery, combat service support, and personnel were hinged to the success of MTDS. Also, the Air Force adopted the follow-on MTDS as their Mobile Tactical Combat Operations System. My own role was also historical, as the first regular officer in today's 7200 field.

Colonel Michael Stankosky, USMC (Ret).

19.

A Soldier's Reflections
by Gilbert "Butch" Hill

I don't think about Vietnam very much. I try not to as images start popping up behind my eyes and I have a hard time stopping it once it starts. Not necessarily images of unpleasant things (like war stuff), but, of people, places, settings, and events. Just once, when I start the news reel rolling, it keeps going on its own.

First, I've always found the airplane trip over and back to be a particularly weird phenomenon. You step on the plane in the U.S. (Oakland for me), then step off in Vietnam. Of course, there were a couple of stops along the way, but you get the idea. Almost living science fiction. A person is living a 'normal' life in a comfortable place, then he steps through the door of the airplane and moves through a sort of atmospheric pneumatic tube into another very foreign place. I don't know if that's a common feeling, but it's always been something I've thought about.

Upon arrival in Vietnam, you step out of an air-conditioned plane out onto the airstrip and immediately are overwhelmed by a blast of heat and high humidity. I mean the most intense heat! Then it gets worse! That feeling is something that sticks with you, and I know a lot of guys feel the same way. The heat is the first thing they remember.

A lot of soldiers were shipped into the country via Bien Hoa air base and were processed through a facility at a large Army base nearby called Long Binh. After I'd been in-country for quite a while I remember being at that processing center for some reason (I can't recall why, picking up some new guys, but I'm not sure). I was standing in a Quonset hut looking out the door. Across the way a short distance was something called a 'lister bag.' These things were large canvas bags held in the air by an overhead cross beam. Each bag was several feet high, a few feet around and they held water. Around the bottom was a series of spouts from which the water could be drawn.

I watched a large group of new arrivals gather around the bag like a herd, their fatigues soaking wet with sweat. They were about two deep, shoulder to shoulder and bent over at the waist trying to reach the waterspouts. There was a sort of pushing, shoving and groveling as they tried to suck water out of those spouts. I immediately had the image of pigs feeding and the associated sounds of sniveling and grunting flashed in my head. The image has always stayed with me.

I don't usually tell war stories. That's just not stuff you want to relive. A few days after coming home from Vietnam I was suffering a sleepless night. I turned on a light next to the bed and on the nightstand was a book. It just happened to be "All Quiet On The Western Front." I picked it up and started reading. Keep in mind I'd just come home so it was all fresh in my mind. In that book Remarque said everything there was to say about it. The lesson is that at a basic level, it's all the same. Technology may change from war to war, but the basic reality is the same. It's timeless.

Having said that, here's a sort of weird event that often comes to me when I think back. This thing lasted about 60 or 90 seconds, though at the time it seemed like many minutes. We were driving on a paved road, like a highway, in a quarter- ton, which is like a pick-up. Me on the passenger side and Billy Farley driving. Billy had a very bad speech impediment, which didn't stop him from talking a lot. We were the only vehicle on that section of the road and going at a pretty good clip, which should have been a red flag, but we didn't notice. Both sides of the road were heavily forested such that you couldn't see through or see much of what was ahead. I was just looking out the window listening to Billy's constant jabbering that I could barely understand. We drove around a curve and suddenly were right in the middle of a firefight. There was firing going on that I think was mostly parallel to the road (not across the road and not necessarily at us). Suddenly there were spotter planes flying overhead and mortars landing in the woods along the road. We were surprised and shocked at first and then driving like crazy as Billy jumped on it. Given our lack of emotional/psychological preparation the needle on our mutual fear monitor spiked past the maximum, burying itself on the far extreme of the dial. Briefly, we freaked out! I was yelling at Billy. He was yelling back at me with that speech impediment, and I couldn't understand what he was yelling. But the whole time he was laughing. Laughing loud and shouting out stuff that was entirely unintelligible. Did I get on the floorboard? I did or I imagined it. But I do remember him laughing even harder.

Here's another story. It's my favorite and does involve the subject of leadership. At one point I was working at/in a communications center for a helicopter battalion. Our leader was a Major named John Holliday, like the famous gunfighter friend of Wyatt Earp. So, naturally his nickname was 'Doc.' No one ever called him 'John' or 'Major.' It was always 'Doc.' Even the Privates called him Doc. He was a long-time helicopter pilot going all the way back to Korea. One of the first. Absolutely fearless. An incredibly good guy. He was the kind of leader that inherently generated respect and didn't need to flaunt his authority. People just naturally followed him.

At one point we were supposed to put up a large telephone pole near the comm-center and install antennas on the top. We dug a deep hole to set it in. But we had no mechanism to place the bottom of the pole in the hole and then put it in a standing position (it was more than 30 feet long/tall and heavy). Several approaches were tried, but they all failed. Well, Doc got increasingly frustrated while this was going on. I think his bosses may have been giving him some grief. One day he gathered us together and said that he was going on R&R and when he returned that pole was going to be up. Period! It's the only time I ever heard him give a direct order. So, he left. Still no luck with the pole. Someone got the idea of using a wrecker from the motor pool that had a short beam. So, we tried that. Attached a rope to the top of the pole and to the end of the beam on the wrecker. Then someone drove the wrecker slowly pulling up the top of the pole while we tried to guide it with other ropes that were attached. Disaster! The pole was about halfway up, and it went out of control and fell with a crash. Now it so happened that the Doc's quarters were located across a patch of dirt directly in front of the comm-center. And, as luck would have it, the pole fell directly on his quarters! Crashed right through his roof, crushing everything in its path.

Doc had a plaque that someone had once given him. It stated:

Major John 'Doc' Holliday
Nothing is Impossible

Well, we found that plaque amongst the remains of his belongings. It was broken in half! Virtually right down the middle! I'm not exaggerating or embellishing in any way. It happened that way. Someone got the Combat Engineers to come over and put up the pole. It took them about 30 minutes. Then they repaired his quarters. We taped the plaque back together and hung it on his door.

Gilbert "Butch" Hill did one tour in Vietnam and was discharged from the Army as a Spc 4. He returned to civilian life having a very successful life in the banking industry in Kansas. These are his reflections on a few incidents. Butch is playwright Harry Kantorovich's cousin.

20.

As I Remember It - 1968
by Steve Hansen

Vietnam – On the Ground - At approximately 11:00 am on 30 May 1968, our Pan-Am commercial jetliner landed at Danang. My first feeling of the country as I exited the plane was it felt like I had just entered a sauna. As bad as the heat and humidity was, the smell was worse. It was like the smell of a musty, dank basement with a good measure of garbage thrown in.

Christmas 1968 - It was in October 1968 that I got tagged to go to temporary additional duty to the 1st Marine Division post office near DaNang through Christmas. This was to help with the huge influx of letters and packages coming there from family and friends. Each day began with these serrated cardboard strips. Our locator "catalog" of names and unit addresses had to be updated daily with all the changes. If a Marine's unit changed, we would tear out his one-eighth" name and address strip and replace it with a new one. The big advantage to being so near the air base at DaNang was there an American style café (it was run by the Air Force) that served real American cheeseburgers, French fries, and such. I do not remember all that family and friends sent me for Christmas then, except for a small humorous mouse and Santa that my wife, Ella, had sent me.

Johnny Walker Black - In January 1969, I was working in the Force Logistics Command's (FLC's) communication center at Red Beach. We worked 12 hours on, 12 hours off. I initially arrived in Vietnam in May 1968 for a 13-month tour. I was a lance corporal (E-3) and a watch stander. FLC had a Provisional Rifle Company (ProvRifle) tasked with security of the perimeter. ProvRifle consisted of three platoons - one each from Motor Transport Co, Supply Co, and Comm Co. Each platoon rotated between ten days of day patrols, ten days of night patrols and ambushes, and ten days of standby.

The sergeant who made assignments to ProvRifle from our communication center tended to play favorites and I was not on his favorites list. Being a "schemer," I produced a plan to get on ProvRifle. I asked the sergeant what was his favorite liquor? "Johnny Walker Black" he replied. I asked him if I got him a bottle of Johnny Walker Black, would he put me on the next assignment to ProvRifle. "Sure" he said, and I was confident that you had to be at least a Marine staff sergeant (E-6) to buy hard liquor and, at the time, I was a mere lance corporal (E-3). After I got off my watch at 08:00 the next morning, I caught a ride to the Freedom Hill PX (Hill 327). I wore my "saltiest" set of jungle cammies. I found an Air Force E-3 in starched utilities and spit shined boots. I asked him if he would buy a bottle of Johnny Walker Black for me if I gave him the money. "Sure, Marine." A few minutes later he came back with a fifth of Johnny Walker Black. I paid him his cost ($1.25) and thanked him profusely. When I returned to Red Beach, I went back to the sergeant's rack and put the bottle under his dust cover (folded blanket) that covered his pillow. The next watch, a very wide-eyed sergeant asked me how the Hell I got that bottle. I told him not to ask. Then he announces "Well, I'm still not going to put you on ProvRifle." I then did my only Request Mast in my Marine Corps career. I requested mast to see the Communication Center Chief. He was a master gunnery sergeant and had been an enlisted Marine pilot. We all thought of him as a "square shooter." When Master Gunny called me into his office, the sergeant followed me in. The Master Guns asked me what this is all about. I refused to talk. He then told the sergeant to leave the office and close the door. He says "Open up. What is going on?" I told him that I wanted to go to ProvRifle. "That's it?" He laughed and said, "You will be on the next detail to ProvRifle." He said he would prefer volunteers anyway. (Side note: I had been on the receiving end of Viet Cong 122mm rockets and 82mm mortar fire before and it left you feeling a bit helpless. I felt like I wanted to occasionally be able to return fire.)

My salty helmet cover - I took with me, to Vietnam, my World War II Marine helmet cover from my Junior Marine days. I always wanted to look "salty" and avoid anything that made me look like a "boot." The helmet cover gave me a salty air. One day on watch at the communications center, I caught one of my sergeants trying to swap out my helmet cover for his. I called him on it, and he put my helmet down with only a mutter or two. I then replaced that WWII helmet cover with the helmet cover I was issued to prevent it from happening again. I still have that WWII helmet cover.

Chevron Bet - "Three up, four down and a bursting bomb" I said as I and another lance corporal were discussing our comm chief's master gunnery sergeant chevrons. "Oh no," he says, it is three up and three down with a bursting bomb. I asked, "Bet?" and he says, "Five bucks says it's three up and three down." I then walked him to a chart that had all the officer and enlisted ranks for all the services. He paid up.

First Patrol - The first patrol I had on ProvRifle was a night patrol. Our Tactical Area of Responsibility (TAOR) extended about three miles around the perimeter of Red Beach. The rice paddies were separated by raised dikes that divided each paddy. Some paddies were filled with water, others were dry. We were going out on a platoon size patrol (three squads). The point man (the man in the front of the column) must have thought he was John Wayne. He was carrying an M-60 machine gun. Our squad was bringing up the rear. After about a half hour, we heard a big explosion. The VC had set a command detonated charge on one of the dikes around the paddies. They waited until the point man reached the charge and they set it off. (No more point man nor machine gun.) We continued the patrol until we reached Temple Island. This was an island in the paddies that had once held a Buddhist temple. It was long since destroyed, but this was the island we set up on. For this patrol, we were also carrying a 60-mm mortar. We were all tasked to carry at least one mortar round for it. Once we were in position and had set up our perimeter, we settled in to see what might come our way. (No civilians were allowed out at night, or they were considered the enemy.) We heard the noise of people stepping on broken tiles on a nearby island. The Staff Sergeant in charge of the patrol was familiar with the 60mm mortar. He coordinated the settings and the charges for each of the fragmentation mortar rounds. He started dropping them in the tube and adjusting as he went. He was landing rounds on that island right and left. Pretty soon, he stopped and all we heard on that island was silence. The next day we walked over to it. We found several blood trails, but no bodies. (The VC were good at removing their dead and wounded.)

This same first patrol had us set up in a 360° perimeter. We were all very much on alert, considering having lost the point man. I looked at a tall black object about fifty yards from our position. I mentioned it to the Staff Sergeant who was leading the platoon. He handed me his binoculars and my "moving object" was a stunted pine tree. Ooops.

First Kill - It was April 1969. Our squad of the Provisional Rifle Company was returning from a night ambush a couple clicks outside the perimeter of Camp Books, FLC at Red Beach. (This was about five miles north of DaNang.) As we were working our way back to camp, we came across a dud 81mm illumination round. The Viet Cong were masters of turning our own ordinance against us. Our squad leader called it in, and HQ suggested we blow it in place with a fragmentation grenade. We were about fifty meters from a small Vietnamese hamlet, so it was decided to dig a small trench in the opposite side of a dry rice paddy dike. I dug it about eight inches deep, four inches wide and around two feet long. We placed the dud round in the trench. I pulled the pin on a fragmentation grenade, dropped it in front of the 81mm round and jumped back on the opposite side of the dike. We all took cover. Then we heard the explosion followed by a "whupada-whupada" sound. Then we heard screaming coming from the hamlet. An old papa-san was rushing toward us. I felt sick as I looked at this old gentleman's arm. Where a normal elbow bends 90°, his had another 90° bend right below it like a stair step. We rushed over to him, and we asked if we had done that to him. He shook his head and with a stick wrote "VC 1965" in the sand. He motioned for us to follow him back to his home. On top of his roof was a rooster with the 81mm illumination round sticking though its middle and it was still kicking its legs. We all reached into our wallets and gave him what piasters (Vietnamese money) we had. He smiled and thanked us.

Vietnam First Sergeant - We had the "Vietnam Leaf" camouflage pattern issued to us for our jungle utilities. They came with rain hats of the same pattern, but no matching utility cover. The Vietnamese that ran the little tailoring shops would make matching Vietnam Leaf utility covers that did match our jungle utilities. We all got them and thought they looked "squared away," because cap, jacket, and trousers all matched. Our first sergeant fired us up for wearing them because they were not "Marine Corps issue." We could not wear the rain hat (bush cover) in garrison either unless it was raining.

Night Ambush – One night we conducted a night ambush. Our patrol consisted of three squads. Each squad set up its ambush in a preplanned location. All three squads were in fair proximity, should we need to reinforce a site in contact with the enemy. Shortly after midnight, we heard a firefight coming from one of the other locations. We quickly moved from our site to theirs. When daylight finally arrived, there was one dead Viet Cong soldier lying not twenty feet from the ambush site. We learned that a group of three Viet Cong were walking along the rice paddy dike and almost walked into the Marines waiting in ambush. There was a blood trail leading away from the site, indicating at least one more had been injured. When we looked at the dead enemy soldier, he did not look real. He had a gray pallor and the one wound we could see in his leg was in the shape of a football about 5 or 6 inches long at the points. The tissue underneath looked like wet gray mattress stuffing.

Night Ambush II - I remember one night ambush where we traded fire with the Viet Cong. A friend of mine was prone and taking cover behind a concrete headstone in a Vietnamese cemetery. The Viet Cong broke off the ambush and skedaddled. My friend behind the headstone noticed that concrete headstone had a bullet hole punched clean through it just above where his head had been. Scary.

Night Insertion - One evening while I was with the on Provisional Rifle Company, we were on our designated ten days of standby. We received word that one of our patrols was in a serious fire fight and needed to be reinforced. It was pitch black. A Huey helicopter arrived, and our squad quickly got on board. In just a few minutes we were where the other squad was that needed to be reinforced. The helicopter hovered off the ground. We had to jump out the sides. We had no idea if we were two feet off the ground or five feet off the ground. I jumped, expecting a long drop. Fortunately, the helicopter was only about two feet off the ground. Even so, that first jump was scary.

Hansen Photography - I was able to get my dad his first single lens reflex (SLR) Petri camera in Vietnam. I also got him a 200 mm telephoto lens to go with it. I started with a 35mm Minolta rangefinder camera but moved up to the same Petri camera as I had gotten my dad before I left Vietnam. Dad soon had his own darkroom in the basement of his home.

Larry Kerr Visits - I had the distinct pleasure to have my good friend, Corporal Larry Kerr, visit me in Vietnam in June 1968. Larry was down from his artillery unit escorting a prisoner to the brig. He stopped by to see his fellow Marshalltown Junior Marine friend on his way back. Larry has remained my best friend. Larry was with Foxtrot Battery, 11th Marines near Chu Lai (M109's) on his first tour March 1966-December 1966. He arrived in Vietnam on his first tour via a troop ship from the U.S. His second tour went from June 1967 to July 1968. This time he flew to Vietnam. He was with Kilo Battery, 12th Marines near Dong Ha, Con Tien, and Charlie 2 near the DMZ. He was an MOS 0811 artilleryman. His battery fired 105mm towed artillery. Larry suffers from exposure to Agent Orange. Agent Orange was a defoliant designed to destroy the dense vegetation in the jungles of Vietnam. The Veteran's Affairs has just recently acknowledged the health problems it caused. Larry has TWO Purple Heart Medals, one for each tour in Vietnam.

Last Patrol - Toward the end of April 1969, our squad (13 Marines) had set up an ambush position. We got word that a decent size force (about two dozen they said) of Viet Cong were heading in our direction. When they were about five hundred meters from our position, they came under mortar fire and faded into a nearby village. It was our job, the next morning, to clean them out of there. When we swept the village the next morning, the VC were gone. (We were glad!) I was told that this was my last month on ProvRifle as I would be going home in June. (No complaints from me.) We did come across a spider hole. This was like a WWII foxhole, but this one had a small tunnel going back a ways. I got "volunteered" to check it out, as I was one of the smallest guys in our squad. I had a .45pistol and a K-bar fighting knife. Luckily, no one was home.

ASP1 - Ammunition Supply Point One was located near Freedom Hill PX (Hill 327). It was about three miles from our base at Red Beach. In

April 1969, a trash fire grew out of control at ASP1 and soon spread to where the ammunition was stored. Everything from small arms ammo to 500-pound bombs were exploding. I was told the bombs that exploded on the ground sent others high up into the air where they exploded. The concussion from the exploding bombs wreaked havoc on the PX and every building nearby. Our corrugated metal roofs on our hooches at Red Beach were being pealed back from the concussions over three miles away. I had seen videos of the shock waves from the atomic bomb blasts at the end of World War II. I was seeing the same type of waves in daylight and later at night. If I remember correctly, we spent most of that day and night in our bunkers.

Orphanage - Our base, Camp Books, Force Logistics Command, Red Beach Vietnam had a clinic/orphanage. The Seabees had built it. We would sometimes volunteer our labor to the Seabees and do odd jobs to help them with the building. The kids had swings and other things to take their minds off the war. Someone told me than when the U.S. pulled out of there, the Viet Cong came in and killed all those orphans. The reason was they did not want anyone who might remember Americans as good people.

Charlie Barrels - In Vietnam they placed large yellow 55-gallon barrels in our living area. This was to keep material, like utility uniforms, boots, poncho liners and such from ending up in the trash (where the enemy WOULD use them). The reasoning was the Charlie Barrels would be taken back to supply and destroyed there. I was always a schemer. I took torn poncho liners from the Charlie barrels back to our supply and they gave me a brand new one. I did the same with jungle boots and camouflage utilities. I didn't do this so often that they would become suspicious, but I sent it all home with my reel-to-reel tape recorder as "padding" for the tape recorder.

Homefront - While I was in Vietnam, my wife, Ella, lived in an apartment across the street and down a couple of houses from my parents' home. She shared the rent with my cousin Larry Robertson's wife, Lynda. Larry was in the Navy. About a month before I was due to come home, Larry had orders and he and Lynda left for California. Ella was working at Taylor's Maid-Rite and could not afford the whole rent on her salary.

My brother, Roy, then about 13 years old, graciously volunteered to give up his bedroom and to live in the little alcove upstairs. Ella was touched by his generosity. She remembers watching TV with my parents. She would catch my dad smiling at her when she was singing with the commercials. She said she did not realize she was even singing until she saw him smiling at her.

Koala Con Job - When my 13 months in Vietnam were ending, I was sent to DaNang to catch my "freedom bird" back to the land of the Big PX (the U.S.). I had taken my R&R in Australia and had bought a "stuffed" koala bear for Ella. It was about fourteen inches tall and I was carrying it with me to give to her when I finally landed in Des Moines. (She would be living with my folks and paternal grandparents.) We were standing in a lengthy line waiting to board the plane. A corporal started counting from the front of the line. He gets to the Marine in front of me and tells the rest of us to go back inside and we can catch the next flight in about three days. I let him have a tirade of my best profanity and tell him "I'm supposed to get married in 3 days!" (The truth is it was like 10 days, but he did not need to know that.) He tells me to "Wait here" and went back to talk to his boss. He came back and told me to get on the plane. (He told me they normally had four extra seats in case they had someone on emergency leave or a very high-ranking officer at the last minute. He said no one in those categories was there and I could get onboard. I went to Vietnam in May 1968, just shy of my 19th birthday which is in early June. Our 13-month tour let me go home in June 1969, shortly after my 20th birthday. I can honestly say I felt twice that old.

Surprise is Not Always Good - A friend of mine told me when he rotated back to the U.S. at the end of his Vietnam tour, he flew home and took a cab to his parent's home. (He did not tell them his tour was ending.) He wanted to surprise his mom. BOY, did he. When the cab delivered him to his mother's home, he knocked on the door. His mom answered the door. When she saw her son (whom she thought was still in Vietnam) she had a heart attack. The intended surprise backfired, and his family was not amused.

July 1969 - Home from the War - When I finally got home from Vietnam, my parents and Ella were at the airport to greet me. When we got home, I do not think my folks knew what to expect from their eldest son. (Weren't all Vietnam veterans a bit psycho killers and all that?) I do remember my brother, Roy, had a small motor scooter. I remember getting on it and feeling the joy of riding it around the backyard of our home.

Steve Hansen, Cpl. USMC

21.

Operation Pegasus – Hill 881

by Colonel Billy R. Duncan,
United States Marine Corps (Ret)
&
Lieutenant Colonel Clyde Woods,
United States Marine Corps (Ret)

Getting Off of Hill 881

Orders came down to retake Hill 881 North outside Khe Sanh and to keep a presence there. Because of its high vantage point and close proximity to the Khe Sanh Command Base, it served as Fire Direction Control for artillery directed toward the base.

On the second day of fighting, a barrage of enemy fire came in as we were digging in. An artillery shell exploded close to our position and shrapnel knocked out one of my teeth. My ears were ringing, my balance was gone, and I couldn't walk. My Corpsman said they were not going to carry me off and that I had to be medevac'd to the medical ship. I resisted leaving my command and my post. However, the lead Corpsman has the authority to override any rank. When you are injured and arrive at a hospital ship, they strip you of all your fighting gear. By the time they looked at me, my head had cleared up some. They cleaned the blood, removed some shrapnel (although some still remains today), and determined I had a concussion. After some time, my balance returned, and I regained the use of my legs.

For the next few hours, helicopters continued to bring in wounded from Hill 881 and other areas. Around 8 pm, I asked if they were finished with me, and they said "Yes" and put me in a holding area. I then checked myself out and made my way to the helicopter deck. I planned to catch a chopper back to my command. I grabbed an M16 rifle, flak vest, a belt of ammunition and my helmet. I strapped it on and climbed aboard a helicopter with my friend Colonel Wilson, the Commanding Officer of the Marine Air Group. Yes…I was AWOL. When I got back to Khe Sanh, I found the Commanding General. He asked if I was sure I was okay. I assured him I was going back in.

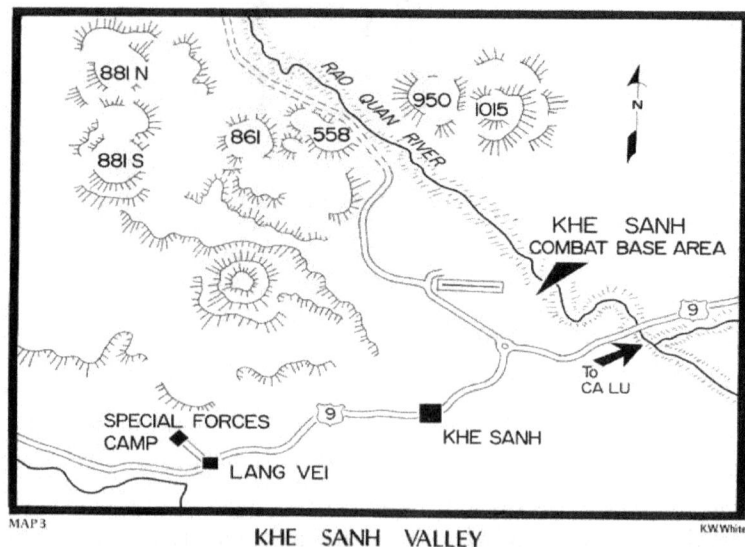

KHE SANH VALLEY

Prior to my return, the General had determined to evacuate Hill 881. Command wanted to send in helicopters to evacuate us, and I advised against. With so many choppers coming in and out, we were bound to lose some to enemy fire. This would cause us to slow down, cause casualties, and we would have to strip the helicopters of classified material, technology, and weapons. I told them we would walk out. The General told me that the enemy had been building up during my absence and we were now outnumbered twenty to one. We knew the NVA was committed to annihilate our forces. I responded that I would trust my men to a higher power than to him or me. We had another full day of fighting to stay alive on that hill.

I talked to our battalion commander about my plan. The remaining battalion on Hill 881 consisted of three companies. The fourth Company, H (Hotel) was left at Khe Sanh to hold down and maintain control of the base. The three other companies with me on the Hill were down to 575 – 600 men due to losses and wounded out of one thousand.

I assigned our most seasoned Company Commander, Tom Lang, of Fox Company, and a communications expert, to lead us north and west. We had put a minefield in that area earlier. We placed artillery fire on our flanks, and ahead of and behind us. My Artillery Officer was Bud McFarlane, (who later became President Reagan's National Security Advisor). Bud said, "I understand what you want. I have seen this maneuver in books, but I don't think it has ever been done." I instructed Bud to help lead us out with survey firing in place and with artillery. Bud drew up our detailed retrograde movement off that Hill by keeping our flanks protected and firing our way out. The plan was for artillery fire to find the minefield by triggering sympathetic explosions. Then we would move over to the left, directing our way out.

We traveled one hundred yards, stopped, fired out, communicated, and then traveled another hundred yards. We traversed through the blackness of night for over nine hours. All five hundred plus men left in a single file line that stretched for about a mile. Our exit was in a controlled distance and direction that would be coordinated by Tom Lan's movement with artillery fire. The artillery fire would cushion the route off Hill 881 N and set the pace for Company Echo with Tom Eagen and Company Golf with Clyde Woods all keeping in a column.

After three days of fighting, we reorganized and made a retrograde night movement with Fox Company up front, Echo mid-section, and Clyde with Golf Company had the racetrack in the rear. For three days we fought and an oversized enemy that had orders to kill every Marine. To my understanding, a retrograde of this size had not been tried since the Chosin Reservoir retrograde during the Korean War. Therefore, the exit was bold, dangerous, unprecedented, and now historic in size. Our movement that night turned out to be a great maneuver: no KIAs and no WIAs.

Many years later I ran across an article written by one of our Gunnery Sergeants where he referred to Duncan's Death March. He said that his men were so tired after fighting on that Hill for three days that when we paused our march to communicate with the artillery, some of his men fell asleep on their feet.

Our Golf Company Commander Clyde Woods wrote the following when asked about Hill 881 North: I can remember most of the events as though it were yesterday. At my age, what I cannot remember is what I did yesterday. It must be an age thing, or my bell has been rung too many times. I don't recall with OpSec that I ever knew that we were going to hump back to Khe Sanh CB until after we had started the movement and "The Word" was passed back from man to man in the column. At the start, Golf was well down the slope of a ridgeline and the contour lines were on top of each other for grid square. We had just been mortared late that afternoon and were able to get one medevac bird in for three or four seriously wounded (the birds were CH-34s) so only a few could go. We had three or four walking wounded, and by the time we were able to go to the top of the sixty-degree slope, I knew they would never be able to make it. I had to "fireman" carry one Marine the last five hundred meters up the slope because at that time he was unable or unwilling to move. He said, "I cannot go any further, but please don't leave me."

When we reached the top, we were able to get another medevac to come in, in the dark, and we lit the Landing Zone with the heat tabs (C4), so the pilot could see the zone. Even so, he had to guess where the ground was. I really don't know how he was able to land without a crash, but glad he made it, because if he had crashed, we would have lost more than I would care to count, including ME! Later, I think the pilot was recommended for a Silver Star. One of the "funny" stories of that memorable night: the Crew Chief of one chopper had bailed out while the medevacs were loaded. I don't know if he was left behind on purpose because of lift issues, or if it was a mistake. He was left on the ground with us and had to walk out. One of my Marines voiced from the dark and was heard by many to say, "Welcome to the war M-F-er." Poor chap had a long night alongside the rest of us!

Now, I was never consulted on the wisdom of the retrograde, so I had no input on the decision. In retrospect, what saved us was that it was done primarily under the cover of darkness. My Marines were on their feet without any rest all day and all night and much of the next day. To this day I do not know how they did it. No one fell out and most of them were malnourished veterans of the bush. I know that The Crucible of today cannot match what those Marines were able to do. Could they have fought their way out of an ambush? I am just glad we didn't have to find out.

This vignette is taken from discussions with Colonel Duncan and from his biography, The Life and Journey of Colonel Billy R. Duncan *with Tamie Nannarone.*

22.

Wartime Notes
by Colonel Billy R. Duncan, United States Marine Corps (Ret)

One evening in January 1968, I made the following notes:

I returned to our Command Bunker to collect my thoughts. The Command Bunker (an area of 15 x 30 feet) was the center of never ceasing activity pertinent to Con Thien. Radios were buzzing like a pack of bees providing specifics on the activity in the TAOR (Tactical Area of Responsibility) 24/7. I was aware of our command's role for today, and I was also aware of just how dark it had become. We were still under heavy artillery and mortar fire. Our gunners were conducting counter battery fire at enemy battery locations. The air was heavy with the smell of gunpowder and explosive ordnance. A light rain had begun which should have provided a sweet smell, yet somehow there was no cleansing from the rain, no washing of today's activity from our nostrils or minds. Our ears were clouded with continued noises and there was no break offered from this madness.

Three squads of thirteen men each, or a platoon-sized patrol (about 38-40) was very active outside and around Con Thien this night and every night, always patrolling. Intelligence reports from Division G-2 informed me of possible enemy infiltration into our TAOR. We had been advised of an assault from the northwest side of our Command Post. And area minefields and protective concertina (or razor wire) had been destroyed by direct and indirect artillery from the North Vietnamese gunners. Time is running out; new challenges surfaced by the minute as we continued to receive casualty reports from Company Commanders. It was hard to keep overall morale and ability to operate as a fighting Battalion.

Despite the continued battery of enemy fire, three companies (Echo, Foxtrot, and Golf) we WILL HOLD OUR CURRENT LOCATION. Hotel Company was briefed to hold their position a quarter mile south of Con Thien. If Hotel Company needed our battalion to reinforce its position, we were ready to provide that help. I thought of the bravery of all the men under my command and how loyal they are regarding the challenges to our position. Three of the four Company Commanders are married, all solid and loyal officers. Each officer is aware of the conditions facing the command, and they strive to keep the cohesiveness for the Battalion.

All movement throughout Con Thien is hazardous, laced with added danger from always exploding munitions and both friendly and enemy fire. Traversing the ground in darkness introduces more challenges. I remember the darkness felt like a heavy blanket, and since we stayed in "Black-Out Conditions," moving around was dangerous. Only the distant sound of vehicle movement pierced the darkness as patrols positioned themselves a mile or so from base camp. Con Thien was void of any animal sounds. The moist night air gave way to rain, a steady pounding on our steel helmets. We scrambled to find cover. The sounds of other voices from The inside the Command Bunker gave evidence that leaders of different units were inside attending the Enemy and Operations Briefings. Sgt. Major was checking off all the reporting units: Engineers, 4.2-inch mortars, medical and civilian leaders of a special laser system that was positioned on OP#2, and three rifle company commanders.

In the Command Bunker we had a good meeting, with specific guidelines on operations for the night and modifications to our combat against the enemy. Specific attention was directed to the condition of trenches, bunkers, and the availability to shift forces inside the compound as the latest information was provided on the NVA's threat to our location. We were aware that the long-awaited TET Enemy Offensive was now underway. Confirmations were made that heavier NVA 152mm artillery was being used against our location. A 152mm artillery round had crashed, without exploding, into the southern side of the Medical Bunker earlier in the day. Our EOD (Explosive Ordnance Disposal) team defused the projectile and displayed it to our briefing team table. All in attendance expressed how good it felt to gather as a Command Unit; spirits were lifted, and the Battalion Chaplain closed the meeting with prayer. [We learned later that this round of explosive made its way all the way to Washington, D.C.].

Following the meeting, team members began to disperse, followed by leaders of attached units, then Company Commanders. I was in possession of a fifth of Jack Daniels bourbon that a helicopter pilot had left for "Texas Pete" (my command radio nickname), and I proposed a toast to each of the Commanders. A shot for each Commander was in order; we shared a silent toast, swallowed the flaming liquid, coughed a little, and then left the meeting. With the last man leaving, I thought how much older and how tired the men looked. Everyone was 10 to 20pounds under their normal weight. Many close friendships were developed under trying conditions - friendships that still exist today some fifty-plus years later after experiencing the activity of Con Thien and the reward of Command in Combat.

During a quiet period, I composed a letter to my wife and two daughters – marked to open only after my death and departure on a new journey. The letter was sealed and given to one of the battalion runners to deliver it to the pilot of the next medevac helicopter. The personal letter was inside another envelope addressed to a close friend in Cincinnati with instructions to deliver to my wife should I die in combat. When I saw this friend months later, he chastised me jokingly, "Do not do that to me again. Give the letter to someone else next time." We both laughed.

From "A Warrior's Walk" *with Tamie Nannarone.*

23.

The Start of the Tet Offensive

by Captain Bob Quinn, United States Navy (Ret)

I was assigned as the operations officer of the 32nd Naval Construction Regiment located at Gia Lei Vietnam. In early January of 1968 units of the Army, First Air Cavalry division were moved into northern I Corps to supplement the third Marine division. These units needed to set up support bases and many landing zones to allow them to operate effectively. To help in preparing these sites for the air cavalry units, Army engineer forces were to supplement the Seabee units found in this area. A LtCol. and a Sergeant Major from the Army engineer organization came to the 32nd regimental headquarters to coordinate what units would do which items of work in support of the air cavalry units.

On January 30th LtCol. Martin, the operations officer of the 45th group of the 18th engineer brigade, and his Sergeant Major George Shepard arrived at the 32nd regimental headquarters. After supper we discussed the general plan to tour existing and future sites for bases and landing zones. The plan was to begin early on the morning of 31 January, fly by helicopter from our headquarters to Camp Evans and then go ahead to other sites, as necessary. The discussions were interrupted by a rocket and mortar attack on the Gia Le Site that evening. No damage was done and there were no casualties. It was our understanding that a ceasefire had been agreed to by all parties for Tet, the Lunar New Year.

On the morning of the 31st heavy ground fog prevented the helicopters from flying. The fog lifted by midmorning, and we took off heading for Camp Evans. To provide LtCol. Martin with an appreciation of the countryside between Gia Lei and Hue, the helicopter flew at a low altitude. Col. Martin was seated on the left side of the chopper facing outward. I was seated on the left end of the bench seat facing forward so the Col. and

I could both see the terrain on the left side of the aircraft and communicate. While I pointed out landmarks as we approached Hue, the helicopter was hit by ground fire with Col. Martin and the Sergeant Major being hit with rounds coming through the deck of the helicopter and traveling up through both of them. They lost consciousness. I saw bullet holes appear in the deck between my feet, but I did not seem to have been hit. The pilot advised that he needed to land the helicopter, and we headed toward a compound flying the South Vietnamese flag. The pilot landed the helicopter in a rice paddy next to the compound with the flag. The compound and rice paddy were located on the south side of the Perfume River next to the south abutment of the railroad bridge that crossed the river along the west side of the Hue citadel. When the engine stopped, we were able to hear significant gunfire. One of the door gunners and I started to unbuckle the wounded Army men. We had not completed releasing the wounded from their seatbelts when the chopper was hit by a rocket propelled grenade. I do not remember an explosion or any large noise.

The next thing that I remember was lying face down in the rice paddy with my left leg numb and unusable. A large piece of my calf had been blown away and another chunk was hanging on by the skin along one side. There were many shrapnel wounds in both my legs and buttocks. I checked my .45 caliber pistol and started to crawl through the rice paddy toward the South Vietnamese compound. My progress using two arms and only one leg was quite slow, but I made it to the edge of the rice paddy. I encountered an embankment five or six feet tall, with the South Vietnamese compound on the upper level. I was not making any real progress getting up the embankment when several South Vietnamese engineers ran out from the compound and dragged me inside.

Once I arrived, all the helicopter passengers except for the two Army engineers who had been wounded had made it to the compound. One door gunner and I were the only two that were not ambulatory. All but the pilot had received minor wounds, but they could return to duty. The South Vietnamese Sergeant Major cleaned my wound as best he could and put the large pieces of what I had left in place. I believe he placed some sulfa powder on the wound and bandaged the calf area to hold all the pieces together. The pilot arranged by radio for a helicopter to land in the compound and take the ambulatory personnel back to the squadron's base camp. He had also arranged for a medevac chopper to come for the door gunner and me. The two of us were placed on the porch of the headquarters building under a canopy to protect us from enemy fire coming from the tall buildings that looked down into the compound.

The first chopper arrived and took all but the door gunner and me from the compound. Shortly afterward, a Medevac chopper arrived, and as it was landing the Army medic on board jumped to the ground and started running toward me. As he did so several mortar rounds impacted within the compound and the medic was blinded. The chopper lifted off and was not seen again. Communications were impossible: the Vietnamese CO spoke only Vietnamese and French the gunner, medic and I spoke English. In addition, the only radio was set for the Vietnamese frequencies and none of us knew the frequencies used by the American forces.

The gunner using the Vietnamese radio tried to contact someone to let the world know where we were. As evening approached, I was placed in a bunker. I must have been slipping in and out of consciousness because I remember some incidents clearly and then there are large blanks of time. I gave my .45 pistol and ammo to the Vietnamese since I was no help in defending the compound.

I do not remember much of anything until the evening of the 2nd of February when Terry Egan arrived. He was an Australian Warrant Officer and the advisor to a South Vietnamese Ranger unit. They had been on a long-range patrol to the south and west of Hue. They fought through large numbers of North Vietnamese trying to get back to their headquarters inside the citadel within the old part of Hue. Terry heard some of the radio transmissions on the Vietnamese radio. From those transmissions he could recognize that there were some Yanks in serious trouble in a compound in Hue. Terry got approval to go and land and he and his crew were able to get into the compound on the night of the 2nd. In addition to assessing the situation he snuck out to the helicopter and confirmed that the two engineers were dead. He retrieved their dog tags to return to the Army to confirm their location and status.

Terry Egan was in contact with 2/5 on the 11th and 12th of February. He knew the location of several Vietnamese boats and ferried F/2/5 across Perfume River to assist us in our movement forward.

The Citadel at Hue -1968.

Later that evening there was a very heavy attack on the compound near the Citadel, but the enemy defenders were successful in holding. Terry was in contact with the ARVN headquarters that were holding out in the northeast part of the Citadel. It had been agreed that a helo medevac should try to extract the Americans from the compound. If that did not work, we were to try to escape down the Perfume River.

Early on the morning of the 3rd Terry had arranged for a medevac chopper which flew up the river and was advised that because there were several compounds they did not know which one we were in. Terry responded that when he heard the chopper coming on the next fly by, he would throw a smoke grenade into the center of the compound to identify where we were located. By this time all of us had been moved under some trucks at the edge of the landing zone ready for the arrival of the chopper. As we heard the chopper coming, Terry threw the grenade into the open area and it just fizzled. That was the only smoke grenade he had, so he requested that the chopper make another pass, and he would stand in the landing area and wave his field jacket.

On the next pass, Terry ran out to the center of the pad and waved his jacket as bullets flew. It was suggested that a gunship spray the tall buildings as the medevac chopper made its approach. The radio began to go bad so it was crucial for the first attempt to be successful.

As we heard the choppers coming, we crawled out from under the trucks and got ready to move to the chopper as it arrived.

I remember putting my arms over Terry's shoulders as we advanced toward the landing area. The chopper rose above the wall and lowered as it approached the landing area. Looking over Terry's shoulder I saw the chopper's skids descending from head high. I was thrown in the chopper and the rest of the wounded piled in. I do not believe the skids ever touched the ground. It lifted with all of us up with Terry sitting on the deck with his feet on the skids firing his rifle at the tall buildings. Once we were at altitude, Terry apologized to the pilot for not getting permission to fire from the chopper. We flew over the city of Hue to an Army medical unit where Terry and I were put on another chopper to be flown to the Navy hospital at Phu Bai.

At Phu Bai I was on a stretcher placed on the tarmac along with lots of other stretchers. I was so dehydrated that they could not do any surgery on me until they had administered both plasma and glucose. While lying on the tarmac being hydrated, I saw the Marine Col. from MAG 16 and hollered to him and asked that he do whatever he could to help Terry. He said that Terry had been terrorizing the Third Marine Division headquarters wanting to get back to his troops in the compound. There was no way the Marines were going to land a helo in that compound, but they did drop a sling with ammo, medicine, and rations. I also talked to the CO of the Seabee battalion located at Phu Bai as he walked among the stretchers looking for any of his troops. He informed Commodore Hill that I was alive and on my way to a hospital. Late in the afternoon, I was taken into surgery for a debridement. I was given spinal anesthesia for the operation and since they would not let me watch the surgery, I asked the anesthesiologist to explain how it worked. He used a felt pen and sketched the spinal column on a sheet suspended above my waist and explained where the injection is made and how they control what part of the body is made numb.

Once the operation was completed, I was put on a stretcher and placed on an inflated fabric structure in the recovery area. There was a mortar attack on the hospital but we sustained no hits. At about 0200 on the 4th, I was medevaced from Phu Bai to a hospital in Danang. I was loaded on a C-141 for a flight to Japan.

The Air Force medevac system was amazing. The wounded were not placed on a medevac plane until a bed has been identified at the receiving hospital. When I got to the stretcher that I had been assigned, the nurse asked if I wanted to be face up or face down. She quickly explained that the stretchers were so closely stacked, turning over was not possible. The nurses walked up and down the narrow aisles keeping the wounded as comfortable as possible.

Upon arrival at Tachikawa air base we were once again lined up on our stretchers on the tarmac and sorted by service to be transported to the right hospital. The Marines and Navy personnel were flown by chopper to the Navy hospital at Yokosuka. Once there we were lined up on the deck in a hallway waiting to be delivered to the assigned bed. While lying in the hallway I saw LCDR Harry Davis walking along. I called to him and asked him to try to call my wife Judy in Wisconsin to let her know I had been wounded but was ok and was in Japan away from the war. Harry made the call, but it was a challenge. Judy received a collect call but refused to accept the call because I was not in Japan. She and the Japanese operator went back and forth but were not making any progress when an American operator broke in and offered to try to get the full story. She shortly explained to Judy that there was a collect call from Harry Davis from Japan for her husband. Judy knew Harry and knew he had been wounded in a mine explosion a short time earlier, so she accepted the call. Judy was all concerned about Harry when he said, "You haven't heard about Bob. She was completely, so Harry quickly informed Judy that I had been wounded in the leg, was in the hospital in Japan and I was going to be okay, and I would be in touch with her as soon as possible.

The doctors performed another debridement operation and asked me if I wanted them to do the reconstruction in Japan or wait several more days till I was at Great Lakes. Since the wound had been untreated for four days or more, it was preferable to start surgery at once. The surgery would involve several sessions with a limited time between operations, so once started, the whole process would need to be done in Japan. In addition, the doctors recommended that I do the physical therapy in Japan so that when the family saw me for the first time I would be walking and not bed ridden.

Thus, we embarked on a series of operations to return as much of the calf that remained to its proper location as possible. The rest would be covered in skin grafts. While they were at this task, they removed many of the large pieces of shrapnel from my legs and butt. Over time, small pieces would be expelled by the body and foreign objects would be encapsulated in tissue. This process continued for over a year. A percentage of each skin graft would adhere and grow, but some would not attach and the failed patch had to be removed and another skin graft put in place. There were quite a few skin grafts performed. Once the surgeries were completed, I was wheeled to physical therapy twice a day. As I improved, the wheelchair was replaced by crutches, and eventually by a cane. I was able to keep track of Terry since he joined each Marine unit that was in the front as they retook the city of Hue and I talked to the new arrivals each day as they arrived from Hue.

On the 11th of March, I was medevaced on a C-141 to Scott AFB in southern Illinois. I thought I would be sitting in a seat but once again I was on a stretcher on the deck in the rear of the airplane. It wasn't bad until we stopped in Alaska to refuel. Once the plane was parked the rear door was opened and since I was dressed in my hospital gown my bare butt was getting frost bitten from the icy blasts coming in the door. The nurses responded to my gripes and covered me with warm wool blankets.

At Scott we were all put to bed for the night and then sent the following morning to the hospital closest to our home. I was flown to Great Lakes where they kept me overnight, did several tests, and then turned me over to my family for 30 days of convalescent leave. I returned to Great Lakes hospital for one night and a round of tests then I was sent home for another 30 days of convalescent leave. After the last set of tests and I was returned to duty with orders to the SHAPE staff in Belgium.

After our adventure, we stayed connected with Terry. Since we were both on active duty and changed duty stations every few years, we would lose contact. Several times I contacted the Australian Embassy in

Washington D.C. and once I told my story they tracked him down and put us in contact again. Eventually we both retired and settled down, making it much easier to stay in touch.

Retired Navy Captain Bob Quinn is the President of the Channel Island Navy League. As a Naval Civil Engineer Corps (CEC) officer some of his assignments included Allied Powers Europe, Joint Chief of Staff, 30th Naval Construction Regiment, 32nd Naval Construction Regiment and Naval Mobile Construction Battalion Forty.

24.

Hue City - January – March 1968

by Brigadier General, Mike Downs,
United States Marine Corps (Ret)

"I have lasting ties to Massachusetts...

I was born in the town of Oak Bluffs on the Island of Martha's Vineyard and graduated from the Oak Bluffs High School in 1957. There were only thirteen students in my class. Martha's Vineyard had just three high schools during my time there; Tisbury, Edgartown, and Oak Bluffs. Martha's Vineyard Regional High School began with the senior class of 1960. I was a graduate of the College of the Holy Cross, which is not too far down the road from Natick, with the Class of 1961 and was a member of the NROTC while a student at Holy Cross.

Having been commissioned a Marine 2nd Lieutenant at our graduation ceremony on 14 June 1961, and having retired from the Marine Corps on 1 August 1992, I served for 31 years, 1 month and 17 days as a United States Marine. Without question, the most memorable and impactful period of those many years was from 1 February 1968 until 2 March, when our company – Company F, 2nd Battalion, 5th Marine Battalion – was engaged in combat in Hue City. There is no group of Marine and Corpsmen for whom I have greater respect than those with whom I was honored to serve in Hue.

I reported to the 2nd Battalion, 5th Marines, on 10 October 1967 and joined Foxtrot Company the next day. Before leaving for Vietnam in late summer of 1967, I attended an "Impossible Dream" Boston Red Sox baseball game with my brother at Fenway Park as they were in contention to win the American League Pennant. Also, on 12 October, the day after joining F/2/5 in Vietnam, I was in the presence of another Marine who had a portable radio and we listened on the Armed Forces Radio Station as

Bob Gibson and the St. Louis Cardinals beat the Sox in the 7th game of the World Series. Ugh!

As you may know, Hue City was actually two cities in one. The ancient Citadel to the north of the Song Huong, or Perfume River, and the "New Hue" with Thua Thien Province government buildings including the Province Headquarters, the Treasury, Post Office, Hue University, multiple elementary and secondary schools, churches, and residential buildings were all located to the south of the Perfume River. All actions by our battalion, 2nd Battalion, 5th Marine Regiment, took place in the "New Hue" area and its outskirts south of the Perfume River.

Now to my direct responses to your questions:

- *What was the significance of the Battle of Hue City?*

Hue, with the Old Imperial Palace inside the Citadel, was the former Capital of Vietnam and was of historic significance for the Vietnamese people going back for centuries. Until the North Vietnamese Army (NVA) Tet Offensive of 1968, Hue had not experienced any noticeable combat activity during the Vietnam War. Of course, that all changed on the night of 30/31 January 1968, when the NVA and Viet Cong (VC) units executed numerous attacks on multiple South Vietnamese cities, including Hue City, in hopes of inciting a citizen uprising throughout all of South Vietnam.

On 31 January, only the Army of the Republic of Vietnam (ARVN) First Division headquarters remained in friendly hands. It was located in the far northeastern part of the Citadel and the U.S. Hue Military Advisory Command Vietnam (MACV) headquarters, was located off of Route 1, about 250 meters south of the Perfume River.

A large enemy flag was flying from a huge flagpole at the Imperial Palace and a smaller National Liberation Front (NFL) flag was flying at the Provincial headquarters in New Hue. While all the South Vietnam city battles were significant, most were of short duration. The Battle of Hue City is "officially" listed as a 24-day battle (although our Battalion was still suffering casualties through March 2nd, and we didn't leave Hue until the 9th and 10th of March) and is considered by many as the United States' longest and bloodiest battle of the Vietnam War. Of particular significance is the fact that North Vietnam's hope for a citizen uprising did not materialize.

- *What were the memorable experiences that you had there?*

My most memorable experiences were:

First, my daily observation of the disciplined courage of the Marines and Corpsmen of our Battalion.
- Our Company's attack on the Treasury Building on the 3rd and 4th of February; the first successful engagement by U.S. forces in Hue.
- Fox 2/5's rescue of 8 or 9 U.S. Army/U.S. Air Force officers and U.S. Government civilians on the 5th of February.
- *Fox 2/5's rescue of LtCol Khoa, the Province Chief of Thua Thien Province/Mayor of Hue City in the Hue hospital complex on the 5th of February.
- Hotel 2/5's successful attack on the jail on the 6th of February.
- Recognition that on 31 January the NVA "owned" New Hue and by 8 February we essentially did! (I'm referring to the area bordering on Route 1, the Perfume River, and the Phu Cam Canal. We had many more serious and costly engagements in the outskirts.
- Hotel 2/5's successful attack of the Province Capital on the 6th of February and the lowering of the NLF flag and the raising of the Stars and Stripes on the building's flagpole.

U. S. Marines with captured NLF flag at Hue City – 1968.

- *This battle was different than others; Hue was a city and others were in the jungle. Can you comment on the difference?*

The Vietnam experience of U. S. service personnel and U. S. units varied greatly according to "When you were there? And, where were you?" Not until well after the Hue Battle did our battalion operate in a jungle environment.

Our Company and Battalion were operating in a place called An Hoa, about 25 miles south of Danang until early January 1968, when the Battalion (and the 5th Marine Regiment, were moved to an operating area (AO) south of a Marine Combat Base in Phu Bai. Phu Bai is located about 8 miles south of Hue. Our actions, especially at An Hoa, consisted of search and destroy operations in rice paddies and small villages, while being shot at from some of the villages. We seldom saw any enemy yet suffered casualties from small arms and boobytraps when maneuvering through these villages. It was frustrating. In the Phu Bai AO, we started to engage VC units and confronted fewer booby traps and our morale improved.

In New Hue, we fought the enemy, which were mostly NVA, among substantial buildings at close range with essentially the same weapons systems as the NVA/VC, rifles, machine guns, shoulder fired rocket launchers, 60mm and 81mm mortars, 106mm recoilless rifles, and hand grenades. Our Marines also had CS gas grenades and E-8 gas launchers which were most valuable as we attacked the Treasury Building while wearing our gas masks. Directly facing the enemy and winning was, despite our casualties, a morale booster.

An important lesson we learned on Day One was not to go down the streets, but rather through the building.

- *From my research, it seems that this battle turned the American public against the war. I would love to know your perspective, whether or not it aligns with that view.*

This opinion was largely attributed to television coverage of a statement by Walter Cronkite, in late February 1968, after he returned from a visit to Vietnam, including Hue City on 17 February. Early, in an hour-long CBS television program of 27 February 1968 entitled; "Report from Vietnam: Who, What, When, Where and Why?" Walter said, "Who won and who lost in the great Tet Offensive against the Cities? I'm not sure, he said. The Viet Cong did not win a knockout, but neither did we. The referees of history may make it a draw."

(Left) CBS Anchorman Walter Cronkite I Hue City – 1968.

I can't believe he could make such remarks. The goals of the NVA (not the Viet Cong) were to start a general uprising among the South Vietnam people. That clearly did not occur. Nor were the NVA able to hold any of the cities they initially occupied. In fact, the attacking units of the NVA Army were thoroughly defeated with many costly casualties. Their remaining Hue elements returned to North Vietnam and these units were not to be seen until over a year later!

At the close of the hour, Cronkite acknowledged that what he is about to say is subjective, Walter also stated that in his opinion, "It seems now more than ever that the bloody experience of Vietnam is to end in a stalemate --- it is increasingly clear to this reporter that the only rational way out then will be to negotiate, not as victors, but as honorable people who lived up to their pledge to defend democracy and did the best they could." Many Americans were surely believers and I'm told the Anti-War activities increased dramatically. Of course, we didn't remove U.S. fighting forces until many years later and the decision to do so was "dictated" by political considerations, not military ones.

- *Any other insights about Hue or Vietnam or experiences that you would be willing to share would be greatly appreciated.*

Unlike today, The Marines (sailors and soldiers) fighting in Vietnam had no electronic devices. All correspondence home was sent via mail. I very seldom saw a newspaper and after listening to the 7th game of the World Series, back in 1967, I never again listened to a radio. Both Martin

Luther King Jr. (4/4/68) and Robert Kennedy (6/5/68) were assassinated during my Vietnam tour and I didn't learn about them until well after the fact. We had no real awareness of the anti-war actions. Our focus was on the tasks at hand, not what was going on at home.

Marines and Corpsmen of F/2/5 during the Vietnam War years have gathered at reunions 18 times since our first one in 1989. In each case they (we) are proud of our service and know we were the ultimate victors in every one of our engagements.

I was proud to have taken part in the U.S. Navy's commissioning ceremony for the Guided Missile Cruiser CG *USS Hue City*, in 1991. It is still the only U. S. Navy ship named for a Vietnam battle. Mrs. JoAnn Cheatham, the wife of our Hue 2nd Battalion, 5th Marine Commander, LtCol. Ernest Cheatham Jr. (now a retired LtGen and deceased), was the ship's sponsor and broke the ceremonial bottle of champagne across her bow at the christening in 1990. Regrettably, ships age and last year I and other Marine Hue City veterans attended the decommissioning ceremony of this great ship. I hope this helps, Chase. If you have any specific questions that I'm qualified to answer please don't hesitate to ask.

Sincerely,
Mike Downs

This vignette comes from a letter correspondence between Brigadier General Downs and Chase Cooley, a 10th grade student at Natick High School, in May 2023. Chase had selected the Battle of Hue City as a project because "he comes from a family of proud Marines." Brigadier General Downs replied, "I am impressed with your Project, It's well beyond anything I ever contemplated during my High School years. You honor Hue veterans in choosing the Battle of Hue. I know the Marines of your family are especially proud of you."

25.

The Big Fight
by John Wentworth

SSgt. John Wentworth, U. S. Army – 1968.

The story of the December 1968, battle near Dong Xoi, III Corps, South Vietnam as told through the eyes of SSGT John Wentworth, Radio Telephone Operator (RTO) - 10 ½ months in country, eight months in the woods with A Company, 2/5 First Cavalry Division.

They smelled something odd. They had attached some kind of magical machine to a helicopter and flew over an area suspected of hosting NVA activity. The machine knew what smells it should smell if it was flying over the jungle. But it smelled of something else; human feces, or it was smoke. Who knows how clever that machine was, but the brass trusted it enough to send two companies, Companies A & C, 2/5 First Cav to find out what was going on. I was, at that time, one of the CO's two radio operators, Apache 6-India.

They blew holes in the bamboo jungle with bombs, close to a trail that they thought, correctly, led to whatever was there. Because of the size of the trail, this thing had to be big and important. We had no idea! We did know, however, that we were in a place that was dangerous for us. For example, we never, ever walked down a trail. Trails were where ambushes and booby traps were. But this jungle was mature bamboo, impenetrable by machetes that handily cut trails through softer foliage, so down the trail we went, prepared for whatever bad was waiting for us.

We had been flown in from the Special Forces base at Dong Xoi and we had made a lot of noise. Many Huey sorties were flown, bringing two hundred men into a usually silent forest, so they were ready for us with Claymore mines hanging from the trees, machine gunners in other trees, and defenders dug into fortifications. Our first contact signaled the beginning of a multiple day non-stop firefight that ebbed and flowed in intensity but ran day and night.

The trail led to the front door of whatever this place was. We slugged it out for several hours. Then, as the sun started to go down, we withdrew, and set up a circular FOB (forward operating base), next to one of the edges of whatever this was.

By now we had come to the realization that we had no communications with our rear. No resupply, no water, no ammo resupply, and no artillery support. Luckily enough I had been hanging around with some LRRPs (long-range reconnaissance personnel) back at Phuoc Binh, flirting with the idea of joining them. I came to my senses, but in the process the LRRP guys taught me how to make field-expedient antennas, cut to resonate with the frequencies we used. I had a couple in my pack.

But we needed to get them up high. Fortunately, we were out of the bamboo and into a regular forest with tall trees. One had a stout limb about 100 feet off the ground. I needed to get a line over that branch so I could pull the antennas up for the best reception. I talked our "chew hoi," SGT Kahn by name, into climbing up the tree to get this done. Before he was more than halfway up, the bad guys, who had snipers at the edge of our FOB, tried to shoot him off the tree. They missed but he came down the tree in a hurry with the line still in his teeth. We suppressed the bad guys, and SGT Kahn got the lanyard over the limb and down to the ground again. We attached a boom with the two pyramid-shaped antennas hanging from either end. Then we could call for help.

I stayed up all night, calling out into the airwaves, "9er, 9er,9er, this is Apache 6 India, does anyone copy?" frequency after frequency after frequency. Finally, in the middle of the night, I got an answer from a random Huey helicopter flying by. He was able to bridge me into our battalion HQ who dispatched helicopters for the rest of the night. Then airplanes came in the morning, circling our position and functioning as radio relays. At last, we had communication.

We attacked again the next day, taking casualties and getting nowhere. At night, a Huey, the last resupply sortie of the day, was shot out of the air by two of the bad guys, one shooting green tracers, using their weapons, and the other shooting red tracers from American weapons they had gathered in some earlier fight. The Huey crew suffered one broken leg and a lot of bruises. It could have been worse: when the bird landed, it hit the ground right on top of one of the white phosphorous trip flares we used to defend our FOB. The helicopter was half full of fuel and sitting on top of the burning flare. One of our quick-thinking guys hit the flare a couple of times with an entrenching tool and it went out.

The bird left its tail rotor embedded in a tree, like a tomahawk, about 75 feet up.

Finally, after what seems like an endless two or three days (I don't remember which) and multiple assaults on their perimeter to no avail, we went out as we went in, back up the trail to the insertion point from which we'd get plucked out of this patch of jungle. My greatest fear, since the CO and I would be the last two people to be extracted, was that the other bad guys would try to pick us off since we would not have the benefit of a lot of troops guarding the LZ, that asset having been extracted already. But they did not. The Hueys and their M-60's were enough of a deterrent. It turned out that 200 of us were knocking on the doors of an NVA divisional supply base, defended by 1200 well-entrenched NVA regulars. We suffered 35% friendly dead and wounded.

But we were not done. We withdrew to a Michelin rubber plantation. This place had the hardest soil I had ever encountered. One of my jobs was to dig the foxhole that the CO and I would share. It ended up being about 4 inches deep.

The next day the ground rumbled beneath our feet. The standoff distance for a B-52 Arclight bombing run is 1 kilometer. We were well inside that click (kilometer). It felt good though as we thought of what the Arclight was doing to the bad guys.

We walked back in, saw some bloody bandages, but no NVA soldiers, and started the process of off-loading our treasure. In the end, we had captured the NVA supply base; RPGs, and ammunition, principally, and to have been the largest ammunition heist of the war. Our CO, who was commanding three infantry companies by the time we got done, was awarded the Distinguished Service Cross for his efforts.

But we still weren't done yet. We had a third infantry company to help with the off-loading. That company set up inside our new FOB and took responsibility for the mortar fire that peppered the perimeter all night long just in case the bad guys decided to come back for a revenge visit. These new guys were green, and so when they fired off a short round, so short that it was going to explode inside the FOB, they delayed calling out the "SHORT ROUND!!!" warning. The result was that a bunch of our guys were still running for cover when the rounds hit and blew shrapnel up and out, which is what mortars do. We were lucky enough to find another middle of the night Huey traveler who was able and willing to pick up the first load of the 13 wounded casualties, and to call for help to evacuate the rest of wounded.

When we finished moving the loot to the rear, the leadership decided the safest way to get out of there was to walk, not take the risks associated with another Huey extraction. Who in their right minds would attack three infantry companies, even as depleted as we were, walking through the woods in three columns.

And so, we set off. Suddenly there were bullets everywhere.

25. The Big Fight

We had walked into the side of a supply company walking perpendicular to us in the middle of nowhere. Someone said that the NVA had a particular rocket launcher, and the CO wanted it. We sustained some casualties trying to take it away from the bad guys, but never got it. We weren't doing that well in general. The other RTO and I were lying on the ground, shoulders touching and bullets whizzing above our ears. They were close and there were a lot of them and there was not time for one of the other companies to trudge through the woods and bring us help.

According to our Forward Observer this happened:

He told the CO, "Captain, I'm going to do something stupid."

"What are you going to do, Paul?"

"I'm going to jump up and down and see if I can draw their fire."

"You're pretty likely to die, if you do that."

"Better chances than if I don't do it, Sir."

So, the FO jumped up and down waving his arms until the other guys shot at him...and missed, blessedly. But now he knew where the shooters were.

He suggested to the CO that he have the point man and the last guy in our line of men to pop smoke (throw smoke grenades). He then told the pilot of an Apache helicopter that was on station but useless because no one knew where he should shoot, that he should draw a mental line that connected the two columns of smoke and shoot at that line but aim at the treetops not the ground. The bad guys were in the treetops; we were on the ground.

The end of the battle. The enemy took their rocket launcher and left.

The next day, as the troops policed the battleground, the CO, and the CP (Command Post) personnel, me included, sat on the ground, in a circle around a dead NVA soldier. The CO instructed us to all rest our feet on the dead guy to "harden us up."

A few weeks later, I went to Hawaii for my R&R, arriving on New Year's Eve, which was celebrated extensively with firecrackers and firework rockets. I spent most of that night under the bed with my wife wondering what in hell was going on. I came back to Vietnam to a job in the rear. I had been quite sure that my number was up, so I used my college degree and ability to type to land a clerks' job. I read a lot of regulations in my down time and figured out how to get a leave in Bangkok and how to get promoted. So, I came home a hard five SGT, the rank having become effective the day before I left country. And that's the story of the Dong Xoi battle, December 1968, through the eyes of an RTO.

John Wentworth is a graduate of Boston University earning a degree in communications. He served in Vietnam, between Tet 1968 and Tet 1969, as an infantry rifleman and as a Sergeant. John founded Wentworth Recruiting in 1982, retiring in 2018. He has served on many local California and national boards in various roles. John is the current President of Warfighter Advance, a non-profit for the successful reintegration of warfighters.

26.

Sergeant Joe
by John Wentworth

His name was Sergeant Joe and we all cheered when he lost his sight.

He was a career infantry soldier and was, as 2nd platoon sergeant whose radio I carried, my boss. He was an E6, a staff sergeant, although how he was promoted to that rank has always been a mystery to me.

One day, I said to him that I was not that anxious to kill anyone. I would if I had to, but I was not bloodthirsty. He immediately demoted me. His dislike of me may have been fueled by my being one of the few college graduate grunts around and probably made worse by my having bailed out of Infantry OCS. I had signed up for Signal Corps OCS but was sent to the infantry school with the promise that I would get a Signal Corps commission. I did not believe that would happen and further concluded that I was not cut out to lead men to their deaths. So, I quit. And I think that cluster of facts pissed off SGT Joe.

But demoting me was not enough for SGT Joe. One morning he took me for a walk outside of the FOB. We were in the mountains close to the DMZ, prowling around the Ho Chi Minh trail, looking for a fight. Walking around the woods outside of the FOB and the one hundred plus weapons on the perimeter for a couple of hours struck me as suicidal, but there I was, carrying SGT Joe's radio, wandering around the woods with our two rifles, and helpless in my situation. That I was still a "newbie" did not help. I had not yet been in a firefight and was scared.

I process fear by turning it into anger. My rage for SGT Joe increased exponentially when he took my radio away and made me walk point for a week. He also took away my C-4 (plastic explosives). I was the explosives guy for the company, having proven that I could blow neat and clean columns up through the canopy, which the Hueys descended in, bringing food, water, ammo, mail, and personnel out to us in the woods.

The hallmark of a well blown chimney was that the trees fell away from center, not crisscrossed, making it easy to get to the helicopter. SGT Joe took over that duty, thinking he knew how to do it. He did not. The trick to doing it well was to know where to place the explosive and to estimate correctly how much C4 each tree needed to fall, intact, where one wanted it to go. The trunk of SGT Joe's first tree broke into several pieces because he used too much C-4, shattering it. The pieces fell all over the place, forcing the men to climb over them to get to and from the helicopter.

The next chimney, and the next, were the same. The troops began to grumble. They wanted "Winnie," my nickname, to blow the chimneys. "Why don't you give him his radio back while you are at it," was their collective comment. . He finally did.

Our CO rotated to the rear. Our new CO was fierce, as illustrated by his having wrestled alligators for recreation when he was a younger man. He had us write RNR on the back of our helmet cloth covers and came armed with a handful of Sharpies to make sure no one had an excuse for not doing it. RNR stood for Results, Not Reasons, and he meant it.

This was too much for SGT Joe. He climbed on a bird, went back to the rear, found the prior CO, and talked his way into a job with him, out of the woods and away from the new CO. The troops, who liked SGT Joe no better than I did, were thrilled to be rid of him.

One day, one of our guys unloaded off the afternoon resupply Huey hooting and hollering that SGT Joe had lost his sight. The entire camp let out a joyful noise. It turns out he drank too much local liquor and went blind. Not a soul in the company was sad to hear about this.

A few days later, another guy got off the resupply bird with a profoundly hang dog look. SGT Joe's sight had returned. A loud "boo" rolled through the camp, following the news as it spread. We should have been ashamed of ourselves for being so happy at SGT Joe's misfortune, but we were not, and especially not me.

Despite my run-in with SGT Joe and his demoting me, I went on to get promoted, working my way up from the platoon sergeant's RTO to the platoon leader's RTO to one of the CO's RTOs. I came home as a

26. Sergeant Joe

Sergeant, a rank I talked my way into to ensure that I would not have to do KP duty if the reserves got me.

I never heard from the reserves. Rumor had it that combat infantry troops had proven to be more trouble than they were worth in the eyes of some of the reserve outfits, including the one I would have gone to had I gotten the orders. The best story I heard, true or not, was of a unit that conducted an exercise that entailed walking through some woods from point A to point B. The grunts added a dog leg to point C, a local bar, appearing late at point B, (the original goal), happy, drunk and with no contrition whatsoever. That is an unauthorized walk in the woods that I would have welcomed.

I never looked for SGT Joe, nor did the organizers of our reunions. It is just as well. He would just have found a way to spoil our fun, particularly mine, 50+ years later. I am still mad at him.

27.

The Queen of Spades
by John Wentworth

The memo had gone out, we were told, directing us to cease and desist the practice of cutting the ears off dead enemy soldiers and leaving them in their mouths. We had never done that, but there was no faster way to get us to do something than to tell us not to. So, when our point man killed an enemy soldier, one of our guys stuck a queen of spades card in his mouth.

We were told the Queen of Spades had a lot of bad juju attached to it in the minds of the enemy, so we didn't actually violate the directive, which was about collecting ears, not playing cards, but we did get the satisfaction of putting a hex on the spirit of any enemy soldier we killed.

We were in a "hot" area. Some of the second and third tour NCOs had told the boss. They had been there before, and it was an extremely dangerous place. The boss heard about this and went forward with his plan anyway.

The boss was an overly aggressive and very accomplished infantry captain who was a graduate of the Citadel, and this was his second tour in Vietnam. His daughter told us this story years later at one of our reunions. During his first tour, he was an advisor to the South Vietnamese Army which meant that he accompanied South Vietnamese units as they performed their missions. On one night mission they had crawled up to the edge of a rural village through the surrounding rice patties. They did whatever they were supposed to do, and were withdrawing when the boss realized that, due to weight loss, his Citadel class ring had fallen off his finger. This would not do, he thought to himself. He loved that ring. He crawled through the mud and found the person to whom he reported and requested permission to find his ring. It was granted. By himself, in the dark, in enemy territory and with no support, he worked his way back to his prior position, scratched around the ground with his hands until he found his ring, then, crawling back in the mud, rejoined his company.

To say that he knew his mind and was not afraid to follow what it told him to do would be an understatement. So, as dangerous as this area was, we marched on, looking for a fight.

It was a week and a day before Thanksgiving 1968, and we had been selected by MACV as the poster boys of Thanksgiving 1968. The battalion commander and a CBS news crew were coming to visit us the next day to film a piece about how well these fine American troops were treated on Thanksgiving. They were bringing a hot turkey meal for us, replacing our normal C-rations. The intention was to shoot the film then rush it back to the U.S. to be shown on Walter Cronkite's CBS news show on Thanksgiving Day.

We were walking through tall grass when our point man and a six-foot-tall Chinese advisor to the VC came upon each other. They played quick-draw and our guy won. He killed the other guy. Then someone had the bright idea of putting the playing card in his mouth and did it. We walked to our objective, circled up, cleared the brush for some distance so any attacker would have to cross an area that provided no cover to get to our perimeter. Then we laid out the white phosphorus trip flares which if tripped, would illuminate an intruder. Then we planted the Claymore mines that would kill anyone in the kill zone when detonated by one of our guys. Behind all this fortification, the guys had dug fox holes that functioned as cover in a firefight. This was done with extra care because of the seasoned NCOs admonition about how dangerous this area was and the certainty of our having really upset the friends of the dead guy.

The next day, half the company broke into small teams and walked cloverleaf patterns in the woods outside of the FOB, in the hope that our guys would run into their guys, should they have decided to visit us for a little retribution. We did not want to be on the receiving visit of a hostile visit when the boss' boss and the CBS news crew were visiting.

We went as far as to put a stationary LP (Listening Post) outside of the FOB, too: four guys with a radio and their weapons whose job was to listen

27. The Queen of Spades

and alert us if they heard enemy movement, then run back to the protection of the FOB.

Being one of the boss' radio operators, I was left back at the FOB to ensure we had good communications between the boss, who was leading one of the small teams, the other team leaders, and our support lifeline. It was incredibly quiet until suddenly bullets, a lot of bullets, started flying through the center of the FOB. We were being attacked. I flew in one impossible leap to get to my radio and call for help. I was quite sure that the next thing I was going to see was a North Vietnamese soldier running toward me, shooting at me. But suddenly the attack stopped.

The only noise was the crackle of the radio. The toll was six of our guys killed, the four in the OP and two in a foxhole on the perimeter of the FOB. To make clear why they visited us that day, they left a pair of Ho Chi Minh sandals, skillfully placed on the edge of the foxhole. The rest of the company hot-footed it back to the FOB. They had been too far out to help, the attack having been efficiently brief, but they were in time to meet the helicopter with the battalion commander, the CBS news crew, and the hot meal. The battalion commander struck a heroic pose, one foot in a foxhole, one on the foxhole's lip, and waxed eloquently about the marvels of air mobility. The sixth casualty, still living at the time, was evacuated to medical help on the same helicopter that had brought the battalion commander and the food to us. Our wounded brother died anyway, however.

The meal was only OK, but welcome, nonetheless. Some of the guys were not too hungry because of being so close to so much death, but only a few. Back in the rear sometime later a guy came up to my, yelling, "Winnie, Winnie, you're on TV." They had been watching film of the CBS news. I was very visible, caught by the CBS cameraman helping to lift one of my dead friends onto a Huey. Six dead in trade for the Queen of Spades did not seem like a good tradeoff. On the other hand, I got on TV and got a small medal for my part. The real recasting of the tradeoff was that a few weeks later we were a key part of an effort that took an NVA divisional forward supply base from them, the largest ammunition cache capture of the war. This only makes sense if one has been in combat and hardened to death, but we were glad that we got our payback and felt that we had won.

Later, in civilian life, many of us came to understand while coping with post trauma issues, that, as necessary as war seems to be to some, it may or may not be, but, for sure, no one wins.

28.

USS Frank E. Evans (DD-754) – The Lost 74

by Louann Sage Withers

I was a 16-year-old sophomore in high school. I came home from school on the afternoon of June 4, 1969, to find my parents sobbing. They informed me that my three cousins Gary 22, Greg 21, and Kelly, 19, had all died. Their ship, the *USS Frank E. Evans* had been cut in half by an Australian Aircraft Carrier in the South China Seas. All the boys were on the side that sank immediately. The worst part was that my Aunt Eunice and Uncle Ernie had heard about the accident the night before while in bed listening to the 10:00 news. It wasn't until the next day that the Navy came out to tell them all three boys had perished, along with another 71 crew members. My aunt and uncle had one son left - Doug who was only 7 years old at this time.

The Sage Brothers; Gary, Greg, and Kelly.

The memorial service was one of the saddest times in my life. In this tiny town of Niobrara, Nebraska, national news cameras - were everywhere. The sadness was overwhelming for everyone. When the flags were given to my Aunt, Uncle, Doug, and Linda (Greg's widow), I knew the service was ending. When the bugler with the trumpet started playing "Taps," I knew my Aunt and Uncles lifetime of grief had just begun.

My cousin and I stayed with Aunt Eunice and Uncle Ernie for about the next three weeks. We helped them on the farm during the day and just sat with them in the evening listening to whatever they wanted to talk about. Aunt Eunice would say over and over, "If I just had a body, just one body to bury." Uncle Ernie would tell how he convinced the boys to join the Navy, because he had been in the Army during WWII, and he felt the Navy would be a safer choice. When the boys got permission to be on the same ship, Uncle Ernie stressed his concern to them that what if something were to happen like the five Sullivan brothers that were on the same ship, attacked and sunk, during WWII. He was so guilt ridden. He blamed himself forever.

They started to receive letters from all over the world every day. We would all go through bags and bags of mail. Most people in this world are kind and have beautiful words to say. One day I opened a piece of mail to read "this did not happen and that they were all living on an island somewhere and it is just a government conspiracy." Some letters were from people requesting money for framed obituaries. We screened every letter, trying hard not to let them see the cruelty.

Aunt Eunice was the aunt we all loved. She had the best sense of humor, talked slowly, and smiled all the time. Her blue eyes "twinkled." Not anymore. They both just existed. I really believe if they did have "just one body to bury" there could have been some sense of closure.

The names of the 74 sailors who lost their lives that night were never included on the Vietnam Memorial Wall. We were always told because the accident occurred outside the designated combat zone of the time, the men who make up the Lost 74 don't qualify for inclusion on the Vietnam War Memorial Wall. My aunt and uncle spent the rest of their lives fighting to get their sons' names along with the other 71 names on the wall. My three cousins and the other 71 who lost their lives still to this day, deserve the honor of having their names memorialized.

USS Evans DD-754.

Louann Sage Withers of Scottsdale, AZ. is a high school classmate of playwright Harry Kantrovich. Together, with her sister Joan and Harry, they have been petitioning to add the Lost 74 to the Vietnam Wall.

29.

Goin' to the Nam - 1969
by Mike Humason

I was sent to Vietnam in the fall of 1969. During my short time in the U. S. Army, I had met a few guys who were really looking forward to going, but I was not one of them. I did not particularly want to go, although there was a sense of adventure around my pending time in a war zone. I was concerned about the dangers, but at the same time, in a way I was excited.

I had been given leave before my departure, which I used up mostly hanging out with my girlfriend. I remember that my Mom was not happy about that, but I was going off to where people get shot and blown to smithereens, so I wanted to fill what might be my last free days on earth with as much sweet female presence as possible.

I took a taxi cab to the Los Angeles International Airport and caught a flight to Oakland. I don't remember how I got to the departure gate – by another cab or bus, Once I got there I was assigned to a barracks, then processed through Supply for a nice new set of jungle fatigues and a pair of jungle boots. The next morning, I was assigned to supervise a squad of enlisted men destined for KP (kitchen) duty. During the course of the morning, a runner came to find me. My father had come to see me off. I went to the main gate, signed him in, then took him back to the staging area, where I showed him around. As we walked back toward the barracks, two of the men I was in charge of came around a corner and stopped dead in their tracks when they saw me. They had ditched KP and had gone to the PX. They begged me not to turn them in. I told them that if they were back on duty by the time I arrived, I would fail to note their absence. My old man thought that was a good technique. He didn't stay long – we had a drink at the PX, and then I went back to duty.

I believe it was that night when we were taken over to Travis Air Force Base to be flown out to Vietnam. We were put on a bus, taken to the air base, and put on a Flying Tiger Airlines 707, where we strapped in and took off into the black sky. I sat next to a guy whom I had met at Fort Ord, a Sergeant Aiken. We shared stories about our leave time, and we wondered where we would end up once we reached Vietnam.

About five rows behind me there was a Private 1st Class who decided that he was in love with one of the flight attendants, named Maria. He became increasing loud as he beseeched her to marry him and to take him "away from all of this." We kept hoping that he would give up, but Aiken finally got up, went back, and put a finger on the guy's face and told him to shut up. He came back chuckling, telling me that guy was a little twerp whose eyes got very big as Aiken chewed his ass. As he turned to come back to his seat, Aiken heard the Pfc. mutter under his breath, "lifer." Aiken told me the only way he would be a Lifer was if he didn't come home at all. Such was our sense of humor.

We landed some hours later at Honolulu Airport. I think it was about 2 a.m. local time. We were allowed to get off the plane as it was being serviced, and as flight crews changed over. I strolled around a bit – and all that I remember about that was getting outside for a while, finding it to be hot and humid. Soon, we got back on board the 707 and once again headed West. At about dawn we landed on Guam. Once again, we got off the airplane and were allowed to stroll around the area. I visited the beach, which was covered with coral and seashells. The ocean was a very light, bright blue. I remember thinking about the Marines trying to defend Guam against the Japanese invasion in 1941, and I wondered if they had fought on the very beach where I stood, enjoying the morning air.

Soon, we were back on board the airplane. Our next stop was Anderson Air Force Base in the Philippines – just another waystation on the long Pacific road to Asia. After another short interlude, we climbed back aboard and went into the sky for the final leg of the journey. The plane became very, very quiet until the moment when we crossed over the coastline of Vietnam. As we looked down at mile after mile of impenetrable green jungle, a loud voice called out from the rear of the 707; "There ain't nothin' down there, so turn this damn thing around!" The entire planeload of GI's burst out in a huge uproar of laughter, and conversations resumed. I saw explosions in the foliage below serval times and felt my nerves tighten.

We circled once, and then went into a steep approach to the last airstrip. We touched down, the brakes lit up, and the men became silent again. We rolled to a stop, the ramp was rolled up to the 707, and the cabin door opened. We stood up and shuffled slowly toward the open exit. I remember the heat and the smell that hit me just before I came to the doorway. We walked down the ramp and the heat struck in full force. My thought was that I would eventually adapt to it, but that it would be miserable anyway. We were taken across the apron and into our new lives, knowing that some of us would never return home.

We were taken by truck to Long Binh, where we were put into barracks and processed in-country. Our 201 files were delivered and we were asked to write down our primary MOS (Military Occupational Specialty) on the 201 jacket. I wrote 11H40, Recoilless Rifle NCO. I had trained on the 106mm at Fort Polk before going to NCO School at Fort Benning, where I took on the 11B MOS, Light Weapons Infantry. 11H was still my primary MOS, though, so that is what I wrote down, without really thinking about it too much. I believe that thoughtless action on my part determined the rest of my time in Vietnam, because several days later, I was assigned to the 101st Airborne Division and was told that I was going to Phu Bai, up north. There was another sergeant I knew from Fort Benning in my group, and we renewed acquaintances on our trip north, which began again by truck, then continued by C-130 to Phu Bai, and extended through our processing into the 101st, then through P-training. I never saw that sergeant again, and wondered once in a while whatever became of him.

From the moment we stepped off the C-130 aircraft, all the way through P-Training, it rained every day. I remember my surprise at this after experiencing the heat of Long Binh, but I soon learned about the Monsoon season, and had to adapt to it just like everything else. From Phu Bai, we were trucked to Camp Evans, where we were placed under the command of an E-6 Black Hat, who took us through the next several days on integration into the Screaming Eagles. It was not particularly fun, but it wasn't very hard. It was cold and rainy, and we got a lot of use from our ponchos and spare dry socks. We learned about Division SOP for everything from smoke color to radio protocol, and we were taught about the proud history of the 101st. We were told that we were now a part of that tradition, and that whether we wore jump wings or not, we were part of an Airborne division, and that we would conduct ourselves as such at all times, especially on the battlefield. We were there to protect the South Vietnamese and to destroy our enemies. I remember a number of cooks and clerks who didn't think much about that message until we went out on a platoon training patrol and got shot at by a sniper. Those of us with combat MOSs took cover and got the men away from the sniper's field of fire while the Black Hat called in a Cobra gunship to work over the sniper's suspected position. I found that I enjoyed the whole thing, since no one got hurt. After all the boredom and drudgery of P-Training it was exciting.

Then came the day that I was given my orders to my new unit, Delta 2/17. I was driven through the mud and rain to Camp Eagle, where I was dropped off at the Troop area. The first thing I noticed was the 106mm jeeps, and the memory shot through my mind of writing "11H40" on the outside of my 201 jacket. I reported in at the Troop office, where I met Platoon Sergeant Walker, who shook my hand and welcomed me warmly. He told me that he was happy to see me, and that they had a job all ready and waiting. He sent a runner to get Sergeant Mike Lafever, who also made me feel at home as he got me a cot and a sleeping bag and explained how things worked. I met a number of other men, and then settled into my sleeping bag to catch up on sleep after the short off-hours P-Training. I didn't know how much time I would have to rest, so I decided to get some sleep. I remember thinking as I dozed off that I didn't have much choice in the matter. I was in a new home and I would have to become a part of the family. I was a long way away from California.

30.

Tet of 1969
- Attack on the Chu Chi Base Camp

by Colonel Douglas E. Moore, United States Army

As the Vietnamese holiday of TET approached, everyone became a little concerned as to the enemy's attempt a repeat the performance of the famous TET attacks of 1968. There was heightened security everywhere and all of us became a little more cautious during the lead-up to TET.

Then on the afternoon of February 25, 1969, I was called fly out to evacuate several seriously wounded soldiers from a furious battle that was raging near Trung Lap and brought them to the 12th Evacuation Hospital at Chu Chi.

About 3 AM the following morning, I got a call from the hospital telling me two of the wounded men we had brought in were "bad bleeders" and that their blood supply was running low. The caller said they would need more blood from the depot at Long Binh within the next 3-4 hours. Since the crew and I were already awake, I told him we would go ahead and fly the mission if the blood was ready for pick-up. He assured me it was, so I said we would return in about an hour. I clearly remember walking to our helicopter that morning because it was pitch-black dark and eerily quiet. The only sound we could hear, other than the crunching of our boots against the ground, was a lone generator running somewhere in the distance. The co-pilot and I climbed in while the medic and crew chief assumed their pre-start positions. When the crew chief spun the blades, I called "Clear" and pulled the start trigger.

I was watching the RPM gauge slowly building towards 6600 RPM when I heard a loud explosion, and our helicopter shook. My first thought was we had blown an engine, so I looked out the door just as the crew chief yelled "A rocket hit right behind us." I told the crew chief and medic to get in and, just as they climbed aboard, a second rocket hit even closer. Fortunately, it came in at an angle and its blast and shrapnel went behind us. I called Chu Chi tower for immediate take-off and was cleared, but the tower operator asked, "Dust Off, are you aware that two rockets landed right behind you?" I told him we heard them but did not think we sustained any damage.

After reaching one thousand feet, I turned back towards the airfield to see if we could figure out where the rockets were coming from. We saw flashes in a wooded area about 4-5 miles northeast of the basecamp, so I called the tower and gave them the map coordinates. I knew the tower had a direct phone line to Division Artillery and that they could quickly start counter-battery fire at the rocket launching positions. We watched more rockets raining down on the basecamp and then we began seeing explosions, one after another, along the southeastern perimeter where the 242nd Aviation Company (Muleskinners) parked their CH-47 (Chinook) Helicopters. An enemy sapper unit had penetrated that part of the basecamp and began throwing satchel charges, filled with TNT, into the backs of the Chinooks.

Shortly thereafter, a tremendous firefight erupted all along our southern perimeter and red and green tracers began flying in every direction. We then saw a fire erupt in one of the "hot refueling" points for helicopters and the bad guys managed to set an ammunition bunker on fire. A minute or so later, I heard the Diamond Head quick-reaction gunship team calling for take-off, so I contacted their flight lead and gave them the location where the rockets were coming from.

By that time, the bad guys had either fired all their rockets or stopped firing because they knew they would soon be attacked. Within a short time, dozens of other helicopters began calling for take-off and the tower operator did a magnificent job keeping control over what could have been chaos. I later wrote a memo to the Airfield Commander recommending the tower crew for heroism awards because they stayed at their stations and kept order while rockets landed all around them and the air was filled with bullets.

Since there was nothing more we could do, we flew to Long Binh and picked up several boxes of blood before starting back to Chu Chi. Along the way back, the night sky was filled with the flashing lights of helicopters headed towards Long Binh and Bien Hoa where most remained until the crisis was over. When I called Chu Chi tower for landing instructions, the tower operator told me the basecamp was closed and that I should divert to some other location. I told him I had several boxes of blood that was desperately needed at the hospital, and they would have people standing by to take them. The tower operator cleared me to land but recommended extreme caution because he said there were enemy sapper teams on the basecamp and firefights were underway at several locations.

I made a high-speed approach to the 12th Evacuation Hospital's helipad and their waiting staff grabbed the boxes of blood and ran for cover. We then headed for Long Binh where we stayed until midday.

When I got back to Chu Chi, I learned the Commanding General had directed all units to conduct a thorough search of their areas because it was believed some enemy sappers were still on the basecamp. In typical GI fashion, my soldiers searched our unit area and reported back to me that the only suspicious thing they found was an old, mangy looking dog in our motor pool tent. They said it could have been a Viet Cong sympathizer because it refused to talk, but they sent it on its way without harm. Everyone joked about the search until, just before dark, four enemy sappers were found hiding in a Conex container about one hundred yards away in another unit's area. As that word spread, the search took on a more serious tone and we, for the next several days, were all more cautious.

Fourteen Americans were killed and thirty were wounded during the attack on Chu Chi basecamp. Eleven enemy soldiers were killed and eight were captured. Nine Chinook helicopters were destroyed, three were heavily damaged, and an unknown amount of fuel and ammunition were lost in our version of TET of 1969.

31.

1970s Random reflections on service in South Vietnam 1970-1971

by Lieutenant Colonel Gil Robinson,
United States Marine Corps (Ret)

LtCol Gil Robinson, USMC.

I arrived in the Republic of South Vietnam from Okinawa having had my orders changed from 1st Amtracs, 3rd MARDIV to 1st MARDIV at my request. I was assigned to G-3 as a Watch Officer and sent to Quang Da Special Zone as the G-3 Liaison Officer. It was made up of an ARVN Corps HQ consisting of the 51st Regiment, 33rd Ranger Bn, and the 2nd ARVN Armored Division.

As luck would have it, I got to brief adjacent Marine Regiments which included 1st Marine Regiment commanded by Col Paul X Kelly, (later to become the 28th Commandant of the Marine Corps) and 2nd Battalion, 1st Marine Regiment, commanded by LtCol Bill Leftwich. After several briefings I spoke with LtCol Leftwich and asked for his help in a transfer to an infantry battalion. Two weeks later I was assigned to 2nd Battalion, 1st Marine Regiment as the S-2 and Scout Platoon Commander.

LtCol Leftwich was an exceptional leader who would later be killed in action in a helicopter crash in the Que Son mountains, while commanding the 1st Reconnaissance Battalion. His leadership is the reason I chose to stay in the Marine Corps and serve for the next 24 years.

On 21 July 1970, the Secon Battalion, 1st Marines, was conducting a Combined operation with the 2nd Republic of Korea Marine Brigade north of Hoi An. Hotel 2/1 was in contact with the VC from the VC R-20 Battalion and had killed 10 VC fighters, captured 1 POW, and detained 13 suspected VC. LtCol Leftwich and I went to the Hotel position on an 11th Motors Huskie (tracked vehicle) and on our return we were hit by a command denotated box mine. I along with LtCol Leftwich and four other Marines were blown 20 to 30 feet away and the vehicle was totally destroyed.

I don't know how long I was knocked unconscious, but when I came to, I saw Leftwich moving toward the wounded Marines, and I followed his lead. When I got to the driver, he had a serious head wound and I was able to stop the bleeding, but he died at the 1st Medical Battalion the very next day. It wasn't until the MEDEVAC arrived that I realized I had multiple shrapnel wounds in my leg, thighs, chest, and face. A Sub Team from 3rd CIT (counterintelligence team), detained several Vietnamese villagers that were in the immediate area. One of these detainees was a young Vietnamese lady who was a messenger for the VC cadre and who ran the war in southern Quang Nam Province.

The Sub-Team Commander, 1st Lt Tom Marino, turned that Vietnamese girl into a valuable asset which led to the famous 4 August Raid. On 7 September 1970, after several successful raids on High Value Targets resulting from the 4 August Operation, I along with 1st Lt Marino went to a meeting at Hill 55. We parked our Jeep next to a 5-ton truck. We exited the jeep and just 15 seconds later the truck blew up and blew us into a sandbagged bunker. We were dazed but the jeep was destroyed. The VC had attached explosive charge underneath the truck with a timer. Lady luck was with me once again.

We organized my Scout Platoon into three Battalion Scout Teams. The Division didn't have enough Reconnaissance assets to cover all of Quang Nam Province. 1st Reconnaissance Battalion conducted a short course for our Scouts, and we performed the reconnaissance patrols in our TAOR (Tactical Area of Operations), which was in the lowlands east of Charlie Ridge, in the Rocket Belt, and South of Marble Mountain.

I was blessed with superb NCO's. My Chief Scout was Sgt Rodriguez. He was on his 2nd tour extension when he stepped on a Toe-Popper booby trap on a night ambush. He was evacuated to the Naval Hospital on Guam. Here is an excerpt from the letter he wrote me:

"Sir, I'm sorry I let you and the guys down the way I did. I never expected to trip the booby trap at the time I did. I guess I just couldn't help it. I'm glad nobody else was hurt. All the VC can rest easy now that I will never return to Vietnam. Tell the guys to give the VC/NVA hell. All of you take care of yourself. Rod." Lord where do we get such men? He lost part of his foot but remained on active duty and retired as a Master Gunnery Sergeant.

I had the privilege to serve with and lead real heroes. To this very day I consider my 16 months the highlight of my life. I would do it all over again.

[Editor's note: First Lt Michael Dan Kellum, USMCR served under LtCol Leftwich in 2/1 in 1970. He is the author of "Books I and II, American Heroes: Grunts, Pilots & 'Docs.'" The books are available through Navarro-Hill Publishing Group, P.O. Box 1088, Longview, TX 75606, or www.MichaelDanKellum.com. 28 LEATHERNECK MAY 2011]

The August 4th Caper

"On 4 Aug. 1970, Leftwich and Major John S. Grinalds, 2/1's operations officer, sat down with the 3d Counterintelligence (CIT) officer, First Lieutenant Thomas H. "Tom" Marino, and 2/1's intelligence officer, Second Lieutenant Gilford A. "Gil" Robinson, to produce what the division called the Cam Sa Raid (Marino favored the more flippant "The August 4 Caper" for the name of the operation).

They planned a daring daylight heliborne raid against an estimated 30 Viet Cong (VC) cadre commanders and their small security detachment. The local enemy leaders gathered regularly in a large field just inside the Republic of Korea Marine Corps' area of operation below Cam Sa, between Phong Ha and Quang Ha, seven kilometers or "clicks" due south of Camp Lauer.

Another one of the keys to success for the midday heliborne raid was Leftwich and Grinalds' decision to leave their Vietnamese counterparts out of the loop. "The major assumption the enemy made was that we would coordinate with Vietnamese authorities, where their spies were located, before we began an attack. We never did that, and, as a consequence, they had no warning," said Major Grinalds. By not coordinating their raid with the local "friendly" Vietnamese hierarchy, the Marines caught the VC commanders completely unaware and so sure of their safety they didn't have the necessary armed escort. Nor could they scurry down into their well-hidden tunnels or melt into nearby forests to await the Marines' departure, according to Grinalds.

"The results were beyond my fondest hopes. Prior to this action, we've played cat and mouse with them for a long time. We've had several unsuccessful efforts to kill or capture these people, and we feel this will have a significant long-term impact on the direction of Viet Cong and North Vietnamese activities in the Danang area," said LtCol Leftwich. The firefight and roundup of prisoners from start to finish lasted only 25 minutes!

It turned out to be a bonanza for 2/1. Golf-3, ITT (Interrogator Translator Team) and CIT (Counterintelligence Team), CH-46s with help from above [Cobras, Huey's, and Sea Knights - CH-46s], cut the legs out from under the VC command infrastructure in that part of the Quang Nam Province for some time. Leftwich later was awarded a well-deserved Silver Star for engineering the bold heliborne attack and its star-studded outcome."

Author's note: This condensed excerpt comes from Chapter 12, "Book II, American Heroes: Grunts, Pilots & 'Docs." *LtCol Bill Leftwich Jr., who orchestrated the Cam Sa Raid, was killed in a helicopter accident in the Que Son Mountains, 18 Nov. 1970. To honor his memory, the Leftwich Trophy is given each year to the most outstanding Marine captain.*

32.

Delta Troop 2nd/17th Operations - June 1969 - November 1970

by Lieutenant Colonel Blair Craig,
United States Army (Ret)

Captain Blair Craig, U.S. Army – 1969.

Background:

In June of 1969 President Nixon began the withdrawal of U.S. troops from Vietnam and established the Presidential Blue Line on the East side of the A Shau valley. By November, in northern I Corps, the only U.S.

Soldiers allowed to work the Roung Roung and A Shau valleys to the Laotian border, and up to the Demilitarized Zone with North Vietnam were elements of 2/17th Cavalry, the 75th Rangers, USMC 3rd Force Recon, and Special Forces.

November 1969 saw Delta Troop change command from Captain Raymond (Fred) Rees to Captain Paul Protzman. Unlike the earlier great commander, the new commander was an aviator, knew nothing about ground operations, never went to the field, and never took part in the missions of the Troop. It was a Platoon level operation and leadership. The mission of the 2d Squadron 17th Cavalry in Vietnam was to provide both aerial and ground reconnaissance for the 101st Airborne Division. The Squadron performed a variety of missions:

> Reconnaissance Bomb Damage Assessments
> Rescue of downed airmen Ranger Team Support
> Enemy snatch operations Marine Recon Team Support
> Support of ground troops by fire Convoy escort
> Search and destroy Perimeter base defense
> Special G2 directed missions Ambushes
> Immediate reaction force OPCON to Infantry Brigades

Delta Troop was the primary ground force used to exploit on the ground what was seen by the Squadron's aerial reconnaissance assets. Quite simply, Delta Troop's mission differed from the Infantry in that we worked in small elements, inserted by combat assault, often rappelling from helicopters 100 feet thru the triple canopy jungle directly into known enemy locations. The mission was to figure out the actual enemy strength by engaging them, or capturing them, and bringing back their equipment and documents.

Operation RICHLAND SQUARE began in August 1969. On the 16th of that month LTC William Deloach turned over command of the 2/17th to LTC Jack Patterson. Six days later, while inspecting the Cav's perimeter defense, LTC Patterson fell and broke his leg. His replacement was LTC Lavere Bindrup. The rest of that year was spent on small unit level operation throughout Thua Thien Province, the Vietnamese and Laotian salient, and northern I Corps area.

32. Delta Troop 2nd/17th Operations - June 1969 - November 1970

The monsoons of November '69 thru February '70 kept the number of missions down. Operation RANDOLPH GLEN began on 15 Feb in response to elements of nine NVA regiments having been identified in the northern I Corps area. In early March 1970 LTC Robert F. Molinelli assumed command of 2/17 Cavalry. He proved to be the finest Soldier and unit Commander, and just what 2/17th needed in this time of daily enemy contact and large NVA movement into South Vietnam.

The 101st Division began another operation TEXAS STAR which ran from 1 Apr to 5 Sep 1970. In May through November 1970, 1st Lt. David Blair Craig assumed command of Delta Troop 8 May 1970. He had been Delta's 3d Platoon leader since June 1969 and volunteered to extend in Vietnam to take command of the Troop. Delta Troop was now being employed often beyond any supporting artillery fan, and could not be reinforced by U.S. ground units, only by a special unit of the 1st ARVN Division known as the Hoc Bao (Black Panther).

On 11 May, three days into a five-day reconnaissance mission, Team Kansas, L Company 75th Rangers, made a 0430 communications check. At 0600, when they failed to again check in, Squadron launched an OH-6 Light Observation Helicopter (LOH) to investigate and found the 6-man team dead. A reaction force was inserted to recover their bodies – all 6 had been shot in the head.

In response to this tragedy, Delta Troop took over all the Ranger reconnaissance, ambush, and sniper missions in I Corps for four weeks while the Ranger Company went into retraining. In June, the Squadron jumped its Tactical Operations Center (TOC) to the city of Quang Tri. The Cav found evidence of a regimental base camp belonging to the North Vietnam Army (NVA) 66th Regiment. Delta Troop was inserted on June 24th and discovered a large hospital complex with supporting bunkers. Most of the enemy had fled, leaving a small security element for Delta Troop to eliminate. Left behind were weapons, medical supplies, surgical instruments, food, and over 100 pounds of documents.

July. Having destroyed a large part of the 66th Regiment the previous month, the 2/17th was targeted against the 9th NVA Regiment believed to have arrived in South Vietnam from its sanctuary in Laos. At approximately 1130 on 8 July, a pink team (light observation helicopters), was conducting a visual recon in the Fire Support Base (FSB) Snapper area, and saw 150-200 NVA in the open, moving along a fresh well-beaten trail. The enemy was engaged by Cav pink teams, Cobra gunships and Aerial Rocket Artillery gunships. In the first engagement 50 NVA were killed. At 1358 8 July, Delta Troop with OPCON of A and C Troop Aero-rifle platoons, was inserted into two locations directly on top of what turned out to be a 600 man North Vietnamese Regiment. In the ensuing firefight 139 enemy soldiers were killed and four captured, along with many documents, individual and crew-served weapons, and elimination of the NVA Command Group.

8 July 1970. On that day, Delta Troop engaged the enemy and did what no other unit in I Corps could have done. On that day, Delta Troop saved the lives of many soldiers, for along with disseminating the enemy, Delta Troop captured all the 9th NVA Regiment's maps and battle plans to attack I Corps American bases. On that Day – Delta Troop lost great men – Cavalry Troopers: PSG Walter L. Walker, SSG Allen R. Stroud, SGT Stanley J. Cruse, SGT Harold L. Frank, SP4 Joseph F. McDermott, and PFC Harry McEwing. They wait for us to join them, in our time, half way down the trail to hell ... at a place called Fiddler's Green.

August 1970. Delta provided extensive ground reconnaissance, downed aircraft crew security and airframe recovery, ready reaction force for ground units in contact, 31 days of convoy escorts, ambushes, and security sweeps around Camp Eagle, as well as providing the Camp Eagle security reaction force with jeeps mounted with M-60s and 106mm Recoilless Rifles. Delta was inserted on 16 August with the ARVN Hoc Bao unit to secure and recover two downed aircraft. Additionally, that month Delta reinforced and extracted 2 Ranger Teams in contact. Ranger team Kenya was inserted on 29 August, 07:50 into a "hot LZ" on top of Dong Mang Chan mountain and sustained severe casualties to the Ranger team and the C Troop insertion aircrew.

The C Troop Aero-rifle reaction force was inserted at 08:22. By 09:25 Delta Troop reaction force of 54 Troopers was inserted, and a sweep was made of the area. At 15:25pm, A Company, 3/506 Infantry was inserted and all elements remained throughout the night. A Reconnaissance in Force (RIF) took place the next day with negative findings.

32. Delta Troop 2nd/17th Operations - June 1969 - November 1970

September saw increased enemy activity in Elephant Valley called for the Cavalry. On 8 September 2/17 elements including Delta Troop, set up a Command Post (CP) at Marble Mountain. The Elephant Valley now belonged to the Cav. On 29 September Delta rappelled thru the triple canopy 12 kilometers south of FSB Fist for a recon-in-force. Enroute radio briefing to Delta's Commander by the Division G-2 reported a 120-man NVA unit on a river, had been located downslope from the insert point, with caution to avoid contact as the weather was closing in and a major engagement could not be reinforced. Several hundred pounds of rice and stores were located. However, the early monsoon did come in and no aircraft could return for extraction. The 101st Division declared "No Fly" for all aircraft.

Delta Troop remained on that hillside for 5 days in continuous driving rain, with only one days ration per man to eat, while also being sporadically probed by the enemy.

On the evening of the 4th day, LTC Molinelli called for Squadron volunteers to attempt to get in to Delta Troop: everyone stepped forward. At first light, without informing the Division, the Cav lifted off for the Roung Roung Valley. A Forward Arm and Refuel Point (FARP) was set up with an Aero-Rifle platoon providing security. Then a single LOH (OH-6) began to maneuver up the river through the rain and fog, and established radio communication with Delta's CO.

At this point, LTC Molinelli declared a "Tactical Emergency" and told the Division the Cav had lifted off to rescue Delta Troop. The LOH had only about 50 foot visibility but was able to take instruction from Delta CO, who could hear the LOH rotor blades and talked the LOH upslope into a clearing. What followed was a string of LOHs and UH-1 Hueys, one at a time, each risking the very hazardous flight in almost zero visibility to come in and recover Delta Troopers (2-4 men at a time) until the two platoons and Command HQ (all 52 Troopers) were lifted to the FARP and transferred to UH-1Hs for the trip back to Camp Eagle. Those glorious pilots and "Men in the Doorway" ---- Cavalry all the way!!

October and November. Monsoons and two typhoons severely restricted operations for both aviation and ground Cav elements. Delta continued to provide daily patrols and nightly ambushes in the foothill region between the mountains East of the A Shau Valley, protecting the area around Camp Eagle (Headquarters of the 101st Division), to the China Sea. It was miserable weather for both the friendly and enemy forces.

In late November, Captain Blair Craig relinquished command of Delta Troop to Captain Robert Thomas.

LtCol. D. Blair Craig United States Army (Ret)
Commander, Delta Troop 2/17th Cavalry, May-Nov 1970

33.

A Day in a Year …. A Year in a Life
by Lieutenant Colonel Blair Craig
United States Army (Ret)

From the China Sea to Hamburger Hill and the Laotian border, from Bach Ma through the A Shau Valley, past Khe Sanh (site of the Viet Min defeat of the French in 1954, and the siege of the U.S. Marines in 1968) to the Demilitarized Zone separating North and South Vietnam, Delta Troop, 2d Squadron 17th Cavalry executed their missions in the finest traditions of the U. S. military.

We served in Delta Troop of the 2d Squadron 17th U.S. Cavalry, a combat unit within one of the most storied Divisions of the U.S. military history – the 101st Airborne Division (Airmobile). We, along with L Company 75th Rangers were the eyes and ears of the 101st. We were called upon to perform some of the craziest missions that came down from Division Headquarters.

Vietnam was a "come as you are" tour of duty. There were few arriving unit formations – only individual replacements. You came in by yourself. And you left by yourself. Going home often to family and friends who couldn't understand where you had been or want to discuss what you did – or why.

The 2/17th Cavalry re-deployed from Vietnam 1 April 1972 to its home station with the 101st Division at Fort Campbell, Kentucky. This historical narrative stands as a tribute to all the men of Delta Troop. It is with all credit to their personal valor, teamwork, and looking after one another, that enabled them to conduct some of the most diverse and dangerous missions during the Vietnam conflict.

Thirty-six Delta Troopers died in combat from 13 April 69 through 11 September 1971, in the Republic of Vietnam. Thirty-six Delta Troopers have died between 19 September 1972 and 25 September 2015, at home.

LtCol. D. Blair Craig, United States Army (Ret)

34.

Delta Troop 2nd/17th Air Cavalry - 1969
by Thom Stoddert

I was just 19 years old when I arrived in South Vietnam, in the winter of 1969, and was later assigned to Delta Troop, 2/17th Cavalry, 101st Airborne Division, found near Phu Bai/Hue, in I Corps. Our primary mission was to be the reaction force for the division whose area of operations included several South Vietnamese provinces and sometimes going into Laos. These missions would be for things such as rescue missions, aircraft and body recovery, reconnaissance patrols, ground convoy escort, and base defense, all with the use of gun jeeps or helicopter transport.

It sounded glamourous at first, but reality soon set in. In between missions were long hot days doing nothing or menial chores. After a couple of weeks of doing extraordinarily little, a sergeant burst into our hootch in the middle of a card game and asked for three volunteers to go out on a mission. I saw SP-4 Don Beghtal immediately stand up. Since he was my mentor of sorts and because I wanted to lose my status as a "cherry" (a new guy), I stood up. A minute or so later another NCO told me I could back off - it was going to be rough, and I was too new. Knowing that I had volunteered in front of everyone, I kept my word. This was my first mission and I needed to be broken in.

The 20-minute helicopter flight culminated with a silent aerial ballet right out of Hollywood, and it was taking place just below us. Looking out of the Huey (UH-1) helicopter I was in; I could see three tight rings of four attack cobras (AH-1's) circling below us. One ring, on top of another and at the same time, several observation choppers (OH-6's) were scurrying all around, just feet above the elephant grass.

In turn, one gun ship, and then another, would peel off from the lowest ring, unload its rockets and machine guns rounds into the jungle from a much lower altitude than expected, and then fly home and reload. Eventually it was our turn. We came in about 10 to 15 feet above the vegetation, the door gunners began pushing us out. They did not tell us that the choppers were being shot up and that was the reason they were not landing. Doing an intense detailed half-second assessment, I decided to jump. All sorts of thoughts came to me after standing up. The most vivid was how badly the place smelled.

On the ground for less than ten minutes, we located what was left of the Marine Force Recon team. Three were beyond help, and two were loaded on medevacs. Looking over my right shoulder I saw one Marine being hoisted into the medevac bird, and a few seconds later I looked again and there was no Marine there. He had fallen off the jungle penetrator and back down to the ground. (Years later I learned his name was Paul Keaveney. Since then, we have called each other on February 7th, the anniversary of that heart-braking mission.)

While this was going on the observation birds raced a few feet overhead and then two more sets of rockets hit close enough that debris hit us. We were only twenty-four men, significantly outnumbered and we knew it.

We tied the dead Marines onto poles to make it easier to carry them. The Marine (James Fuhrman) whom I carried had his hands tied together to the pole a few inches from my face. His wedding band kept reflecting the sun into my eyes. The whole time I kept thinking, why did he have to die? He had a wife and a family. I was a much better candidate. I had little – I never even had a girlfriend. We had to put his body down at one point to catch our breath. I was carrying my rifle and two of the KIA's rifles plus Jim's web gear. A deep realization overcame me for the rest of that year: somehow, there was a God. He was not a kindly white-haired gentleman, and He was very much involved in the affairs of countless people.

After carrying the dead up a knoll and loading them onto a Huey, they were flown back to the 85th Evacuation Hospital at Phu Bai, as was the wounded Marine. The remaining two Marines were taken somewhere; we were never told where. Finally, it was our turn to get out of there. Except for our individual fears, it was all so impersonal.

Years later after reading a sample book from Amazon on my tablet, *"Force Recon Diary, 1969,* by Major Bruce "Doc" Norton, USMC, I realized that he had written about that mission. His publisher at Random House Inc., very quickly put me in touch with "Doc" and later we were able to meet at a Cabela's in Olympia, Washington. During our meeting I invited Bruce and anyone else from 3rd Force Recon Company to come to our reunion which we hold every two years, in Nashville.

Back then in Vietnam, Delta Troop would be scrambled in response to a variety of other missions. We almost never saw the end results of what we did, because it was all so impersonal. Missions were usually a 30-minute helicopter ride accompanied by a certain amount of fear and trepidation. After each mission, anywhere from an hour to several days were spent on the ground. On the day I experienced my first extraction, we recovered three American bodies and rescued three Marines. We did not know who they were, their names, or whatever happened to those Force Recon Marines. Our meeting with them was very brief, intense, and impersonal.

I often reflected on what happened to me in Vietnam. When I returned home, my sister told me for that year she had said a prayer for me every day. One night, she woke up sensing I was in trouble. That was the night our four-man team landed on Fire Support Base Ripcord, not too far from the A Shua Valley where I had carried out Fuhrman's body. We were rushed into FSB Ripcord, unprepared to support the infantry company already in place. There was no food, and no protection from the mountain weather. We were socked in by fog for over a week. None of the casualties could be flown out and no food or ammunition came in.

When the weather did clear, we were mortared. I watched a group of men, who had been working in a circle, go flying in the air after a mortar round hit in the middle of them. History books never mention the efforts that were made in the first half of April 1970 that prepared that base for the big battle. But there are books and videos telling of the fight months after we had secured that base.

Many years later, when the 3rd Force Recon Marines came to our reunions they said, "thank you" and told us about who they were, and what they had done with their lives after Vietnam. For the first time, a mission came full circle for me. There were finally faces and names to connect with what we had done that day.

Ironically, at another reunion, a fellow trooper, Bob Primeaux, a 100% Lakota Indian, (who was also on that mission in the A Shua), and I were sitting at the hotel's bar. We were invited to a table with two other gentlemen about our same age who asked us what we were all about. They were salesmen, from Nashville, Tennessee, here for training. They began sharing jokes with us. It was all friendly, and then somehow the conversation turned to Vietnam. Bob and I shared a few stories we thought were very amusing. We left out the blood-and-guts stories, yet that humorous stuff seemed to have rattled them. I can only imagine that they were comparing themselves with what we had done, with what they had done at 19- years of age.

35.

"Choppers"

by Mike Humason

The most enduring symbol of the Vietnam war is the helicopter. Vietnam was the first time that the helicopter was used so widely and effectively in battle, and the sights and sounds of helicopters will forever be a part of that experience for those who served there. To this day, when the circumstances are right, the sound of rotor blades punching the air can make the hair on the back of my neck stand up. For good and sometimes for ill, we rode those aluminum-skinned birds for all they were worth – and more times than we thought about, they were worth our lives.

Our Division, the 101st Airborne, was an Airmobile division. Along with the 1st Air Cavalry Division, we formed the two large units that relied on air transport as the foundation of our battle tactics. Other divisions were mechanized, using tanks and armored personnel carriers to get around, while still others got around in a combination of methods (as we did, also), but massive quantities of helicopter units formed the basic tactical and logistical elements for Airmobile units. We moved very fast, and we delivered a rock-hard punch in a very short period of time because we were Airmobile.

Within the 101st, our unit, the 17th Air Cavalry Squadron ("the Cav"), came from a horse-cavalry and armor tradition. I had been trained at the Infantry School at Fort Benning, Georgia, and was outnumbered by most of the other sergeants around me, who came from the Armor program at Fort Knox, Kentucky. We all had to adjust to a new style of warfare when we came to Vietnam. All that we had been taught was to be adapted to the helicopters. We were an Air Cav unit, which meant that when we left our base camp to go deep into the interior of the country, we went by air. We were able to get down to the Troop helicopter pad in five minutes, ready to go into combat, and at all times there was one platoon assigned to "reaction force" standby, calling for exactly that state of readiness.

My first real mission was one of these. One day after police call and chow, I was sitting around the 1st Platoon NCO hooch playing cards with Bob King, Mike Lafever, and Grady Walton when the door opened and Lieutenant Rausch stuck his head inside. "Get down to the pad now" he said, "the Rangers are in contact!" We dropped the cards on the table, stood up, put on web gear, and grabbed our M-16's, then each of us headed out to the other hooch's where the rest of the men were. We quickly passed Lt. Rausch's order and trotted down to the pad. I remember checking over my men to see that they had all their gear in order, when John Oakley strolled by. I think Oakley had been in-country longer than anyone else in the Troop. He gave me a long look and said, "You be cool out there." The Hueys came in quickly and settled down for just a moment while we boarded, sitting on the steel floors. I was both nervous and excited, and my heart rate picked up as the chopper lifted off the pad and into the sky. As we rode up into the sky, I noticed the air turning cooler, and as I went on succeeding missions, that was one element I looked forward to. A chopper ride was the closest thing we had to air conditioning. And the view was always spectacular.

We turned west and flew for what seemed like only ten or fifteen minutes, then we began to circle, getting lower and lower. My heart rate sped up, my eyeballs were about twice their normal size, and I remember what I had been told about getting off fast and getting out to the edge of the LZ (landing zone).

In the Cav, we had our own Air Force, which included not only transport, but fighters, and there they were - the Cobra gunships were working both sides of the hilltop LZ as we came in, and rockets were exploding in the jungle just below us. The ground came up very fast, we hit and I jumped off. I landed on my feet, and I ran as fast as I could to the outer edge of the LZ, where I dove on my belly into the dirt behind some dead tree branches. I kept my head down and waited for the choppers to clear off and for the rocket shrapnel to stop flying through the air.

When it started to become quiet, I raised my head up and looked around. I saw other troopers to my right, and a Ranger to my left. I also saw a dead NVA soldier lying on his back about 20 feet away. He seemed like a wax dummy, not really real. I had never seen a dead man before, and I was surprised that he really had no effect on me beyond simple curiosity. Then, I recognized the Ranger coming toward me; his name was Ed Miller, and he had trained me at Fort Benning the year before.

"Hey, Ed," I said, "what are you doing out here?" He shook his head and apologized for having us come out. "Do you have any extra magazines? I gave him two or three magazines, and then asked him what had happened. Ed had been out with a six man LRRP (Long Range Reconnaissance Patrol) team and they had been taking a short break in the bush just below the hilltop, when someone began to toss rocks at them. He said the NVA knew they were around the area but didn't seem to know exactly where or how many they were. They figured that the average Mark I GI would bitch, "Hey, who's throwing rocks?" Instead, the Rangers stayed down until the NVA got close. There had been a short fire fight, and a couple of Rangers had been hit. They had been Medevac'd before we got on the ground. When the Cobras and the Cav showed up, the NVA left the AO (Area of Operation).

A couple of Rangers had stripped the clothing from the dead man, which they bundled up to be taken back for intelligence evaluation. PSG Walker took a recon team down the hillside that led away from the LZ. They had been gone for about five minutes when there was a sudden burst of automatic weapons fired from their location. It lasted only a few short seconds, and then there was silence. I had no idea what was going on down there, and I began to wonder if we were about to have more action. Nothing else occurred, however, and soon the recon element returned, telling us that the fire had just been a recon-by-fire action in a particularly dense area. They had seen blood trails, but nothing else.

We gathered up our gear, the choppers came in, and we flew home. The hilltop and the jungle were left behind. I don't remember the location at all now, it was just another hilltop in Vietnam, where something once happened. That night we were back in the hooch and resumed our card game. I remember Bob King talking about the recon-by fire episode, which had startled him quite a bit. Other than that, it was as though nothing much had happened to change our routines. In one day, we had gone from a card game into a hot combat operation, then came back to resume the card game that evening. Only in a helicopter-borne armed unit could such a story be told.

UH-1 Huey Helicopter.

36.

Freedom Bird

by Mike Humason - Delta Troop 2nd/17th Air Cav

Every Vietnam veteran remembers the day he came home. In the same way you might remember the day that President Kennedy was shot, or the events of September 11th, 2001, you will always remember Freedom Day. This was the magical day when you climbed up the stairs and into the 707 airliner that would take you away from Hell and back to "The World."

Some of my friends did not get to ride the Freedom Bird. Mike Lafever was shot through the leg while on a helicopter taking him back to our base camp, on his last mission. He was flown straight to the 85th Evac Hospital, where he went into surgery, then did two days in ICU, then off to Japan, then eventually home. Other friends like Mike Frank and Walter Walker died in Vietnam, so they never got to take that Ride.

When I hit DEROS (date of estimated return from overseas), I left Camp Eagle for the last time on a truck, spent a few hours in Phu Bai processing paperwork, and then flew to the huge depot at Cam Ranh Bay. Cam Ranh Bay was another world. It was a highly secure area, and we were far from the Cam Ranh Bay perimeter, so we never actually saw it. They had running water and flush toilets. The first time I was able to visit a real flush toilet, I just sat there enjoying the clean coolness of the bathroom. It's hard to describe just how special something like that is, but when you have been surrounded by heat and dirt and foul smells for months at a time, a real bathroom with a real toilet is a sensuous luxury. There was also sand in the compound at Cam Ranh Bay. It was on the ocean, and I found time just to lie down on the sand, to wriggle my feet into it and let it cradle my body. I grew up in Santa Monica, California, and I spent many happy summer days on the beach, so the sands of Cam Ranh Bay were a welcome foretaste of home and freedom. There was also a PX (post exchange), which I visited to buy some gum and a book.

I went through more processing, and was assigned to a group, with a group number. We were allowed to go to chow in groups, and all our movements were staged by group numbers. There was a loudspeaker system at Cam Rahn Bay, and at random hours all through the day and night, announcements would be made telling one group or another that such-and such had been laid on for them. It was difficult to sleep, because there was always a commotion going on, with troops moving, and announcements coming over the loudspeakers. The only announcement we really wanted to hear was the one that directed us to the airfield for the Ride.

There were two places to find peace and quiet: the latrines with the flush toilets, and the Chapel. On my last day in Vietnam, there was an announcement that came over the loudspeakers that a nondenominational service would be held, and that anyone who felt the need could attend. We were to tell our group leaders if we wanted to go, so I checked out and headed to the base Chapel. I was not raised in a particular religion, but I had found myself taking stock of the past months, and I thought that going to a service might be a very good thing. The Chaplain was a very plainspoken man, and though I felt that he said the same things to various groups of men heading home, his words seemed heartfelt. He seemed to genuinely care for and respect the troops, and I still remember the lesson he gave us. It has helped me to cope with death, not only then, but over the years, and I'm very glad that I went to that service.

37.

"Days to Come"
by Mike Humason

Vietnam changed all of us, in ways both good and not so good. In the end, it helped form us into the men and women we are today, and one hopes that it helped us to become better fathers, mothers, husbands, wives, workers, and friends to those we've met along the many trails we have walked since returning to the World.

One story will help to illustrate the inner difference that Vietnam made: After returning home from Vietnam, I had a friend in the 1970s and 1980s who had made his living for a while as a fur trapper in the coastal mountains of California. He also hunted deer, upland game, and the occasional wild pig. One day, he invited me to go pig hunting with him. I hadn't hunted since I was a kid, shooting at jack rabbits in the desert, but I thought it might be an interesting thing to do. I agreed. We got up well before dawn the next day and drove into the mountains of Santa Barbara County, arriving at a turnout in the road at about daybreak. We grabbed our packs, water, and rifles, and began trudging through the tall wet grass and over hills covered with scrub and oak trees.

About three miles in, I heard a grunting sound off to the left in a hollow below us. I signaled to my buddy and we began a slow sweep down through the bush where the pigs had been. There was fresh scat on the ground and freshly broken grass where they had walked away headed downhill.

My buddy and I came out of the tree line and I signaled while he swept around counterclockwise to cut the pigs off. Suddenly, the pigs broke from their cover and ran across my front, and then back up the hill that we had just come down. My friend fired his rifle. The report was so loud (a 30/06 rifle shot across your front makes a tremendous amount of noise), that I was on my knees before I realized it. I heard a huge screaming squeal from the edge of the hilltop, then a crashing in the brush as the pig worked its way into cover. We followed him in and finished him off. He was a very large boar – and he had made the mistake of stopping to look behind himself as he crested the hill. My buddy had shot him square in the butt.

We butchered that hog there in the brush, packing the meat into burlap sacks that we carried in our packs, and carried the meat back to the truck. Wild pigs have extremely tough hides, so it was hard working getting this big guy cut up, and soon we were headed back to the truck. I soon realized that my pal was being very, very careful, looking around a lot, moving from tree to tree, then pausing before moving on again. When I asked him why, he told me that we were on private ranch land, and that the local wranglers had a reputation for rounding up hunters and taking them to see the sheriff. I wish that he had told me before, but there we were, so I began to skulk around as well, overlapping his field of view and his path through the woods. This went on for about ten minutes before I began to chuckle. I sat down under a big oak tree and found myself laughing even more. My buddy looked at me with alarm and asked what I was laughing about. I told him, "You know, I just realized that the last time I did anything like this, there were people in the woods who wanted to kill me. Somehow, I just can't take this very seriously."

We made it back to the truck and back home without incident. The hog became barbequed ribs, chops, steaks, and carnitas for burritos, as wild pig is a very good meal indeed. That was the last time I went hunting; my curiosity about wild pig was satisfied. More than that, though, it made it clear to me that there were things in this world that would never be able to make me nervous, no matter how anyone else felt. I had been inoculated by Vietnam.

I can only speak for myself, but I believe that I am right in guessing that my experiences after coming home were common. I had my share of bad dreams and my share of silence from those who were supposed to care for me but did not know how to ask; my everyman's ration of trying to understand the age-old question so well asked by Admiral James Stockdale in another context: "Who am I? Why am I here?" It has been 35 years [written in 2003] since I came home from Vietnam. I have done and

37. Days to Come

been so many things and have gone far beyond the young, inexperienced kid that I was in 1969, but my time in the service and my time in Vietnam are a very large part of what formed me into who I am today. And I suspect that is true for most of us.

We as individuals did not know, and our country did not know, what lay in store for us in 1970-something. The term PTSD had not yet been coined. Our turmoil was wrapped up in the political and cultural upheaval of that time, so the twists and turns that befell us were often intertwined and confused with other issues. Some of us moved on, and some of us dragged the anchor of Vietnam around with us. Each man and women dealt with life in the way that God wired us to do so.

So here we stand, 35 years later, having loved, hated, laughed, cried, had children, and in some cases grandchildren, having coached baseball, basketball, football, hockey, soccer, and God only knows what else – in short, having lived our lives as all of us do – and in doing so, we have fulfilled the answer to Admiral Stockdale's questions. We have only to see our children hit a home run, kick a goal, come home with a straight-A report card, or just hear them say, "I love you, Daddy," and the answer is there just as plain as day. The things that happened to us all those years ago have made us, in part, the men we became, and the men who we became are the men who have shared our gifts with our friends, co-workers, our wives and sweethearts, and especially our children. We changed the lives of those around us, and we will continue to do so.

And so, the balance of our lives was tipped. There was great pain and suffering on one end of the beam, but there was strength and wisdom on the other. There was fear and guilt and nightmares on one end, and joy, life, and creation on the other. Like everything in life, our time in the service came with darkness, but also with light. And, it came with a brotherhood that nothing can break. In an instant, in a sudden burst of gunfire, or a quick glimpse of an approaching enemy, a group of men became ready to fight to the death – not for God or Country, but for each other. Each man becomes transformed into a new thing that he was not before, in the space of a heartbeat. And that thing is never lost. It is what makes us different from other men. It is a very special gift, the bond that we share, that is still strong in us 35 years later.

I hadn't started writing this with the intention of getting overly serious or philosophical, but somehow it always seems to drift off in that direction whenever there is a discussion on Vietnam that lasts over ten minutes. In the end, it seems only right to say that I would give my life for my children or for my wife, without hesitation. But there was a time when I might have been asked to give my life for you, so I understand better what that willingness means. Thank you for your sacrifice, and for the gifts you have brought to the world.

May God bless all who served – those who came home and those who were not so fortunate. War is a hard and cruel teacher. May its lessons be remembered and used to make the world a better place.

38.

With 3rd Force Recon Company – 1970
by Rick Jenkins

We had been patrolling in the A Shau Valley since early December 1969, and we had been lucky with suffering no casualties. However, that was about to change.

It is February 1970. Team Box Hill is on the X-Ray/Zulu radio relay site doing their 10 days of Radio Relay assignment. I am a 2533/8654, which means I am a Radio/Telegraph operator with a full Force Reconnaissance MOS, being both "Jump" and SCUBA qualified.

LCpl. Harry Doan and Cpl. Rick Jenkins, USMC.

During our time on the relay site, two of our Force Recon teams were ambushed by the NVA. The first one was on February 5th, when one of the teams came into heavy contact. I communicated that fact to our Commanding Officer Major Alex Lee and also had the duty to relay to Major Lee the initials of the team's KIA's. The second ambush occurred on February 7th. Again, I had to communicate to the CO the initials of those KIAs. This laid heavily on my heart because I was well aware of who these individuals were. Out of the 12 people on the two teams seven were KIAs. They were Marines that I associated with and greatly cared about.

We shortly came off the relay site and prepared to go out on patrol. We were pissed that our fellow Marines had been killed. On our patrol we were operating in extremely heavy foliage. This was the start of our patrol. Suddenly there was trouble. Three of my team members had fallen off a cliff and were lying below on the side of the cliff. The patrol leader was Corporal Jim Vinyard; our point man was Jimmy Keysacker; and he was lying below with a Marine named Cooper. The foliage was cleared enough that I could see the side of the cliff, and I had to find another way down to these injured men. I took Harry Doan and our "Tail-end Charlie," LCpl. Steger, with me as we found a safer way down. There was a dried up stream bed at the bottom of the ravine, large enough to serve as a landing zone, and I immediately called for a medivac helicopter.

We were waiting for the medevac helicopter with our three team mates still on the side of the hill and were sprawled out on their backs. A rock rolled down and hit Keysacker on the top of his head and had knocked him out cold. Finally, we got the remaining Marines off the side of the hill, including Keysacker.

The medevac chopper finally arrived and sent down a Jungle Penetrator to lift the men out because the canopy was too thick for the pilot to land. At that point I got the three injured Marines on the penetrator and put Steger on the chopper.

That left me and Harry Doan to get on the penetrator. I got Harry on and when I tried to get myself on, I got the extraction strap caught around my neck but wasn't able to get myself up and onto on the two steel bars of the penetrator. The chopper started to take off and my M-16 was still lying on the ground. At that point I had a decision to make. I could grab my rifle and wait for the chopper to pick me up alone on the ground, or I could hang on to the penetrator and leave the rifle. I chose to stay on the penetrator. Apparently the chopper pilot got nervous and took off leaving us hanging on for dear life. We were dragged through the trees but finally we cleared the branches.

As the Huey pulled us up we finally got ahold of the skids. Harry was on one end of the skids, farthest from the crew chief, and I was on the opposite end and the crew chief had held onto my pack. We were heading toward a hilltop where the chopper could set down, but we didn't know that, because we were too scared to look down.

Harry could hang on no longer and he fell off the skid. We figured he fell between 15 and 20 feet. I, on the other hand, continued to hang on a little longer. Then, neither the crew chief nor I could hang on any longer and I fell from the skid. The only problem was that I still had the heavy nylon strap around my neck. As I fell, the strap violently jerked my neck upward and as I fell, I could feel the vertebrae in my neck crack. Then I passed out.

The next thing I remember was rolling on my side and releasing the quick release strap on my pack. Then, I remember being stood up and I thought I was a bird flying. Unbeknownst to both Harry and I, the command helicopter was still overhead and Captain Hisler landed with the chopper and was helping both Harry and me to get on our feet. We managed to get on board the chopper and headed to 85th Evac Hospital in Phu Bai. There the entire team was checked out for injuries. There was no blood on me and I remember the doctor saying I was fine but that I was going to have trouble later in life with arthritis in my spinal column. This was one of the last patrols into the A Shau Valley. It was a good thing because for the next few weeks I wasn't able to move my neck.

The Company was moved down to DaNang and part of our company was moved to 1st Force and part of us became a cadre that was going to train South Vietnamese Marines and Royal Korean Marines down in Hoi An.

In retrospect I wouldn't have changed a thing. Our company was tight knit and our leaders were the best in the Corps. The team members from our Corpsmen, officers, platoon leaders, and team members were the very best and I would not have traded my experiences as a team member for anything in the world.

Richard Jenkins – 3rd Force Reconnaissance Company in Vietnam - 1970

39.

Long Binh
by Charles Jameson

Before I marched for high school graduation, I was drafted. I was sent to basic training at Fort Campbell Kentucky on May 13, 1970. There I spent two months of hard physical training with many mental tests and left with an M-16 sharpshooter rating. I was offered warrant officer training with helicopters and planes, but it required signing up for six years of service in the Army. But that was not to be, as those six years were not in my plans. I was sent to air-conditioned classrooms for Advanced Individual Training at Fort Sill, Oklahoma with a MOS of 13E20 Cannon Fire Direction Specialist. After completion of training, I got two weeks at home with orders to report to Fort Ord, California on Oct. 07, 1970, to await orders to Vietnam.

I arrived in Vietnam Oct. 14, 1970. My rear area was Long Binh and I was assigned to the 11th Armored Cavalry. I arrived with two other men, both college graduates, and was told this story by one of the men we would be replacing. He told us if we were not "service oriented" then we may want to consider extending our time in Vietnam, because if we returned to the states with less than five months' time we could get out of the Army. He then explained that we would be working on the same thing he did and he had extended for two months. But because it was close to Christmas, he was getting a one month Christmas drop. So, he only had to pull one extra month of duty. We all three did this when we got the opportunity. Immediately I was trained and became the Armored Personnel Carriers Driver. We also ran our missions out of the APC.

As time went on and due to those leaving, I became section chief of a five-man crew on a 12-hr. shift. All went well until the 18th of January 1971. I was off duty and our person on the radio-watch hollered out: "Contact, Fire Mission," I stood up to holler out for those on duty and I saw our sergeant come through, holding his side from a wound. Those not on duty headed to the bunker and awaited a clear call. I then noticed blood running down my cheek from the side of my head. The wounded, including me, were gathered up and were airlifted to nearby hospitals.

I went to a head trauma unit. I can remember someone working on me that night as I faded out. My injury was not that bad, because I was told to catch a ride back to my rear unit. I waited outside, in front of the hospital and told people in charge where I needed to go. It worked and I got back to my unit.

Later in February we headed for DaNang for cleanup of the 11th Armored Cavalry's equipment before returning home. For those guys such as myself who had not finished their tour, it was a couple of days of waiting at China Beach, sleeping around the airport until our flights came up for our next duty station.

Finally, flight came up and I was assigned to Firebase Charlie 2 on the DMZ with the 1st/5th Mechanized Unit, again with 155-mm self-propelled howitzers. I know now no one else was as far up to the north. Quang Tri was our rear area. As a new man introducing myself, I may have introduced myself as Chuck (never really had a nickname) so one of the guys who we would be replacing says, "how about Cherry Chuck"! I said, "No, I have been in the country for four months and I'm no cherry!" He said I was a cherry to him because he had been there 12 months. So, Cherry Chuck it was!

39. Long Binh

I also again became the driver of the APC when we went out on missions. When we were on base, we operated out of a bunker. Also being a new guy, I got called for guard duty when the infantry was out. I was the first one out to the bunker that evening and immediately there were incoming artillery rounds hitting and exploding in front of me. At this point I was hunkered down with my M-16 watching the rockets overshoot our base and worrying if the other guys would make it to the bunker. I worried about having to stay awake all night by myself. Finally, they got there, and we made it through the night. Shortly thereafter Cherry Chuck once again became section chief of a 12-hour crew figuring the deflection, elevation, and charge. This was during the time that was known as Lamson 719.

At Firebase Charlie 2, we could expect a rocket attack around four and five o' clock nearly every day. Mess halls were not protected by sand bags and sometimes soldiers would have to scramble for a bunker during mess time incoming. Now I understood those 122-mm rockets were very inaccurate and thank goodness for that! On May 21, 1971, the NVA started shooting their 122-mm rockets on the infantry side of the base. A bunker close to the mess hall took a direct hit and 52 soldiers were buried under sandbags and other debris. Twenty of the soldiers were saved, but 32 died. (While at a VFW meeting last year I had a fellow Vietnam veteran who I knew, a helicopter pilot, ask me where I had served and when had I gotten to Firebase Charlie 2 and Lam Son 719. We had this eerie connection as he said he was one of the helicopter pilots who had gotten shot down that night while searching for the rocket location.

We had many fire missions, some just coordinates to shoot into, but also fire missions with Forward Observers who could give us corrections for more precise and accurate fire.

Another memory on Firebase Charlie 2 was when a South Vietnamese base was overrun by the VC. They were too far away, and we could only shoot illuminating rounds, But, the next morning, we did see a couple of B-52's that blew up the hill with their fire power. Here again after five months in country, I was going to Danang, part of the way by barge, to help clean up the unit's equipment before its trip back to the states.

But not Cherry Chuck, my service in Vietnam was not done and I was being transferred to the 101st Airborne Artillery. We were airlifted and dropped into several areas; this time along the Laotian Border, still trying to blow up the Ho Chi Minh trail. I was again assigned as the section chief. My sergeant major had wanted to recommend me as the "soldier of the month," but I kept telling him I was not going to be around much longer because I would be getting that one month Christmas drop.

On our last night before we were airlifted out, we did no firing. What was happening was our unit was transferring our established positions to the South Vietnamese Army. That night the person on radio watch hollered out around 4am that he saw an arm come around the bunker door trying to pick up our raincoats at the entrance. As we all got up that morning and started moving our material out of the bunker and into Conex boxes to be airlifted out, while the ARVN soldiers just milled around our area before we could get out. I always wondered what happened to this group.

Recently I found on the internet that the ARVN's were encircled by the NVA after just one month as two-thirds of them were taken as prisoners. It took 30 days for those South Vietnamese soldiers who escaped from the NVA to get back down south. This was my last mission, and I got that one month Christmas drop. The day I was leaving Vietnam, November 16th,1971, was the Soldier of the Month competition. I returned home and school had started, so I went to work with my father who retired the following year. I was diagnosed with a Pituitary tumor in 2003 and retired in 2010.

While I was in Vietnam, I served with three units; the 11th armored Cav, 1st of the 5th Mechanized unit on the DMZ, and finishing with the 101st Airborne on the Laotian Border. I was awarded three Bronze star Medals, the Purple Heart, three Army Commendation Medals, a Good Conduct Medal, and the Vietnamese Cross of Gallantry, which was a unit citation.

Charles Jameson, born in Culpeper Virginia. He graduated from George Washington Carver Regional High School. Charles is a 1970 Graduate of Virginia Commonwealth University. He earned a B.S. in Education. His service in Vietnam was in the United States Army as a Specialist 4.

40.

United States Air Force Security Service
by Harvey Goldstein

In addition to marching everywhere and doing some light exercises, we were given a battery of tests, one of which was a made-up language. I scored well, which put the wheels in motion for me to be assigned to the Air Force Security Service. Those of us who tested well were given a "dream sheet" and listed the five languages we would like to learn in order of preference. I picked Russian, Mandarin Chinese, and three Eastern European languages. North Vietnamese was not on the list, but that is the one I was assigned to learn.

Language school was at a civilian contract school in Rosslyn, Virginia, a section of Arlington and home for the Defense Language Institute East Coast. We were housed at Andrews AFB, and bussed into Virginia Monday-Friday for classes from 9:00 a.m. until 3:00 p.m.

The written Vietnamese is the same, whether it is North or South Vietnam. The difference is in the pronunciation: the North Vietnamese dialect is the proper way of speaking; the southern version is slow and more of a drawl. We were to learn the nuances of the North dialect. We started with a book that might be compared to the old "Dick and Jane" series that many of us old-timers had learned in first grade. Our early lessons were to become familiar with the alphabet and diacritical marks.

While we were learning basic conversational Vietnamese for nine months, the FBI was investigating us to be sure that we could be trusted with highly classified information. Our schooling continued with radio school at Goodfellow AFB in San Angelo, Texas for five months, learning North Vietnamese military terms, and listening to actual combat tape recordings. We prepared for our overseas assignment, after training, by attending various survival schools, simulating being a POW, living in the mountains, water survival, jungle survival in the Philippine. I arrived at Tan Son Nhut Air Base outside of Saigon, Vietnam in mid-July 1970.

I was going to be flying on an EC-47, which was a C-47, or civilian DC-3, that had been reconfigured and loaded with equipment to eavesdrop on the Viet Cong transmitting Morse signals and North Vietnamese voice targets on the ground. Each day there were many missions, beginning early in the morning, usually before sunrise, and some take-offs were as late as 8:00 p.m. If there was a linguist on board, the missions would be five hours in the air. If the aircraft carried only Morse Code intercept operators, the mission would be seven hours in the air. These times did not include the two pre-flight briefings and the one post mission de-briefing. Some of our missions were over the Delta, but most of our missions took us over Cambodia, with hot targets over the Parrot's Beak, Phnom Penh, Kampong Cham, and Kampong Som, also known as Sihanoukville. While serving temporary duty in Nakhon Phanom (NKP), Thailand, we flew our missions over Laos. The flight personnel consisted of one linguist, two Morse interceptors, a Morse analyst and one who helped the navigator fix the position of the targets on the ground. It should be noted that we flew at altitudes between 5,000 and 8,000 feet; our airplanes were not pressurized. We had to fly above 11,500 feet when we flew over Laos to be above the mountains; the non-mountainous area was the Plain of Jars (PDJ), which was a stronghold for the North Vietnamese and the Pathet Lao communist forces.

My flight days began at least two hours before takeoff. It was a ten-minute walk from our barracks to the 7th Air Force Headquarters compound, which was where our office was located for the first briefing. The sergeant in charge would tell us what our mission was and where we would be flying. Following the briefing at our headquarters, we were driven to the flight line where we would pick up our .38 caliber Smith & Wesson pistol, meet with the pilot (Aircraft Commander/AC), co-pilot, and navigator, and have another briefing. This briefing was by an officer who explained what weather we might encounter, the terrain we will fly over, and the possibility of enemy guns. There were now eight of us as we walked to the revetment where our airplane was parked. If our parking space was too far to walk, another Air Force vehicle would drive us along the taxiway to our parking space.

When the initial pre-flight was complete, the engines were shut down and we climbed the three steps into the airplane. Once aboard, we walked to our positions (I was up front over the right wing) and placed our holstered guns over the back of our seats. We were now ready for the final pre-flight to begin and we could hear the entire checklist of the pilot and the co-pilot through our headsets, with the AC and co-pilot double checking everything. Then it was time to start the engines.

My next five hours were spent rolling a radio dial seeking North Vietnamese voice communications, while the other enlisted personnel on board were listening to the Viet Cong's Morse code. They had lots of dits, dots and dashes to listen to, while I spun the dial looking for North Vietnamese voice targets. There were some voice targets in the Mekong Delta, but there were more in Cambodia. When I picked up a viable voice target, I alerted the pilot and navigator, turned on the tape recorder and recorded his coded message for 20-30 minutes while we got a triangular fix on his location below us. The Morse interceptors picked up valid information in real time. The voice targets always spoke in coded messages, using four or five-digit numbers. We had learned that if it was a five-digit coded transmission, it was just chatter, but if it was four digits, it was hot and needed to be transcribed, decoded, and translated as soon as possible. The Morse targets on the ground were also fixed, so that we knew where they were and where they were traveling from and to. The voice targets were transmitting from heavy equipment that was not mobile. When I left, my voice targets were in the same locations as when I had arrived a year earlier. That was important information.

Our primary function for our missions was to find the Viet Cong and North Vietnamese on the ground, gather the information, and bring it back for evaluation. Our organization, the 6994th Security Squadron, flew 10-15 missions every day out of Tan Son Nhut, as well as similar numbers at our detachments in Danang, which covered the northern sector of Vietnam, including the DMZ, Cam Ranh Bay, which covered the central part of Vietnam, and Nakhon Phanom (NKP), Thailand, which flew over Laos.

Before my first flight in Thailand, I paid serious attention to the briefings. The first briefing described the possible Morse Code and voice targets. The briefing with the pilot, co-pilot and navigator was about the terrain and guns on the ground. We were flying in a non-pressurized aircraft, designed to go no higher than 10,000 feet. The mountains we were supposed to fly over were 11,500 feet, which meant that we would be spending the better part of five hours at 12,000 feet or higher. We were not to waiver from above the mountains because the area next to it was the Plain of Jars (known as the PDJ to the Air Force) which was a Communist stronghold and had a lot of big guns that could easily blow us out of the sky.

Even though I had been flying in Vietnam for almost two months, it was standard procedure to have an instructor go up with the new guy on the first flight. As my instructor napped on the floor, I worked the position. At one point I looked out my window over the wing and didn't see any mountains – at all! I woke up the instructor and asked him if he thought we were where I thought we were. He called to the navigator, "Do you have any idea as to where the f**k we are?," to which the navigator answered, "No." EC-47s are not known for speed, but we may have broken air-speed records getting out of there. We were flying over the PDJ. I couldn't wait to get back to base for a drink (and clean shorts).

After 45 days in Thailand, I returned to Tan Son Nhut and finished my year in Vietnam flying missions at only 8,000 feet over hostile targets. We were easy targets flying so low, but we were only fired on once, to my knowledge, during a night flight over Cambodia. I thought we had flown through a cloud, but the pilot nervously reported to us that, "They are shooting at us! We're going back to Tan Son Nhut!"

40. United States Air Force Security Service

Harvey Goldstein & Crew U. S. Air Force.

Harvey Goldstein served with the United States Air Force from 1968 until 1972 and was assigned to the Security Service. He studied North Vietnamese at the Defense Language Institute in Arlington, Virginia, and served in Vietnam from July 1970 until July 1971. He completed his Air Force years at the National Security Agency in Laurel, Maryland. Harvey participates with a veterans' writing group that has recounted their stories for a book that is scheduled for publishing in 2024. The book, with stories from all branches of the military from veterans from World War II to the present, will be distributed to middle and high school students. Harvey and his wife, Nancy, live in Branford, CT.

41.

"Short"

by Harvey Goldstein

"Short" was a term everyone used when you did not have much time remaining in Vietnam. It was usually reserved for those of us with 30 days or less left before going home. We adjusted it to almost short when we reached the less than 90-day mark. We were not "officially" short, but we were getting close.

On the days that we flew, we got up in the morning, had a can of Coca Cola for breakfast, reported to operations for our first briefing, grabbed a cup of coffee for the briefing and our boxed or C-ration lunch, jumped on the van for the ride to the flight line and our second briefing and then boarded the airplane for our five hours patrolling the skies of South East Asia.

Even though they were more than 30 years old when we flew them, our airplanes were dependable and very safe. A C-47, also known as a DC-3 or as they were more affectionately known, "Gooney Bird," was our flying office. Because of their wingspan and aerodynamics, we were told that even IF we lost both engines, the Gooney could glide for another twenty-five miles until the pilot could find a safe place to land.

C-47 Gooney Bird.

Two military terms that we were looking forward to having applied to us were DEROS - *Date Eligible for Return from Overseas* and ROD – *Relieved of Duty*. By mid-May, most of our group had received their DEROS dates. We were now under 60 days of time remaining in Vietnam. I had felt safe and confident after almost one hundred missions over Vietnam, Cambodia, and Laos; now that my time was starting to get short, I was becoming a little apprehensive. Nothing had changed with the pilots, there were always new ones, and nothing had changed with the area we flew or the aircraft we flew in. I was in as much or as little danger now as I was 10 months before, but now I was looking forward to going home and I wanted to return to the United States in one piece. The day I received my return date of July 5, 1971, I considered myself "Officially Short." I just had to make it through the next 45 days.

We were usually relieved of duty seven days before going home. I am not sure how I did it, but I informed those scheduling me for flights that I was ROD on June 22, almost two full weeks before I was due to come home.

My "Fini-Flight" was coming up and I was excited. There is nothing better than to know that you have only one more mission and you are done. For my last mission, I was going to be flying over the Parrot's Beak in Cambodia, which was one of our hot voice areas. My final flight unofficially became known as *Soul Patrol* and *Yid Kid* on fini. The back-end crew was Sergeants Lynwood Odom, Frank Morman and Troy Quinn. I had flown with them at other times, but this was the first time I flew with all of them at the same time. Three African Americans and the only Jewish person in the squadron on Harv's fini-flight. We worked, but we had an exciting time.

One of the traditions that had recently been banned at Tan Son Nhut was that aircrew members, upon completion of their final flight, (or "fini flight") were met and hosed down with water by their squadron comrades and friends, and a bottle of champagne popped. I think it was Frank who called in to the people on the ground, as we started to head home, that Soul Patrol and Yid Kid on fini were returning to base, and to remember that the fire trucks were no longer allowed to hose down Yid Kid. I think he did this a few times.

After we landed, as we taxied to our parking space, I could see the fire truck. As I walked down the steps from the plane, I got ready to brace myself. When I was clear of the airplane's open back door, they opened the hose. The power of the water knocked me off my feet and it felt GREAT! I was done! As Tony Orlando and Dawn sang, "I've done my time, I'm coming home...." I finished my year with 105 missions; it would have been more, but the Air Force kept me in Okinawa for three weeks while my orders were in Vietnam. I was grounded in Thailand for a few weeks after an ear block and was grounded again in Saigon for a month for not following orders. I could have ended up with 180 missions or more. As it was, I received the Air Medal and two or three clusters. Each time we approached the number of missions for the Distinguished Flying Cross (DFC), the Air Force increased the number of missions, so it always eluded me.

My last two weeks were spent filling out forms and packing things up. I wanted to surprise my family, so I contacted my stateside girl about picking me up at the airport when I returned to Connecticut. My flight back to the States was through Hawaii, so I landed about an hour after I took off. All I saw of Hawaii was a red or yellow line at the airport that took me in a circle. When we landed at Travis AFB, I did that corny old thing, and I got down and kissed the tarmac.

They had buses waiting to take us to San Francisco International Airport. As soon as I landed and knew when I'd be at Bradley Airport in Windsor Locks (located just north of Hartford and a little south of Springfield, Massachusetts) I called my girlfriend so she would know when to pick me up. I was excited about coming home. I think the five-hour flight from California to Connecticut felt longer that the 20-plus hour trip from Saigon to San Francisco.

It was Monday, July 5, 1971, and I knew that my family would be celebrating Independence Day with a picnic at my aunt and uncle's house in West Hartford. I was still in uniform, summer khakis, known as 1505s in Air Force jargon. We parked the car on the street, and I walked up the driveway just as my father was walking into the house from the back yard.

My mother followed the war very closely and she obviously talked about it a lot. Dad spotted me and came outside. He was not usually a very demonstrative person, but he hugged me, kissed me, and we shed a few tears. Then he told me, "You had it easy, you only had to fight a war; I had to put up with your mother for a year."

42.

Melody in the Dark Vietnamese Night
by Dell Pendergrast

The distinctive tonal melody of a Vietnamese language song drifted across the rural village square in Tay Ninh province 60 miles north of Saigon. The petite young woman in graceful Vietnamese *ao dai* attire delivered a plaintive theme of loss and despair common in 1971 across the war-ravaged country. Lan, the singer, was a member of a Vietnamese Government Cultural Team seeking to connect with a rural population with skits and songs and also courted by the communist Viet Cong. She was young and quite beautiful.

As a civilian advisor to the provincial government, I regularly went with the Cultural Team on its performance trips that merged propaganda and entertainment.

The Team's performance ended with modest applause from the 200 village residents. They were predictably wary of showing too much enthusiasm before the watchful eyes of Viet Cong supporters. My Vietnamese assistant, Vinh, and I tried to park our pickup truck for the night at the edge of the village. While only ten miles from the provincial capital, risking the dark roads at midnight was a choice we hesitated to make. In the absence of a Motel 6 equivalent in the rural village, we settled for the night into the pickup's open storage bay, relying on folded military flak jackets for pillows and smothered in insect repellant.

After falling immediately into deep slumber, I was jolted awake by Vinh pulling frantically on my arm. "Co Van (advisor) Pendergrast, wake up, wake up. We must leave! Now!" His muffled voice projected alarm bordering on panic.

"Vinh, what is it?" "VC, VC, sir. They are entering the far side of village. We must leave! Now!" Suddenly in the distance I heard the recognizable, staccato signal of a semi-automatic Russian-made AK-47: ack, ack, ack, ack. That was followed by a response from the old-fashioned U.S.-provided carbines which armed the village self-defense militia. Flashes of gunfire pierced the sky above the village. Vinh was right. We had to leave.

Braving the dark roads back to Tay Ninh City was now less intimidating than waiting for the Viet Cong in the village to find us. I jumped behind the steering wheel, and with adrenalin rushing through my veins, roared into the night. At high speed, impervious to VC and livestock on the road, we successfully navigated our way to the safety of the provincial government compound. The next day I learned that a VC force had penetrated the village, killed four local militia soldiers while suffered three casualties themselves. Intelligence officers told us the VC knew our Team was in the village and were particularly interested in capturing the American who went with them. Our midnight escape foiled them. The Cultural Team itself also fled into the night and escaped with one exception. Lan, the pretty young Vietnamese singer, was led away by the Viet Cong into the jungle. She – and her haunting, melancholy voice – were never heard from again.

Dell Pendergrast did his undergraduate work at Northwestern University and received a master's degree from Boston University. He began a career as a Foreign Service Officer with the State Department in 1965 and was assigned to tours in embassies across Europe. He was assigned to the embassy in Saigon in 1969 at the height of the Vietnam War. Dell is also an actor in the Washington, DC Metro area.

43.

His name is Ben
by David Draper

Team A La King – 1970 – 1st Force Recon Company.

My name is Dave. Beginning in March of 1969, I spent my first six months in Vietnam in the grunts – Marine Corps infantrymen. I transferred to 3rd Force Reconnaissance Company for the next six months. It was in February of 1970 that I decided to extend my tour for an additional six months. I was now running long-range reconnaissance patrols for 1st Force Recon Company. Both recon companies, 3rd and 1st Force were made up of superb Marines and Corpsmen.

My first patrol with 1st Force was into the Thuong Duc River Valley to find and observe any foot or vehicle traffic that the enemy might be using along a section of Highway 14, which ran from East to West, toward the village of Thuong Duc.

On this particular mission, I walked point, and walking in the second spot was 1st Lieutenant Steve Corbett, our patrol leader. Rich Gable, a superb recon Marine, followed behind Lt. Corbett and was our primary radio operator. Next came Sgt. Hamilton, our platoon sergeant. Behind him was "Doc" Harrison, our corpsman, followed by 2nd Lieutenant Spruell. Corporal Tommy Sexton, who had been with me in 3rd Force Recon Company, was next in line and was our secondary radio operator, and John Gulda was last as our Tail-End-Charlie, providing rear security for the team. This eight-man team was a very experienced Force reconnaissance team.

It was early summer, in 1970, and the days were already getting very hot, cooled only by an occasional night rain. Our team flew the 35-40 miles out to Hill 510. Once there, we climbed out of the CH-46 chopper and onto a flexible ladder, which dangled below the helicopter, for a short trip over to Hill 487. The chopper expertly lowered our team, code-named A La King, through the trees and finally onto solid ground. Another CH-46 brought in our radio relay team of ten Marines, all from 1st Force Recon Company, and they too were safely lowered onto hill 510 to establish long-range radio capability back to Danang, using a 292 field radio.

Force Recon Team Extraction using the ladder.

After a quick radio check, Team A La King began its descent to the valley floor. The initial movement was steep and precarious, and finally by late afternoon, the ground began to level off. We found a concealed area to rest and we were able to eat. At dusk, we entered an area with heavy vegetation which provided us with concealment for our nighttime harbor site. At 21:00, Lt. Corbett set the security rotation and the rest of us quickly fell asleep. During that night, an artillery mission had shells landing dangerously close to us. I woke up Lt. Corbett and he said, "Don't worry about it" and he went back to sleep. I tried to do the same, but now the rain was coming down very hard and thunder and lightning began to join in. On top of Hill 510, the lightning was intense and both Marines Vernon Rojek and David Wickander were struck by lightning. David Wickander later succumbed to his injuries.

The 292-radio antenna.

Daybreak came much too early. The rain had ended and sun was warming us up when we heard voices. Lt. Corbett and I crawled as close as we could possibly get, to within 100 feet away from the chatter. There were at least two voices and we could tell by the smell that they were cooking something, probably vegetables. We tried to get closer but the voices ceased as quickly as they started. We grabbed our gear and headed in an easterly direction. We had not gone far when we found a well-used trail. We then headed north along the trail, which was something we were taught not to do when we were in 3rd Force Recon Company. "Never, ever, walk on a trail. If you didn't make it, the enemy did. You can cross over it, and examine it, but stay off of it." This sage advice constantly was drummed into our heads.

We soon found an enemy mortar pit. It had a 61mm mortar and base plate, but no mortar rounds. We made a security stop to pack up our new found mortar. Lance Corporal Gabel and I were assigned to frontal security. We sat on either side of the trail as it disappeared into the tall elephant grass. We had only been there a minute or two when we heard a voice close to us; it was very close. Suddenly, a NVA soldier came through the elephant grass. I'll never forget the look of horror on his face as he turned to run away. Gabe and I fired at him at the same time.

A 61-mm Russian mortar.

I got up as fast as I could and followed the NVA soldier's blood trail into the darkness of the thick elephant grass. Within five feet, the trail opened up to a shallow stream bed. There, sitting in the creek bed, barely six feet away, was the wounded NVA soldier. He had four of his NVA friends with him and when they stood up at my arrival, they were all killed with a burst from my M-16.

Lt. Corbett arrived within seconds. We searched the dead NVA soldiers for any intelligence information: maps, notebooks, or papers, but only found one back pack that had a food bowl, along with a spoon inside of a little cloth pouch with a drawstring.

Soon we heard voices coming out from under a concrete bridge that was part of Highway 14. The bridge, overgrown with vegetation, was only 30 feet away, making it nearly impossible to see. Lt. Corbett threw a fragmentation grenade, followed by a white phosphorous grenade, hoping to give us some additional time to get away from where I had killed the four enemy soldiers.

We then turned our attention to the wounded NVA soldier. His face was pleading for mercy and Lt. Corbett asked me if we could take him as a prisoner. I told him "He looks pretty bad." He said, "Go ahead and kill him." His life ended with a short burst from my rifle. War can be so cruel sometimes and one small mistake such as a lack of noise discipline can cost you dearly.

We had been in that area much too long and we needed to leave. We headed off in a southerly direction and then moved easterly along this same trail.

Later that afternoon, we sighted two more NVA soldiers walking on their trail. They sighted us at the same time that we saw them. They retreated the way they had come and we left the area as quickly as possible. Not a shot was fired but we knew they were looking for us. This was a "point-to-point" contact without shot being fired by either side.

L-R: HM3 "Doc" Harrison, Cpl. David Draper, and LCpl. Rich Gabel.

After three more days of uneventful reconnaissance, we headed to the extraction point. We got an early wakeup call on the 24th of June. We would be extracted as an emergency extract. We were all fitted with our Swiss seats (15-foor sections of nylon rope that every man carried), which were used for just such an extraction on the SPIE (Special Purpose Insertion & Extraction) rig. The Cobra gunships were the first to appear over our location. They came in low over the trees firing their rockets and mini guns. The CH-46 helicopter lowered the SPIE rig through the trees. When we were all hooked up and had given a thumbs up sign, up through the trees we went.

It was only 35 miles to DaNang but it seemed much longer. At last, we landed at Camp Reasoner and we were glad to have our feet firmly on the ground. It was time to get cleaned up and ready for the next patrol.

Force Recon Team using the S.P.I.E. rig.

Over the years I've spent hours and hours thinking about the situation I was put into. Was the NVA soldier married? Did he have children? For sure, he was someone's child. In my thoughts I began to ask him questions about his life. Where did he live? What was his vocation? Was he married? What did he think about this crazy war? I could only imagine his answers. This has been going on for over 50 years. We aren't friends, only acquaintances, but I have never forgotten him.

My name is Dave and his name is Ben.

[David Draper served with distinction in both 3rd Force Recon Company and 1st Force Recon Company from 1969-1970. After returning home, to Sheffield, Alabama, he worked for the Alabama Highway Department, while attending college at Jacksonville State University. Following graduation, with a degree in accounting, he was employed with the Alabama Department of Revenue.

David retired in 2010 and enjoys playing golf, racquetball, and tennis.]

44.

In My Viewfinder: The Epilogue
by William Vander Ven

Sunday, September 3, 2023

Dearest Son:

Having deployed several times down range and now a respected Army Instructor, I thought I would share with you a bit of my personal history in another equally dangerous and hated war, the Vietnam War. A twist to my story, however, is that I fought in another, less known parallel war, the war in the adjacent countries of Laos and Cambodia. We, who flew our missions in that conflict, were not supposed to be there and hence there was this "stench" of illicitness to the whole damn mess. However, know this son, your Dad and many of his compatriots are damn proud of our missions and accomplishments defending first our servicemen, followed by our allies the Hmong, other Hill Tribes, followed by the Royal Lao military and the remnants of the Royal Khmer Armed Forces.

Today, that "Secret War" as it is now being called, was NO SECRET to us. Unfortunately, like so many other narratives from the "official" war, many stories, some good and many bad, are beginning to surface. I don't wish to dazzle you with war stories - hell, you have plenty of your own to share. But I do wish to give you a hint of what your Old Man felt, experienced, and triumphed in the fulfillment of his Tour of Duty.

With a deep breath, here is a short story in a long war:

When my brother-in-law, Carl, a retired Navy commander, came to visit us in Sacramento, I naturally took him to see the state's Vietnam Veterans Memorial. Although the memorial is a short drive from our house, I had visited it only twice since its dedication in 1988, and until that day never had the urge to go back. In my short visits, I completely missed the large bronze sculpted map of Vietnam and the surrounding countries of Laos, and Cambodia that I had flown over.

Today, for some reason, I took the time to study the memorial, its statues, and especially, that map.

As I looked down and read the names of features such as the Plaine de Jarres, or "PDJ" as we called it, "Roadrunner Lake," the mass of the Bolaven Plateau, with its misty mountains; places, such as Pakse/Pakxe,'

Mukdahan & Savanahett and numerous other towns and villages with their unpronounceable names.

Certainly, I'm not forgetting the name and first view of the Angkor Wat temple complex, from 8,000 feet Above Ground Level (AGL); a flood of memories and mental pictures washed over me. I shook my head, and with a smile recalled the difficult contortions of having to climb that flimsy step ladder into the back seat of an OV-10 "Bronco" or the tight entry opening of an O-2 Skymaster, wearing a safety harness and survival vest, stuffed with anticipated survival gear, especially the two PRC-90 survival radios and their spare batteries. I was further hampered by the deadweight of two frozen water bottles thawing in each leg pocket of my flight suit. Once I was strapped in, sweating from the effort, I had a decision to make - either drink now from my water bottle, as I waited for engine start and taxi clearance, or wait a bit longer.

Other thoughts ran through my head as well: *"Radio check,"* remembering our call sign for the day; the short banter between the pilot, his crew chief and myself; recounting and verifying, one more time, my photo gear and location of the lenses and film. That wonderful feeling of a breeze on my face as we started engines with the canopy in the up position of the "Bronc" as we taxied on the apron to the main ramp; I always licked my lips from nervousness and, as a result, suffered from painful chapped lips.

I can still feel the "push back" of my body against the harness as the pilot started full throttle and began his taxi down the runway. Upon takeoff, I waited for the comfortable "Klunk" of a successful "Wheels Up" of our landing gear. I remember looking out the side of my canopy as the base retreated; I immediately began to quelch any of those "little nagging thoughts" such as *"Will we ever see the base again!"*

I recalled the lush emerald green of the rice paddies, stretching for miles during the wet monsoon and the golden hue of those same fields in the dry season. *"Crossing the Fence," "feet wet"* entering *"Indian Country"* as we flew over the chocolate brown color of the Mekong River, into either Laos or Cambodia.

We were now under the protection of the orbiting C-130 Hillsboro aircraft with its callsigns of "Cricket" by day, and "Moonbeam" by night. Looking down on the bronze etching on the map marking the Mighty Mekong River, I smile grimly as I recall how it's brown colored presence, from the canopy below me, [flying my first PsyOp mission in an O-2B aircraft,] brought a dose of cold reality of being bodily present in a war.

The miles of rice paddies that were Thailand, once we had crossed into Laos, gave way to a combination of rice paddies and jungle, tall multi-canopied forests of various darkened hues; broken suddenly by a meandering river or a towering waterfall rivaling Niagara in its beauty. Occasionally, as we passed overhead, we would look down on a startled flock of brightly colored birds.

As the pilot jinked our aircraft in an unpredictable manner, I cringed in an unpredictable manner at my attempt to focus on my map as he shifted our flight and altitude. The bouts of nausea and head sweat were dripping onto my map sheet. For us, to fly a predictable path, would have brought a day of "No Joy." As the clear bubble "greenhouse" canopy of the Bronco heated up, I still smirk at the small openings that made up our internal "cooling system." Those pathetic flow ducts were given the laughable term: *"ram air."* That term brought back more unpleasant memories of having to endure the stench of our sweat and farts generated by a day's flying in a plexiglass bubble canopy with no air conditioning and constant humidity. I can vividly recreate my attempts to unzip the zipper of my leg pockets, fumbling for the plastic water bottle. Subconsciously, licking my lips, 30+ years later, I can still feel and taste that first sip of cool water or Kool Aid that I first poured then froze the night before, into white plastic containers.

Continuing with my thoughts, I recall the feel of a wet brown or green terry cloth towel placed around my neck as part of my routine to keep cool; but at the same time, I also remember that constant itching from the sweat throughout my body. Those infernal itches began on the small of my back, then traveled all along my backside; I had no way to scratch them; I had to endure them and continue with the mission. The only redeeming quality was our amount of dehydration also prevented us from having to urinate. Subconsciously, I reach back and massage my rear end as I recall the numbness of my butt pressed against the seat bucket for hours on end. Passing billowing banks of huge rising clouds, whose presence may dictate a mission's success, or not. Coupled to those images was a tangible fear of having to fly near those clouds and endure the violent turbulence they generated.

"Karst Ridges"! Beautiful spires of jungle covered limestone, whose peaks rose out from dense layers of mist. Their beauty hid the danger of losing our situational awareness and flying into the side of one or, as bad, encountering streams of lethal AAA from Pathet Lao/NVA gunners hidden in the many caves surrounding their flanks. Thinking about those hidden gunners brings back other memories from that same flight. I naively raved about the colorful "flashes" that sparkled below as we passed, saying that they reminded me of fireflies. I still blush at the pilot's dumbstruck expression and his droll response: *"...those aren't "fireflies" sergeant, they're gun flashes from the "bad guys"!"*

My mental dam had begun to crack as more memories, held back for so long, began to spill over and fill my mind. The sound and staccato of long forgotten chatter from the multiple radio bands of our three radios, filling my headphones. Unfortunately, I never flew long enough to discern which communique came from what radio.

I remember flying a loose pylon turn while the loudspeakers of the O-2 blared their music and propaganda messages to the villagers below and the whip snap of the propaganda leaflets leaving the chute of the aircraft, followed by their falling onto the grounds of the village and villagers, as I photographed the event. This was followed by eating our lunch as the tape ran its course, and then sharing stories of home.

Flying backseat on a photo reconnaissance mission in an OV-10A Bronco brought a deep satisfaction I still feel today, when we found a hidden water crossing or camouflaged truck parks. This satisfaction was quickly tempered by the metallic taste of fear knowing we would be dropping closer for me to photograph those targets. I still cringe and take deep breaths remembering the aggressive maneuvers, the feel of "G" forces on my body as the pilot placed the aircraft in a proper, and hopefully "safe" flight path, for me to take my photographs. I also recall the level of concentration and the running thoughts of leading my camera onto the target, keeping my hands off the aircraft's interior, firmly but steadily, pressing the shutter release button, focusing the lens as needed; all the time, whispering: *"no fuckups, no fuckups."*

My face lights up at those memories that came from accomplishing those photo runs that showed exactly what we hoped to find and having crisp, clear photographs for the intel guys to plot a future target or call in nearby aircraft to immediately hit the target. My face is well lit now as I bring back the fond memories when on the return leg, upon entering Thailand, the pilot shows off his skill or better yet, says: *"Wanna fly her"*?

Many years later, when I was living in Sacramento, California, I became a docent at the McClellan Air Museum. On my lunch break, I used to drive over to the CAL FIRE section of the base and view the rows of newly refurbished OV-10A Broncos and the occasional O-2 Skymaster. As I ate my lunch, I would wonder how many of those firefighting aircraft I had flown in.

I still recall that tingle of dread, fear, and excitement many years later, when I remember spotting my name on our mission board as the still cameraman on the then very secretive callsign: SPECTRE.

AC-130 Gunship mission, titled Gunship II and flown by crews of the 16th Special Operations Squadron, 16th SOS. I still take a deep breath recalling the preparation work to achieve a successful photo documentation of a SPECTRE mission.

Because the aircraft had a crew of up to 14, and the length of the mission was eight or more hours, (depending on weather, availability of targets, fuel reserves and the usage of ammunition). Most overriding, of course, was the political/tactical importance of the operation; consequently, the means of getting a slot on a mission was very formal; and required a set protocol established between the 16th SOS and my unit, the 601st Photo Flight. There was only one photographer on an aircraft, either a still cameraman such as me, or a motion picture cameraman (MOPIC). ALL photographers had to be fully qualified as aerial crewmembers; all having gone through air crew training at Fairchild AFB, Spokane Washington, and Jungle Survival training (Snake School) located at Clark AFB, in the Philippines. On our first training mission we were evaluated by the crew and conducted during daylight hours; if we passed their evaluation, we were cleared to fly operational missions at night. We cameramen were NOT crewmembers but "observers." The more we flew with the 16th SOS crew, the better we were received and trusted, making it easier to complete our mission.

I will never forget the trepidation I experienced, arriving at the 16th SOS Operations building, to sit on my first operational mission brief, and introduce myself to the crew I would fly with that night. Luckily, I had Sgt Allen Hammer escorting me to the brief, but he would be gone when I sat down, and the rest was up to me. I had already flown several day missions, passed the crew evaluation, and managed to not embarrass myself; more importantly, I took some good quality photos. The copies of those I personally delivered to the pilot and First Gunner for dissemination to the crew. This started out as a task to maintain favoritism, however, as I flew more missions, it became a matter of pride to pass on to the crews, photos they would seldom, if ever, have the opportunity to receive.

By the time I began flying operationally on the gunships, I had already completed several missions as a backseat aerial reconnaissance photographer. I flew in the right seat of the O2B Skymaster on Psychological Operations flights, and as the backseat documentary photographer, in the OV-10 Bronco aircraft; used primarily for Forward Air Control (FAC).

I prided myself on not being a "newbie" and as nervous as I was at that first operational brief, I still believed I "knew the ropes" as to what to expect when we flew "across the fence." I was determined to obtain as many quality photographs as possible; subsequently, I was determined to share some of the photos with the crew. Was I ever in for a humbling surprise!

We completed the crew brief, and I could not help but feel I was in a briefing like what the B-17 bomber crews had in World War II, with similar briefs on weather, target area, potential threats, radio frequencies and escape/evade info for the area. I sat back and took copious notes; later as I became more familiar with the missions, I only copied pertinent data on radio frequencies, the aircraft number and call sign and the area of our operations. The one thing different about my notetaking was that I copied the names of all the crew on my flight and left it with my personal gear in the locker assigned to us. This list would aid me when I printed the crew photos.

Shaking my head in wonder, I recall running around the aircraft, in the heat and humidity, taking photos of the outer fuselage, the gun types, nose art and any other interesting angle I thought worthy of a photograph. At first the crew was too busy to pay attention to me, but they enjoyed the attention when I began taking photos of their preparation.

44. In My Viewfinder: The Epilogue

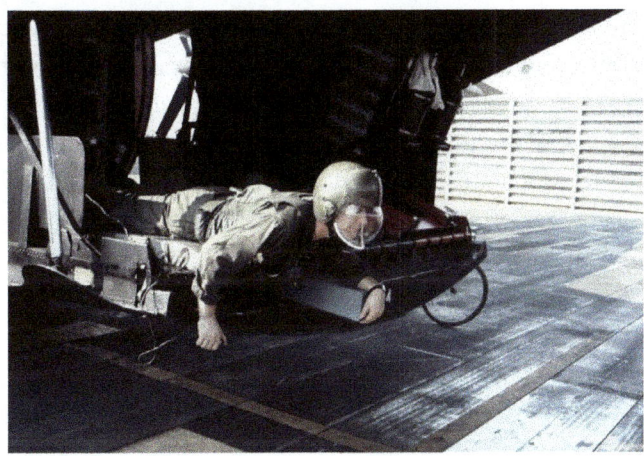

They really got a kick when I "staged" them in their operational positions; these were photographs I could not take in flight.

It was at this time, before the officers arrived and I had to begin photographing their preflight checks, that I found the senior gunner and informed him that when we went into "combat mode," and I could no longer take photographs, he was to put me to work wherever he thought I would be useful. This was not an "ego" thing but a way for me to learn how the aircraft operated and to obtain a solid feel for the mission; and yes, it helped to gain a positive image from the crew.

Sweat dripping down my nose and my entire flight suit damp from all the preflight photography, I approached the aircraft commander (AC), introduced myself and asked his permission to photograph him and the other officers at their stations. I really did not have to ask his permission as this was part of the mission, but the formality created a better rapport between me, the aircraft commander, and the other officers.

Upon completing the preflight check and the crew at their stations, we were beginning our taxi to the main runway. On a very naive whim, I went on the crew intercom and asked permission to take a photo of the aircraft beginning its taxi. There was a long pause, the entire crew was waiting for the AC's response. I will never forget the answer, nor the laughter and banter that followed: *"Master Gunner the photographer has three minutes, if he is not back, close the ramp."*

I remember jumping out the lowered rear ramp, almost falling on my knees as I touched the concrete apron, and sprinting out to where I believed

I could get the aircraft in a full frame. In rapid succession, I snapped two frames, and without hesitation, sprinted back to the retreating aircraft; with seconds to spare, I gladly reached for the helping hand of the First Gunner. I was told later that the entire crew placed bets as to whether I would make it back in time; as a bonus, that stunt earned me my "bona fides."

Once airborne, on my first mission, I quickly and without thinking stowed my camera gear and parachute near the aft 40 MM gun station before I began to take photos of the crew and the aircraft. Time flew and we approached our crossing point over the Mekong River between the Thai town of Mukdahan and its Laotian counterpart, Savanahett.

Once across the river, the crew became busy preparing for the night's hunt. There was enough daylight to conduct a gun check; something I was told makes for exciting photographs. We passed a stream and located an exposed tree trunk sticking out on a mudbank. The AC initiated a left pylon turn and gave permission to load the 40mm guns. With quick succession the gunners loaded the magazine, and the pilot initiated a firing sequence. All this time I was happily running from gun to port, first photographing the loading, followed by capturing the spouts from the shells bracketing the log. The same goes for the forward 20MM rotating gun station. With the gatling gun however, the best photograph was from the side of the gunport with a view of the rapidly spinning barrels, well-lit from the exiting bullets.

From the gunners, I visited "the Box" where all the sensor operators worked, to take a few photographs of them at their stations wearing their full combat gear, minus the parachutes, which were stowed on hooks nearby. All this great photography was about to come to a grand halt as the command "switch from white to red light" was given.

My first mission, and I had already allowed myself to become carried away by the excitement of my photography at the expense of following the crew in their preparation for the work ahead: aerial combat! It wasn't long before the pilot came on the intercom and gave the command to switch from interior "white lights" to combat mode "red light." I still shudder remembering the full panic mode I went into as it dawned on me that somewhere on this now darkened aircraft was my parachute and my camera gear, but I had no idea where! Before my panic really took hold of me, I felt the hand and heard the voice of the First Gunner as he asked,

"Do you still want to help?" Without any hesitation, I agreed, and he thankfully sent me forward to the 20mm station. As I fumbled my way in the darkened gunship, I began to calm down and started paying attention to the reality I found myself in.

I first saw the red beam of the 20mm gunner's flashlight, then saw his grin as he stood with a flashlight in one hand and an enormous coal shovel in the other. I plugged my comm into the outlet and I could first hear his breathing before he told me his name, followed by a "quick and dirty" description of what was about to happen, and my job afterwards. The twin barrels of the 20mm Vulcan rotate, creating an enormous amount of fired bullets; subsequently, hundreds of spent brass casings and broken clips were dropped into the metal pan covering the 20mm station floor. If not picked up promptly, their buildup would create a hazardous environment to work in and if the aircraft had to make any sudden evasive maneuvers, these casings would be tossed onto the floorboards throughout the aircraft.

It was a thankless, sweaty job, but somebody had to do it; that somebody was me.

While we waited for the 20mm to come on station, the gunner explained to me that it was the pilot who initiated the firing of both the 20s and the 40s; the gunners maintained the ammunition feed, freed any jam, and made any repairs when the system failed to fire. Usually there are two gunners to each of the gun stations. We, however, were short one gunner, and I was to be his replacement conducting the "easiest" job on the aircraft: brass shoveler. But if I did a good job, he would put me in for a Shovel Qualified patch, a patch I proudly still display. We heard on the crew comms that a group of NVA trucks had been located and we were initiating our flying position to bring our guns to bear on them. The pilot initially asked for the 40mm to be loaded and soon he began firing the Bofors. Even with the helmet and headset, I could feel the recoil and hear the rhythmic "***boom, boom, boom***" of the guns.

My gunner nudged me, anticipating the use of the 20s and sure enough we were warned to prepare for their action. I really did jump when the six barrels began their cyclic rate of 2,000 rounds a minute; a very distinct "***BRRRRT***" filled my ears, a sound I will never forget. At the same time, I saw flashing images of spent casings and their clips, lit by the dull red

44. In My Viewfinder: The Epilogue

light as they flew onto the floor of the aircraft; it was time to go to work. If the gun operated in a smooth feed, the gunner assisted me by holding the large cotton bag for me to shovel in the brass. When a jams occurred, and they did, I was left alone to shovel, open the bag, drop the casings, and repeat the process as needed.

As long as the aircraft's maneuvering, as unpredictable as it was, maintained a certain rhythm, I could keep my feet braced enough to continue shoveling. However, it was the rapid, evasive maneuvers, to thwart the aim of the enemy gunners, which made all our jobs difficult. Although we had scanners whose primary task was to locate approaching AAA and warn the pilot well ahead of time, sometimes a round or stream of bright light would approach without warning, necessitating an instant response. When this happened, the pilot may have had time to warn us, and then again, he may not have. A good crew can almost anticipate a sudden *"break right,"* *"break left"* or a drop in altitude and be ready. I was too new and too tired. I heard a distinct *"break..."* on the net. As the aircraft banked sharply, gravity took hold and down I went onto the floorboard amongst the empty brass; the "G" forces pinning me to the floor. The gunner himself was holding onto the 20mm belt and could do nothing to assist me; I just lay there remembering my instructor back at George AFB giving us a lecture on the effects of positive G, and negative G forces; I now understood exactly what he was talking about.

When we regained the "normal" combat flight pattern, the gunner helped me up and with a big grin welcomed me to the "club." Unfortunately, on another flight. I experienced a similar occurrence when helping the 40mm Bofor team before I began listening carefully to the crew communication net to gauge any surprises ahead. By now I had forgotten my plight of misplacing the parachute and gear, as I committed myself to helping a fellow airman and gunner.

To this day, when I hear metal-on-metal, it reminds me of the sound a metal coal shovel makes as it screeches over the aluminum floor of the AC-130.

As the Bofors began to be engaged more than the 20's, we were able to catch up on the shoveling and I soon took a break and began monitoring the crew net. I was astounded how calm the voices were, either announcing a target, mentioning a new position, or even hearing the sudden description of approaching AAA; all was done using short clear sentences in a normal voice.

My mind is now as clear as when I stood at the side scanner's opening, looking down, as the inboard prop, only feet away, thrummed in my head. I viewed bright blinking flashes of enemy guns fired from pitch black darkness, followed by the lethal beauty of their tracers rising to meet us; afterward, smelling the stink of cordite from nearby exploding AAA bursts.

Further thoughts of "working" the 40mm Bofor stations brought back memories of wrestling 55-gallon red painted drums filled with spent 40mm brass casings to be lashed to the bulkhead; all the labor was done under a dull red flashlight held firmly in my mouth. Working at high altitudes in an unpressurized aircraft rapidly dissipates one's mental and physical energies; the crew knew this, storing yellow colored oxygen canisters throughout the aircraft. They were not shy about using them either. The gunners quickly taught me how to properly use the oxygen. I remember the metallic taste and cold feel of the gas as it entered my lungs, followed by an almost instant burst of energy.

When we disengaged from our hunt due to lack of ammo, the pilot turned our bird toward Ubon. Upon crossing the Mekong into Thailand, we went to normal "white" light, and it wasn't long before the crew intercom came on and the First Gunner announced that he had the photographer's parachute and camera gear if he wanted to claim them. The intercom went full static from all the laughter, but it was OK, I had passed their test and that comment was a way of showing it.

I smile openly, recalling the exhausted but proud faces of the aircrew as they gathered around on the homeward bound flight, sharing in that unspoken sense of accomplishment of a successful mission, with enemy trucks destroyed and the ammunition status as "Winchester" (empty of ammunition to be fired). But most of all the knowledge that the mission produced: *"No casualties or battle damage to report."*

All these thoughts and more flashed in an instant of time as I stood there looking down onto the bronze surface of the map. The faces of many aircrewmen, pilots I had the privilege of flying with, the cameramen I worked with, joked, and stood Alert with: *"I thank you Brothers; one and all."*

Well, Pete, this personal share of a few moments in time are part of what many of us experienced and endured. We both are now men who know war, and each, in our own way, have learned how to cope with our memories. I, through my writings, and you as a good and loving Father and Husband to your Family.

May our legacy be the last regarding having stories of death, injury, and mental breakdowns to share with future generations.

With All my Love and Respect,

Your Father

Bill joined the Air Force in 1968. After basic training at Lackland AFB, he received his technical training as a still photographer at Lowry AFB, in Denver, Colorado. Upon graduation, his first duty station was with the 15th Reconnaissance Technical Squadron at March AFB, California. Upon attending all the mandatory survival schools, Bill landed at Ubon Royal Thai Air Force Base.

During his tour, 1971-1972, Bill flew backseat as aerial reconnaissance photographer. He documented the AC-130 gunship operations and the many CIVIC ACTION Programs run by the joint USAF/Thai Government; he completed his tour as the photographer for the base paper: The Phantom Flyer.

Upon leaving the Air Force, he received his teaching degree, re-joined the army reserves where he finished his military career in Military Intelligence and Psychological Operations. He and his wife of over twenty years, Louise Ann, an army veteran, and a former career employee with the Social Security Administration have two sons, Eric the oldest is a veteran of ENDURING

FREEDOM: the initial invasion of Iraq and is now a career Defense Civil Servant. The second son, Peter, is career Army with multiple deployments to Iraq, Afghanistan, and Korea.

45.

The 85th Evacuation Hospital, Phu Bai - 1971-1972

by James Slack

September 1st, 1971

"I'm twenty-six hours from Houston and still have four hours to go. There were stopovers in Honolulu and Okinawa. One hundred and sixty-eight of us (mostly officers and senior enlisted) on an American Airlines 707. We are all very tired.

It was about midday when we flew over the coast, and I recall an uneasiness as the jet slowed and things below began to come into focus. I vividly remember seeing thousands of circular spots that I could only assume were bomb and artillery craters, and my predominant thought was, *I don't think I'm going to like this place very much.*

We landed at Bien Hoa Air Base just outside Saigon. I suppose all newbies were processed through the personnel facilities there. As we taxied to a stop, the flight attendant, who was about the age of our mothers, came on her mic, pointed out a hanger-style building, and directed us to double-time into it when we disembarked due to concerns over snipers. Stepping off the plane, I remember being accosted by the overwhelming sensory assault of the noise of helicopters, Skyraider fighter planes, and diesel vehicles along with the smell of aviation fuel, and just as we had been warned in our stateside indoctrination, the smell of burning shit. We soon learned that flush toilets were rare, therefore most toilet facilities were latrines. Fifty-five-gallon drums caught the waste under the two-holers and when full, they were picked up by "hump squads," trucked to designated locations, and incinerated with diesel fuel. The stink permeated the entire country.

We finally arrived in Bien Hoa at 10:00 AM. It was now 5:20 PM and had begun to cool off. All our baggage got rained on earlier today so most of my things were wet. If my writing seems bad now it is because I'm sitting on a sandbag in front of my sleeping quarters trying to keep the flies off me. I was very depressed when we first landed and even more so on the bus ride from Bien Hoa to Long Binh. Everything is ratty and temporary. There are no trees on the base; watch towers and barbed wire and helicopters are everywhere. I can't remember ever being so tired. Tomorrow morning, I should find out what my assignment will be. I am presently at a transient replacement battalion in Long Binh. We are all waiting for assignments or flights to assignments. Most of the bases seem to be on alert due to increased actions generated by the Vietnamese elections. I'm sorry this letter is so short. I had a lot of things I wanted to say, but they all sounded the same. I'm afraid (depression and despair), and all I can think about now is finally having a place to stretch out, even if it is hot and muggy. We are eleven hours ahead of Houston."

While at Long Binh, I recall, we were given our new uniforms, two or three sets of fatigues, a pair of jungle boots, and some olive-drab T-shirts and boxer shorts with a duffle bag to put it all in. We had each been allowed to bring a small suitcase of toiletries and some underwear, and most had been wearing khakis the entire trip. I think we had to take our new fatigues to a Vietnamese shop to have our name, rank, branch, and insignia patches sewn on.

"This replacement station is every inch the hole, Jimmy Curtis said it was. The sheds we sleep in hold about 40 men each, double bunked. I doubt the mattresses have ever been sunned. It's too hot to sleep during the day and we are restricted to this area, so about all there is to do is go to the Officer's Club and drink beer."

I found it tiny, dark, and crowded with guys I didn't know, getting drunk. Not my airport. I bought a paperback book because it caught my attention picturing a guy pulling back on a bow and arrow on the cover. It was *Deliverance*. Not what could be called a feel-good mood elevator. It was unbearably hot all day and the smell of sweat, urine and vomit was overwhelming. We just lay in our sweat under mosquito nets until we fell asleep from fatigue or too many beers. Welcome to Nam.

"The drug program is the big thing here now. It gets priority on all incoming medical personnel. I don't think I want into that. I'm a little anxious about what kind of job I will get up north. The letter Colonel McCall wrote seems to have done a really good job lining me up for a position at Bien Hoa, but the personnel officer got me confused with a captain who had my job at Fort Campbell. Anyway, he got the job and I am still in the melting pot."

I was relieved to finally see my name on a list to board a C-130 headed to Danang. That was about a two-hour flight on the loudest and most uncomfortable airplane I ever flew on. Upon landing, I was picked up and delivered to the 95th Evacuation Hospital. That was nice. The 95th was built on this site in 1968 and had about three hundred and twenty air-conditioned beds in white single-story wings. It was able to provide neurologic, dermatologic, psychiatric, and radiologic services, as well as all surgical specialties. I remember feeling better about things there. These were "my people."

"I am now in Danang and just processed through the personnel funnel shop that Jimmy Curtis used to oversee. Six of us arrived together and spent last night in a ward at the 95th Evac. It was wonderful. Air-conditioned and clean sheets!"

I remember Jimmy telling me most Captain MSC assignments would be pretty good and the only one I should really try to avoid was the 85th. It was the pits.

"Jimmy's friend who replaced him, and who Jimmy promised would give me a good job, left yesterday for 14 days leave in the States, so I never got to talk to him.

I fly out of here by chopper tomorrow morning for Phu Bai and the 85th Evac. It is a 100-bed hospital, and from what they told me here, I will be the adjutant and detachment commander. My address will be the same as on this envelope. Hopefully, you will have gotten it by telegram before you get this letter.

What new tricks can baby daughter Shannon do now? I can honestly only begin to let myself even think about her. I don't think anything has ever so deeply upset me as when I had to walk out of her room that last time. This all seems so useless and senseless. I must say that we do appear to be pulling out quickly, though I'm sure it won't bring me home any earlier. No medical facilities are left except the larger hospitals, with a few exceptions. I may even see the close of the hospital I'm going to.

I heard that letters take about seven days to reach the U.S., but only about three days to reach Vietnam – figure that one out. I'm really looking forward to hearing from you. I know that isn't easy for you either. I love you, darling. Please get a kiss from Shannon for me."

The next day, I caught a ride on a Huey with a colonel who was the CO (commanding officer) of the 67th Medical Group, which was responsible for all medical activities for the northern sector of Vietnam. We flew to Quang Tri, which is the northern most U.S. base, just below the DMZ (Demilitarized Zone, the boundary between North and South Vietnam). There was an aid station there, and the colonel wanted to check the damage from a rocket attack the previous day. There were several damaged buildings still and a lot of smoke, but I don't think anyone got injured. I quickly determined the first order of business upon landing in a new territory to learn the location of the closest bunker. From there, we flew back down to Phu Bai and landed at the 85th Evac helipad.

The official name of my new home was the 85th Evacuation Hospital, SMBL. The acronym of SMBL stands for "Semi-Mobile." That means that we had (or should have) the capability to load up and move the entire hospital within twenty-four hours. Therefore, we had a few trucks assigned to us and maintained on our campus. Several of the hospitals in Nam were SMBLs. This contrasts with MASH units (Mobile Army Surgical Hospital) that moved frequently in Korea to stay close to the action.

85th Evacuation Hospital. Phu Bai.

45. The 85th Evacuation Hospital, Phu Bai - 1971-1972

The mention of MASH units reminds me that there were two movie theatres at Fort Gordon that typically showed latest releases with discounted tickets for soldiers. I remember there being lots of complaints when the Army banned the showing of M*A*S*H at its post theatres. It was one of the top grossing films in 1970, but it was deemed a thinly veiled slam on America's involvement in Vietnam. Of course, that made it even more of a "must see" for all the soldiers. The 2nd MASH Unit served in Nam only from October 1966 until July 1967 before being replaced by the SMBL evacuation hospitals as the war expanded. The advent of "Dustoffs" allowed casualties to be transferred rapidly to the better equipped evacuation hospitals.

Medivac choppers were known universally as Dustoffs. They swooped down, got wounded loaded on, and were gone quickly, usually in a cloud of dust. They have large red crosses painted on them and are not armed, as opposed to the "slicks," which are the same type of helicopter (UH-1 or Huey) and which often had M-60 machine guns mounted at each side door. We often had patients brought in by slicks, which often was a sign of a "hot pickup" (under fire).

All established helipads were made of Perforated Steel Planks (PSPs). These planks could be snapped together and would create rapid paving for roads and landing pads (as well as footpaths to our latrines). Ours had "Phu Bai Dust Off 47.40" painted on its surface in large white letters. The numbers were on our radio frequencies so that any chopper could communicate its landing intentions if they needed immediate help. Unannounced helicopters were not appreciated.

The term "chopper" originated with helicopters in Korea due to the distinct chopping sound their big blades made in flight, especially during lift off and sharp turns. The term became generic for all helicopters but be assured that every veteran of Vietnam can still identify the sound of a Huey from any other aircraft.

"Phu Bai is about 50 miles north of Danang and is the base camp for the 2nd Brigade, 101st Airborne Division. The 101st are the northernmost U.S. ground forces and our protectors here at the hospital. I think this is a safe place to be, as we treat a lot of Viet Cong (VC) and a few North Vietnamese Army (NVA) prisoners, so they are not apt to shell us.

Our perimeter is constantly patrolled by the 101st and the hospital is next to an airbase which houses about 400 aircraft, including 100 Cobra gunships. The 101st is expected to leave Phu Bai within a year and I've been told the VC and NVA seem to have taken the attitude that there will be less wear and tear on everyone if they leave us alone and let us leave. With all the firepower around here, I think I would too."

October 15$^{th.}$ "For some reason, we have suddenly been receiving a lot of battle casualties, most of them very bad, with a lot of traumatic amputations. I think of the last twelve, three have been 1st lieutenants. At 7:00 a.m. today, I was going to breakfast when a dustoff landed with one, a terrible way to start the day. This lieutenant had his leg blown off at the hip, plus chunks of his other one, as well as his right hand. I won't describe the details, but I will say that seeing these horrors leaves a feeling in me that defies description and leaves me subdued for the rest of the day. We always go through the wallets of the wounded to learn all we can of them as well as to secure their valuables. This lieutenant was a 1970 graduate of West Point. He had a family portrait with him in his cadet uniform, his two younger brothers and his parents, all with such proud looks on their faces. I guess it was that picture that made this case get to me worse than most.

Yesterday, we got another lieutenant with both of his legs gone, plus an EM (enlisted man) with one leg gone and the other mangled. I find it hard to understand how a man can force himself to keep going out, knowing that something like that could happen to him. If they saw many of these injuries, I don't think they could. I know that I couldn't.

Today, the company commander of the lieutenant missing both of his legs came in to find out how much his wife had been told of his injuries. The lieutenant was planning to call his wife tonight, and the CO wanted to be sure he wouldn't have to be the one to tell her that he had lost both of his legs. Can you imagine the nightmare that would be? When we call in to the USARV (U.S. Army Republic of Vietnam) headquarters in Long Binh (they relay our information to the U.S.), we always are required to give the most complete diagnosis and prognosis possible. I'm sure it's best that the next of kin know as much as possible to preclude something like the above from happening.

Also, last night, a dead guy, who had been shot as he slept, was brought in by someone on the patrol with him. An autopsy was requested on him and a big investigation is starting about this.

Don't feel bad if you sounded depressed in places on your tape because I know that I do, too. I don't see any real reason for us to put up fronts to each other. The same goes for the personal part of the tape. But I see no reason we shouldn't say those things. We are husband and wife, and those things are strictly between us. We've said and done them with each other, and they were wonderful then, and for that reason they still mean a lot, or should, to us. It's just that they were and will be beautiful times again, and the thought of them helps me to blot out some of the vision of the present. I hope this all makes sense, Darling, for I feel it is very important for us to put our personal thoughts in the open. I think that this will become more important as time passes, for as you said, it's the personal parts of the letters and tapes that mean so very much, no matter how interesting the other stuff might be."

Nov 10. "We had two deaths last night, which kept us busy today. One of them was the lieutenant who got shocked by the hot wire. The other was a 'skag freak' (heroin addict) who developed septicemia (a type of blood poisoning) from unsterile needles. He came in yesterday evening and was dead within three hours. Deaths generate a lot of work for us, as we must notify USARV Casualty in Long Bihn (Saigon) for further notification of kin, notify the Chaplain, call Graves Registration to pick up the body, prepare autopsy requests (when required) and have them signed by the CO, being sure that all death certificates and other reports are properly prepared, plus a few other minor details.

Yesterday, a doctor asked me to go out to the "dead shed" and help him complete a death certificate on a GI. The deceased was very stiff and had been shot through the right cheek with an M-16. I had to put my arms under his back and neck and lift him up so the doctor could look for any other wounds. The bullet had blown out of the back of his skull and I got his brains and blood all over my arms. Turns out he was returning to his perimeter after relieving himself. It was right at dark and a Puerto Rican kid had just assumed his sentry position and gave the challenge password when he saw him approaching from the bush. The accent was heavy enough that the deceased didn't understand and kept coming, so he got shot. At least that was the story we got from the dustoff crew that brought him in. Typical of war!

Also, last night, we received a Captain and a First Sergeant who had been shot by one of their men in their company, so all day long the CID (Criminal Investigation Division) was in and out getting statements and copies of records. Yesterday the MPs brought in a lineup for a warrant officer to pick out the addict who stabbed him in the heart. He is being medevaced tomorrow. Seems like we're doing ourselves more harm than the enemy, since we've only received one battle casualty in the ten days.

Since there has been so little action lately, things have been getting increasingly irritating. We've been getting a lot of static about reports, who we can air evac, haircuts, uniforms, and the like. I don't think we can get out of this environment soon enough. The more these guys are harassed and the less they must do, the more they drink and shoot up heroin and the more trouble they get in.

Bill Green just told me that the hospital XO had finally decided that I was to be the new registrar. There had been some question about it since Burt was more experienced and in the Regular Army. He was a career officer. I'm a reserve officer, although I am more senior in grade. This will be a lot of responsibility, but it should be a good experience for me."

December 25. "We had a floor show last night with free drinks, then a mail call at midnight. I was thrilled to get the card of the 17th and your letters of the 18th and 19th. I wrote back to you at 1:30 a.m.

My men woke me up at 3:30 a.m. to get me to come out and drink some more with them, but I wouldn't. Then, I had to go to the office at 9:30 a.m. and set up an evacuation for twelve patients. A clerk usually does this, but he didn't make it in.

We had the basic turkey dinner for lunch, which means leftovers tonight. The floor show was Korean and very good. Everyone was in the spirit, and we all had a pretty good time. Your letters coming at midnight finished it all off on a great note.

Also, all of us received sacks of various little gifts from church and military wives' groups. I got a nice leather wallet and a key ring. We got piles of homemade Christmas cards from several sororities, too. It's good to know that so many people still put forth the effort for those of us still left here.

I was in the ER a while ago and there was a drunk all strapped down and threatening to kill everyone. The doctor told the MPs to take him to jail, as he was only drunk. He calmed down and promised to behave, so they didn't cuff him. He immediately spat in the face of one of the MPs and then kicked him in the lower stomach. The other MPs grabbed him, and the sergeant who runs X-rays slugged the guy. They cuffed him and threw him to the floor of a jeep and hauled him off. He'll get worked over a little more at the jail. The MP was taken back to the ER in severe pain but proved to be OK. We x-rayed the sergeant's hand but nothing was broken.

The drunk said he had been run off by his parents at the age of 13. *What a sad case he is, with no friends and threatening to kill people on Christmas Day.*

Homecoming:

January 10, 1972, was the last letter I sent home from Vietnam. What follows are my memories of the whirlwind of events that ensued in the next few days.

On January 11, I got a call from Burt Wilde who I believe was preparing to board a helicopter that would begin his journey home with the flag of the 85th (to Fort Campbell, Kentucky, if my memory serves). He saw my name somewhere on a list of approved drops and called me with the news. He also told me a chopper was leaving for Danang in about two hours, and he would try to hold a spot on it for me. I don't remember what all happened in that short time, other than me throwing what few things I owned into a suitcase Janie's folks had sent to me for Christmas, bidding a few farewells, and racing towards that chopper.

I landed at Danang air base which housed the out-processing center for those leaving Vietnam. I was then assigned a bunk in a huge barracks and instructed to check twice a day for name on the latest flight manifest. That was a popular spot! I had no opportunity to call home and alert my family. I think it was two days before my name appeared for a flight leaving at dawn the next morning. After chow that evening, we were confined to an open-air pen of hurricane fencing and locked in. It had a tin roof and several picnic tables to sit on, but it was very open to the chilly ocean breeze that blew all night. We had all exchanged our fatigues and boots for short-sleeved khaki uniforms, and none of us had jackets, but we didn't complain. Dog handlers and their German Shepards patrolled the perimeter all night long. In the early hours before dawn, we lined up in a single file and had to open our trousers and submit to a pat-down search. The intent was to be sure we were not smuggling weapons, souvenirs, porn, or drugs. Once we got our pants pulled up, we were lined up and prepared to board a Flying Tigers DC-8 commercial airliner. I will always remember sitting on the tarmac and watching a flight of four F-4 Phantoms take off in a group with a tremendous roar and orange fire shooting from their engines in the early twilight. I was glad they were on our team!

As one might imagine, there was a concerted roar of elation as we lifted off the ground, and I must say I've never experienced any desire to set foot in that country again. Our first stop was in Japan, I believe at Yokota Air Base. I bought a Miranda SLR camera at the PX during our short layover there.

We flew all night toward home, and just as dawn was breaking, Mt. Rainer's peak came into view, protruding from the thick clouds and illuminated by the rising sun. What a beautiful and welcoming sight that was! We landed at Sea Tac International Airport outside Seattle in a heavy fog and then we were loaded onto buses for the trip to Fort Lewis, Washington (the final leg of my military career). It took all day to out-process out from the Army, and I must have walked miles visiting all the clearing stations.

I finally got to call Janie later in the afternoon, and I really wish we had a recording of that conversation. I remember her first words were, "Where are you? Your voice is so clear!" When I responded that I was in Washington, she exploded into happy tears. Fortunately, she and Shannon had stayed in Houston after her parents had tried their best to get her to accompany them to Austin/Lakeway for the weekend. I would have been so lost if I had not been able to reach her on that call!

By the time I finished processing out of the Army, it was late, and there were no more flights headed toward Texas. My seat on the U.S.-bound plane had been in the front of an exit and could not be reclined, and

I had been unable to sleep on the flight. We had been up for a full day and night before we boarded, so I had not slept in at least sixty-five hours. I was exhausted but determined to get home, so I caught a cab back to Sea Tac and began searching for flights going southeast. I think it took three flights on regional carriers, but I finally arrived at Houston International on Sunday, January 16th, 1972, about 6:00 a.m. As I cleared the gate into the giant hallway, I spotted my beautiful girls headed toward me - the happiest day of my life! Janie asked Shannon if she knew who I was, and she said, "Da Da" and toddled right up to me.

The people walking past us were no doubt oblivious to the young family in their joyous embrace, and this scene had happened a million times during the days of Vietnam. All major airports seemed packed with servicemen back then, but it struck me that most of us were invisible to our fellow countrymen who couldn't imagine the life-changing experiences from which we were returning.

The Dallas Cowboys were playing the Miami Dolphins in the Super Bowl that Sunday, and I tried to stay awake to watch it, even though I'd had no sleep in seventy-six hours. I suffered from malaise and a cough for about a month after my return, which was related to the constant dampness, the all-night exposure to chilly sea breezes in Danang, and some serious jet lag.

Registration at Stephen F. Austin State University began Wednesday, January 20, 1972. Janie and I raced to Lufkin, found a two-bedroom mobile home to rent, and got our utilities connected. As of that morning, I was a registered graduate student. It was a surreal transition from being a soldier in a war zone 8,900 miles away to being a college student in Texas studying parasitology and biogenic amines within a week. I remember how difficult it was to focus on my studies which had no pertinence whatsoever to our new life. Dumping servicemen (and women) abruptly into civilian life, straight from war, seems archaic and even unappreciated, at best.

During the semester at SFA, I was hired by the Upjohn Company as a pharmaceutical sales representative – a job I loved. That came about largely due to my Army experience and especially my time at the 85th Evac.

Janie and I have been married now for 53 years and raised three beautiful daughters: Shannon Hofmann, Jessica Nester, and Cameron Bradley. They each married fine men and gave us seven terrific grandchildren. Certainly, the hard times made us appreciate the good times better and especially strengthened our love for each other. We are very much aware of how blessed our lives have been and give sincere thanks to our Lord for the plan He so obviously had for us.

James Slack was a United States Army Medical Service Corps (MSC) officer when he was assigned to duty in Vietnam in 1971 and 1972. In 2023, James authored a book titled; Letters to Janie, which describes his pre-Vietnam days, his entrance into the U.S. Army, his Medical Service Corps training, and eventually his tour of duty at the 85th Evacuation Hospital, in Phu Bai, and his return home to his wife and his infant daughter, Shannon, in Lufkin, Texas. With his permission, I have taken a few excerpts of letters from his book, which describe his arrival in Vietnam, a few nights of duty at the 85th Evacuation Hospital in Phu Bai, and his arrival back home to the United States.

46.

Letters
HMM 362 "Ugly Angels"
Ky Ha, Republic of South Vietnam
by Richard Lester Houghton

25 September 1966

Dear Mom, Dad, & Kids,

This will be a rushed job.

Guess I'd better say I'm sorry for forgetting your Birthday, Elizabeth. I don't even know how old you are now: 13 maybe? Happy Birthday!

As of tomorrow, I'll be a section leader, with five more aircraft, and many more headaches. It's a Staff Sergeant's job, so my position is only temporary. We are so bad off that I am the senior man in the section. It's a good section, 6 birds, 4 crew chiefs no first mechanics. Guess how hard we work.

I'm also up for some sort of medal. I believe it's a Navy Commendation. It seems that I did an act of heroism or something last night. It's another long story, but it boils down to me getting out of my helicopter named "Teri," and helping a recon Marine in (he was about 50 yards away). The thing is, it was an emergency extraction, and the shit was really hitting the fan in that landing zone. I don't know why I did it, I just went suddenly. I fired almost 1,800 rounds between the two M-60's and I unloaded my .38 running around in the damned mud. He was a mighty grateful guy, but I was one awfully scared one. The thing I can't believe is that "Teri" didn't get a scratch, and rounds were hitting all over that rice paddy.

Glad to hear my camera is being fixed. I hope that it won't take too long. The latest is that we get aboard the *USS Valley Forge* (CV-45), on 3 October.

Signed this pay roster for a $75.00 check and $36.00 cash. I goofed. If you would please send me back that Navy jacket with the patches on it. It gets terribly cold this time of year here. And I don't have a thing. Today was really busy. I flew just better than eight hours. Then "Teri" sprung a beautiful oil leak – what a mess. At least I'll get tomorrow morning to fix it and straighten her out.

Take care all, With love,
Richard "Lester" Houghton Jr.

47.

A Letter to the Editor

The following letter, written in 1967, was sent to a resident of Cecil County in Maryland who then obtained the serviceman's permission to have it reprinted in the "Cecil Whig" newspaper, from Cecil, Maryland.

"… The hot and humid days that sometimes get up to 125 degrees don't seem that hot and the chow we get tastes a lot better when we know there are people at home like yourself backing us.

It sure gives us a lot more encouragement than looking at a stateside newspaper, if you know what I mean. Draft card burners and race riots are not exactly what I came over here to risk my life for, not to mention everything else that is going on. It has really made us guys stop and think for a minute. I am here so that my future wife and children can continue living in a free and peaceful country. Believe me, when the going gets rough, which it does quite frequently where we are, and we know that there are people back home like yourself appreciating what we are doing over here, we get back up on our feet and drive on."

Pfc. T.R. Addis – 3rd Force Recon Company
3rd Marine Division
Vietnam

Terry Addis – Far left & friends.

48.

Letter from a U.S. Army Infantryman
by Annette Langlois Grunseth

1 October 1968

As we moved down a narrow road leading into dense foliage, the whole world suddenly opened fire on the tracks. To be exact, the tracks were caught in an ambush. The enemy had our position on the road zeroed in for mortars. The ambush was sprung by simultaneously firing mortars, RPG's (rifle propelled grenades), and heavy small arm and machine gun fire. One mortar landed in front of our track and another behind it. Bullets were ricocheting off the armor and cracking over our heads. Within seconds, our radio was crackling with screams of "medic, medic – I need a medic fast. Then,

"Hold your fire – don't shoot the fifties – you'll hit our own troops."

"For Christ's sake get a medic, we've got a man bleeding to death."

"The sergeant is hit – his face is covered with blood. God, someone get the medic."

"We're receiving heavy fire – we need the fifties." "Hold your fire, pull back."

As we pulled back from the ambush kill zone, we opened fire with everything we had. The track ahead of us had taken a direct mortar hit the fifty-spraying the gunner and driver with shrapnel. Back at the edge of the rubber, we formed a small tight perimeter. Everyone was still firing full volume as the bedlam continued.

The driver of my track jumped out of the driver's hatch and climbed on to the track that had been hit with the mortar. The fifty gunner was slouched over the remains of his gun. Our driver lifted him off the track and managed to get the wounded man behind the vehicle for cover. The gallantry was futile. The mortar had blown away a bicep, part of his head, and had made his chest crimson mush. As our driver laid the wounded gunner on the ground, his eyes rolled back and cast an icy white stare. He was dead.

The wounded driver managed to get off the track but he had to be led to cover because blood was running over his eyes. At this point, our element had one KIA and three WIA's. One of the wounded was a sergeant who was shot through the side of his face. His eyes were bleeding and swollen shut. One cheek was just a gaping red hole.

Our platoon sergeant started calling for a "dust off" but when the medevac chopper started to approach about 30 minutes later, it suddenly dropped out of the air from enemy fire. Another "dust off" made it 40 minutes later.

It seemed like an eternity waiting for air support. Finally, gunships and several new Huey "Cobras" slammed machine gun and rocket fire into the enemy positions.

The dismounted troops were pinned down. While we waited for the dust-off, our platoon leader kept calling us on the radio, fearful we would get overrun. But we couldn't move until the wounded were taken care of.

Just before dark, the tracks circled back through the rubber trees, crunched through several hedgerows, and approached the pinned down troops in a wood line across a clearing. Once in the open, we opened fire, and roared into the edge of the woods. The whole area was a maze of red flashes in the dim light. About an hour later, our superior fire power overwhelmed the enemy. By now it was dark and we had to keep firing aerial flares so that everyone could find his way back to the tracks. Sniper fire continued and several enemy soldiers caught crawling in the light of the flares were quickly disposed.

At 8:30 p.m. we started driving back through the rubber. Choppers dropped flares for illumination. Back on the main road, casualties were totaled – five KIAs and 15 wounded. We finally got back to our battalion logger at 1:30 a.m. One track was left behind – blown apart in the ambush site.

Annette Langlois Grunseth is a poet and retired from a career in marketing and public relations. Her book, Combat and Campus: Writing

Through War *is written in honor of her brother Peter, a journalist and soldier with the 25th Infantry Division who passed away in 2004 at age 59 from a rare Agent Orange related cancer. From his letters Sergeant Langlois chronicles the smells, sights, and sounds during some of the darkest days of 1968-1969 Vietnam. Annette's book may be found at www.annettegrunseth.com*

49.

My Letter Home
by Paul Keaveney

Ol' Man Paul Keaveney, 3rd Force Recon Company - 1969

15 February 1970

Dear Mom & Dad,

I hope this letter will find you doing well and enjoying those sunny days in Florida. I am fine, but I am dictating this letter to a Navy nurse who has been kind enough to listen to my story and write it down for you.

I am a patient at the U.S. Naval Hospital in Yokosuka, Japan, and being treated for some injuries that I received on the 7th of February. Our team, Snaky, was inserted by helicopter into the A Shau Valley that morning to conduct a reconnaissance of an area used by the NVA. We had only been on the ground for less than an hour when our point man began walking down a trail made by the NVA. This was a deadly mistake.

I told the Marine in front of me to tell Cpl. Bishop to stop this action and to get off the trail, but no sooner had he moved forward when the NVA sprung their ambush on us. I was the first one hit, taking a bullet just a few inches above my knee on my right leg, and down I went. Then all hell broke loose. Sgt. Garcia, the point man, returned fire with his M-14, but he was killed, then Bishop was shot and killed. I told Lance Corporal Fuhrman to get the radio from Bishop's body so I could call for air cover and an emergency extraction. As Fuhrman moved to get the radio, he too, was shot and killed. That left Lance Corporal Silva and Private First Class Murray and me to stay in the fight.

I had my M-79 grenade launcher with me and began to fire at a machine gun position, but then I was hit in the right arm, just above the elbow. I was still able to reload and continue to fire, but then I was hit in my left arm, making me useless. I was able to use the secondary radio and got an immediate response from U.S. Army helicopters still flying near our area. They came in with rocket and machine gun fire to suppress the NVA company that we had walked into.

While waiting for an Army "Blue Team" to arrive from Camp Eagle, I was hit again, and this time it was on my right side with the bullet exiting out near my spine. Last, but not least, I was hit for a fifth time, but that round hit my holstered .45 and set off two rounds in the pistol's magazine.

The most incredible thing to happen was when three NVA soldiers ran up the hill toward me, all carrying AK-47 rifles. They stood in front of me, looked at me, and then ran back down the hill to wherever they had come from. It happened so fast that neither Silva nor Murray fired at them. They certainly could have killed me.

The Army's "Blue Team" arrived about two hours later, coming with a reinforced platoon of trained infantry from Delta Troop, $2^{nd}/17^{th}$ Air Cav. Slowly, they made their way to our position and called in a Huey helicopter and lowered a jungle penetrator to hoist me up and into the Medevac bird. When I was about ten feet up, I fell off and landed in a heap on the ground. They tied me in a little better and the second attempt was successful. I was taken to the Army's 85th Evac Hospital in Phu Bai, and into surgery to remove two of the three bullets that had hit me. Two days later, I was able to attend a Company Memorial Service for eight Marines from 3rd Force Recon Company who had been killed within a week's time.

Today, I am doing fine. All my wounds have been addressed and are healing and I'll be leaving here soon for the U.S. Naval Hospital in Key West, Florida.

Please, do not worry. The tough part is over, and I'll be home soon enough. But please say a prayer for the 3rd Force guys who are still there, as they need all the help they can get.

I'll see you soon, Love,
Paul

Paul Keaveney receiving the Silver Star Medal.

Paul Keaveney of New Smyrna Beach, Florida was a 3rd Force Recon Company teammate of playwright Bruce "Doc" Norton. Upon his return from Vietnam, he was awarded the Silver Star and the Purple Heart for actions during the Vietnam War.

50.

An Australian Infantryman's Letter Long Khanh Province - 1970

by Garry Adams

February 28, 1970

On the morning of February 28, 1970, the 6th Battalion were operating against the North Vietnamese Army in Long Khanh Province. Signs of the enemy were everywhere, all the tracks in the area were well used by the enemy force and it was only a matter of time before there was a major battle with the NVA (North Vietnamese Army) in this area. This however was not to be, there was an "O" Group giving a warning order for a move south to an area east of Nui Dat 2. The impending move was brought about by an agent report which said that a large enemy force consisting of NVA and Main Force VC (Viet Cong) had left their sanctuary near the May Tao's. This force was in full strength of a battalion plus and had been recently armed with additional 12.7 mm heavy machine guns and RPG-2's and RPG-7's.

RPG-2.

Now, we had heard all this before and each time the information was always wrong, so, there was little concern about the report. The battalion plan was to insert A Company west of the Suoi Giau Creek where it would move into a blocking position while the rest of the battalion would move south to engage the enemy battalion reported to be in the area. A Coy flew south from Long Khanh Province and landed around 11:45 hours at Grid 582702. 2 Platoon headed due east, and 3 Platoon headed northeast and later was to swing east and parallel Second Platoon's route. 1st Platoon and CHQ would remain at the landing zone, securing it for Mortar Platoon who were to fly in later. 2 Platoon moved east toward the Suoi Giau where we were to check for any sign of enemy and to check the suitability of the cut off position should the enemy be driven towards us by the rest of the battalion.

The move was about two thousand meters through scattered bamboo clumps and old, long deserted paddy fields. The midafternoon move was hot, it had not rained for months and the area was dry and dusty. Five Section was in the lead and we finally reached the bank of the Suoi Gia Creek, where a steep dry bank led to a dry creek bed.

**And now I will continue
the story in my perspective as the forward Scout:**

In the bottom of this dry creek bed was a trickle of water. While I checked the crossing Geoff Edwards gave me cover with the rest of the platoon spread out in single file behind. So down into the creek I went and there I saw a small rock dam, which had created a pond about a meter long by a meter wide. On a large flat rock next to the dam was a wet bar of soap and a wet handprint. The water was still milky white with the soap and this meant the enemy were close. I gave "the enemy" thumbs down sign to Geoff and moved across the creek. Under the lee of the far bank was a track, hidden from view above by overhanging bamboo clumps. This track was so heavily used there were hundreds of footprints visible and the track had turned to bull dust.

I knew it was only a matter of time before there was a contact and indicated to Geoff, asking which way he wanted to go. He indicated left so away I went. The heavily used track followed the creek bed for a further sixty meters, then it swung right and came up out of the creek bed, went through a small clearing around which there were small saplings, and with knee-length grass along the left side of the track.

On the right, there were scattered bamboo clumps and behind that heavier scrub and forest. When I moved forward there was a jungle chicken up to my right front which had been caught in a snare. I knelt while the rest of the section came out of the creek and all I could see coming in from the right were fire lanes, where the undergrowth had been carefully removed to allow the bunker occupants a clear view of the track we were on... It was one of those "Oh, shit," moments and I knew trouble was not far away. To the left-hand side of the track was an enemy shit pit, freshly used.

Then, I had to push forward again to let Platoon HQ out of the creek and then twenty or so meters away to my right front a transistor radio blared out with Vietnamese music. A curt command in Vietnamese, twenty meters to my left front, quickly had the radio turned off. It was obvious we had found the enemy that the rest of the battalion was looking for, further north to attack.

Still, by some miracle we had not been detected, even when Peter Hill was trying to free the now squawking chicken from the snare. Again, as I knelt, all I could see were more fire lanes cut in the scrub. We moved quietly back and dropped our big packs. The Third Platoon had been stopped and told to head south towards us. And at 17:15 hours, more than three hundred meters away from us they hit a sentry position on the far side of what appeared to be a very big bunker system. They killed the sentry, but had two wounded who needed to be dusted off (medically evacuated).

All was still quiet in our sector, but there had been a bit of movement as the enemy in our area stood to, and we could hear them rushing to take up their fighting positions in their bunkers. The "chink" of metal-on-metal and then the distinctive "clunk" of a 12.7 HMG being cocked was so close to us.

To our north, Third Platoon's "dust off" went without incident and then all hell broke loose as they started to move south towards us. Heavy machine gun fire, RPG fire and numerous AK 47s could be heard, as the enemy were in the process of hitting 3 Platoon hard, who now had several wounded and could not maneuver. At this time 2 Platoon was ordered to move to join 3 Platoon to stop them from being overrun. We knew we would be engaged when we moved but these were our mates being hammered by a continuous roar of gunfire several hundreds of meters away. It was time to move.

Some of us were standing when a shot rang out. One of the riflemen had spotted a VC, who had obviously seen us and was trying to position a D-10 Claymore directional mine and shot him and with that shot, the enemy opened up as one. The first burst of fire had the small saplings to my left being chopped down and I watched as the seed heads of the grass were clipped off by bullets ripping past just below knee height. It was as if we were watching all of this unfold in slow motion. I turned to Geoff Edwards to see if he was still standing and watched the large green tracer from a burst of 12.7 heavy machine gun fire zip in between us. Then there was a lull for a second and it was time to get on the ground. There was a 12.7 heavy machine gun off to our left front and another one off to our right that was firing short bursts.

At one time a couple of RPG rounds flew through the scrub but did not detonate, we were so close that we were inside the arming range and these rounds detonated only after they had gone past us. The 12.7 Heavy Machine Gun to our left front was so close that in brief lulls the brass could be heard falling after a burst along with the excited chatter of the gun crew, and these rounds were cracking only a foot or so over our heads.

12.7 Russian Machine Gun.

(We were to find out the next morning that they had put a large log in front of the gun as camouflage but the same log was saving our lives because in prevented the barrel from being depressed.)

The roar of gunfire somewhere to our front showed that 3 Platoon was still in heavy contact and in big trouble. We were in a similar position, but at this stage no one had been hit. We had an ace up our sleeve: our FO, (forward observer) Bombardier Reg Shepherd, who was without a doubt one of the best FOs the artillery had ever produced. In a short time, Reg was calling in "less than danger close" fire missions, these 105-mm shells were falling with pinpoint accuracy less than fifty meters to our direct front.

The artillery would lift while the RAAF "Bushranger" helicopter gunships came in, often firing only twenty meters to our front with their spent 7.62 mm casings showering down though the bamboo. And during these firing runs Reg Shepherd was organizing artillery covering fire for 3 Platoon, using their contact grid and laying down protective fire to their east.

At one stage in the battle the enemy put half a company into the creek bed some distance from us, and a passing U.S. Army Cobra gunship that had obviously seen the smoke of the battle came to have a look, spotted them, and was fired upon. He retaliated with his nose mounted mini gun with great effect. Since our backs were to the creek bed, had they got behind us we would have been caught between the proverbial "Rock and a Hard Place." Another attempt by six enemy soldiers was made to get behind us along the creek and was repulsed by the rear section. Not long after this the Platoon Commander, who was well and truly out of his depth, told Peter Hill to conduct a right flank attack with his six-man section. A brilliant idea - throwing six men away in a futile assault into a reinforced battalion's position. I remember Hilly answering in colorful language that it was too thick to assault through and the suicide charge never took place.

With the platoon commander out of the picture and not issuing any practical orders the battle was run by our illustrious Platoon Sergeant who came crawling up to me to have a chat, all very matter of fact. "Garry, what do you think these bloody blue flashes are?" "12.7 tracers, Lou, or they are the RPG boosters detonating as they go past." With that sorted out, he gave me a pat on the shoulder, "Kill them if you see them" and crawled away to have a chat with another mate one under fire. He was our rock, all through the tour.

The firing in 3 Platoon's area increased as they were probed again, and orders came from CHQ, some distance away, that we had to link up with them lest darkness see major assaults on both 2 and 3 Platoons. 3 Platoon now had a further nine WIA including Owen, Fang O'Reilly, who had previously been with 2 Platoon. Fang had been shot under the right eye with the bullet exiting below his left ear...and he survived.

That put 3 Platoon's fighting strength down to eighteen men.... 2 Platoon entered the battle with twenty-three men and would soon be down to twenty-two. As darkness was falling, we made our move again... this time an RPG detonated on a tree next to Doug Sorenson who was hit in the face with shrapnel. There was a brief exchange of fire with the left front 12.7 as Doug's number two gunner took over the M-60. After his return fire, the 12.7 fell silent and this gave us an avenue to get out, get into the creek and move towards where we thought 3 Platoon was. The enemy could be heard moving only meters away and there was one more brief clash, and then, nothing.

In the darkness, our navigation was not good and we did not know where the enemy was located. This slowed us down and then Corporal Hans Fleer took it upon himself along with Ted "Pop" Merritt to come out through the enemy camp and guide us back in. There was nothing subtle at all with Han's calling out, "2 Platoon, this way!" ...and with that we linked up and made it into 3 Platoon's position on a small knoll surrounded, as we found out later, on three sides by enemy bunkers.

In the darkness we were put down, but not before there was a quick chance to grab ammunition from some of the wounded's webbing. I did "Fang" laying there, under flare light, looking very much like he was dead. We were in position around 2000 hrs and out in the darkness in between artillery rounds falling, I heard an English-speaking enemy soldier say, "Uc Dai Loi." (Australian) "Surrender, you have no hope, you are surrounded." Geoff came down to where I was and asked, "Did you hear that?" "Yep." And in came another round of our artillery shells and the caller was not heard from again.

Around midnight the medevac helicopters came in and an absolute ton of guts was shown from both the American and Australian "Dust Off" pilots, hovering with their spotlights on and winching out the wounded one by one as they were always a sitting target for the 12.7's. Then, after 30 minutes or so all the wounded had been winched out and were headed for the U.S. Army Evacuation Hospital at Long Binh and it was all dark and quiet again in our position.

Sometime, around 0200 hrs that night, we could hear mortars being fired and the general reaction was "Oh, fuck...here we go again." but then the mortars could be heard impacting south of the bunker system on any enemy withdrawal routes. It was not long after the mortars stopped firing that the clink and jingle of pots and pans could be heard, and with that we knew the enemy was going to abandon their bunker system.

Just after first light the OC turned up and had a mini dummy spit (aka a hissy-fit) about a dead VC still lying beside the track. A couple of us dragged the corpse into a nearby bomb crater and buried him in the bottom which saved us a bit of digging. Then it was time to go back and search the bunkers. I knew where the 12.7 had been, and its tripod was still there, but it had been hit by a burst of fire from one of our M60's and was useless. In the back of the bunker, I saw what I thought would be a prized souvenir - an NVA pith helmet. When I picked it up, it proved to be a throw away. The previous owner's cranium was glued inside by blood and brain matter and it stank.

Another large bunker that I searched stank of blood and rotting flesh... one of our Regiment's artillery rounds had gone through the entrance and detonated inside, leaving bits of bone embedded in the earth walls along with uniform scraps and flesh. The whole interior of the bunker looked like it had been spray painted with blood and gore. Another bunker was found soon after in the same condition. After the search the CO, Lt Col. David Butler and (Chaplain) Padre Mills came in to visit. As he was talking to me the CO mentioned that a Coy 8 RAR had been hit hard by mines in the Long Hai's with 10 KIA and 16 WIA out of a platoon. Then he was gone and the good padre stayed with us for another week.

*From documents captured it showed the enemy force we had fought was a battalion reinforced. It was D445 Battalion, reinforced with NVA regulars to bring it up to full strength. And in the system at the time were:

D445 HQ, C1 D445, C2 D445, C4 D445, C6 D440 and C7 D440 Ba Long Provincial HQ plus an attached Rear Services Group Giving them a strength of over six hundred men. Casualties were unknown apart from one body and the human debris found in the bunkers. There were sixty plus sets of stretcher poles found to have been cut on the withdrawal routes to the south and southwest.

* When the "Dust Off" helicopter landed at the U.S. Field Hospital at Long Binh in the early hours of March 1. Fang O' Reilly was one of the last men taken off on a stretcher and covered with a poncho. There was an American priest at the LZ and this kindly soul started giving the poncho covered body the last rites, when Fang sat up and said, "You can fuck off. I'm not dead yet!" Or, so the story goes.

** For his action and outstanding bravery during the battle Cpl. Hans Fleer was awarded a well-deserved Distinguished Conduct Medal. Second only to the Victoria Cross for "Other Ranks" Hans had rallied the troops after the Platoon Commander had been wounded, went forward, and dragged in the wounded and organized the defense that repulsed several enemy counter attacks.

*** I was speaking to our Company Commander, Major Peter Belt, one Anzac Day a few years before he died. He told me that the sound of heavy machine guns, RPGs and small arms fire was so great, coming out of our contacts, he thought he was in danger of losing both platoons.

Casualties: 2 Platoon, one WIA and 3 Platoon 11 WIA Enemy casualties unknown, two bunkers full of bits and pieces, one helmet complete with cranium, three VC bodies and sixty plus sets of stretcher poles cut and removed.

**Private Garry Adams (Age 20) Unit: Royal Australian Regiment 6th Battalion, A Company, 5 Section, 2 Platoon
(Left and Right, in Saigon years later).**

51.

Stateside

The Stamp
by Steve Smith

Vietnam, as we know now, was a very unpopular war for Americans. Now we know it was entered by the U.S.A. under false pretenses of an attack on our military in the Gulf of Tonkin. This attack was used to play on the emotions of the American people and to justify us entering someone else's conflict.

I was attending North Junior High School in the late 1960s and there was a teacher there, Dr. Shockley, a Korean war vet, which saw the anger and resentment Americans had for the war and that it was being mis-directed toward our servicemen.

Dr. Shockley hatched the idea that we should honor our servicemen no matter if we agreed with the war or not as it was not necessarily their choice to be a part of the war, so he started a campaign to do so. As a result, North Junior High sponsored the issuing of a postage stamp proclaiming our appreciation for our servicemen. To commemorate this stamp, I was selected along with Dr. Shockley to attend a conference by the Freedom Foundation in Washington DC. It was an honor and thrilling for me to have an opportunity to visit many of the historical sites in our Nation's capital and represent our school and community to raise awareness about how rotten our nation was treating some of our own citizens who were asked to make the ultimate sacrifice, in another country, to protect what we considered important values in another country.

By the time I graduated from Central High in Sioux City, Iowa, the war had become very unpopular and the draft had been replaced with a lottery that determined the eligibility of 18-year-olds to be drafted based on their birth day. I vividly remember my freshman year in college the day the lottery was drawn and the fate of every one of my male classmates hinged on the luck of the draw. Many of us had gathered in the TV lounge in the student union building to watch the drawing and the anxiety in the room was palpable. The idea that someone's life hung in the balance of what number they drew was just absurd to me. So, as luck would have it, I drew a high number, #253, and was given the opportunity to have a choice as to whether I wanted to serve or not, which was an absurd luxury.

The war had found its way to that student union lounge that day. It dictated to many young Americans what direction their lives would take from then on and whether they would live or die in a foreign country and how they would be treated by their fellow citizens if they got drafted. I chose not to serve but was painfully aware of the unfairness forced on many by a simple drawing of a number. From that day forward, I always tried to honor and appreciate the service of those who served the greatest nation on Earth, whether it was their choice or not.

I honestly don't think the postage stamp had much impact on the sentiment of the average American at the time but it had a profound effect on me and helped me understand that all American servicemen deserve our honor and respect. GOD BLESS AMERICA!

Steve Smith calls himself a skeptical optimist, or is it an optimistic skeptic? He has always tried to hold honesty and truth as his guiding principles. This story is from a time when Steve attended school in Sioux City, Iowa with playwright Harry Kantrovich. He studied music at the University of Louisville and now lives in Colorado with his brother Mike.

52.

The Lottery

by Steven Cramer

    My story is quite different from so many others because I never went to Vietnam. I won a Lottery. It was just as life-changing lottery as any you might win today, and yet there is some regret, some shame, that I did not serve my country while others did.
    You see, my father was a pilot in the Air Force. He had been barnstorming around Ohio when he wasn't playing trumpet with some Big Band. But when World War II began, he signed up, leaving his trumpet behind, never playing it again. He flew C-47's, among other aircraft, mostly delivering supplies. I learned later in life the significance of him "flying the Hump in Burma." Somehow, with an 80% mortality rate, he

survived. And then I was born just before he was recalled to serve in Korea.

He stayed in the Air Force, and had an interesting career, but never talked about either War, never went into detail about all the medals on his dress uniform that were more than anyone else I had seen, regardless of rank.

At 12 years old we were stationed in Berlin, Germany, two weeks before The Wall divided the city. I know very little about what he did every day. He only said that "He played Chess with the Russians, the British, and the French all day long." After 3 years, we moved to St. Louis, and I knew even less about what he did there. Then to Andrews Air Force base, where I graduated from the third high school I had attended.

So, my story isn't that different from most other 'Brats.' Then, there was Vietnam. Now, I was quite aware of what had been going on. In 1966, I attended an 'Up With People' concert, and the song, "Freedom Isn't Free" made it clear that is why we were there. We were fighting for Freedom. And I figured at some point, more than likely, I would be going to Vietnam. But my father suggested that I enter the ROTC program at the University (My mother, on the other hand, insisted that "If they ever drafted me, that we would all be moving to Canada, because No son of hers is going to die in Vietnam"). I followed my father's suggestion.

I did feel a bit like a 'fish out of water,' because by then I suppose I was a bit of a 'Hippie,' with longish hair and a very liberal attitude about a lot of things. But I knew how to polish my shoes better than anyone else, and received a quick commendation because I knew how to 'talk the talk, walk the walk,' or more precisely, march. I was in a few different marching bands in high school.

Most of my friends in college were in the visual and performing arts. And they were Anti-war. They often poked fun at me on the day I wore my uniform, but otherwise they were very respectful toward me. I think everyone realized that it was a good idea that, "If you are going in the military, at least go in as an officer." As for being in college, that is what gave me a Student Deferment. Otherwise, my Draft Card would have listed me as 1-A. (Actually, I knew that there was a good chance I would be considered 4-F since I had severely flat feet, horrible allergies, color-blind,

52. The Lottery

bad eyesight, and rather frail body—the proverbial '95-pound weakling' that always came in any race in last place, never good at any sport, and always chosen last. But I decided I would never use that as an excuse. I kept my infirmities to myself, covering them up quite well, but mostly being embarrassed.)

I did quite well in ROTC, and had great grades, even though I was always sparring with the instructor about "What do we do if we know our leader is wrong?" It was November 1969, and reports of the My Lai Massacre became well known. The instructor insisted that we 'follow our leader, no matter what.' So, I began listening to more of my friends who insisted that the war in Vietnam was "Immoral." Of course, I was also involved in protests about the racial conditions in the U.S., which, again, were molded through experiences living in the South and were being pulled away from "Colored Only" water fountains. And again, an Up With People song, "What Color Is God's Skin?"

And then December 1, 1969, the first Draft Lottery came and everyone immediately lost all of their deferments. Everyone was considered 1-A.

Now, I don't know how 'popular' the Vietnam War was with the soldiers who readily volunteered long before anyone was drafted against their will. I just seemed to remember that no one wanted to go to Vietnam, no matter how Patriotic they had been, no matter what the family tradition might have been to Serve in the Military. This was different than World War II, and everyone knew it. It seemed a lot more like Korea. We were "Fighting the Spread of Communism." That was supposed to be enough information. We were told that the dominos would surely fall if we didn't draw that line in the sand and fight and die to stop Communism from spreading.

The nightly news was showing the bodies coming home. Mothers, especially MY mother made it clear that, ROTC or no ROTC, Lottery or No Lottery, there was 'no way she was going to allow me to go into the military, which it was assumed would definitely send me to Vietnam, where I would surely die.'

The dates, including February 29th, were written on slips of paper, and put in capsules and pulled out in random order. September 14th was the first number to be drawn. Anyone with that birthdate was told they might as well get things in order, and drop out of school, because they would be getting their draft notice and ordered to report for military service.

I watched it all on TV. Holding my breath. Having such ambivalent feelings that while I just dodged a bullet as each date that wasn't mine was called, it meant someone else received horrible news. I've always wondered how many veterans did the same thing and felt the same way, and what they felt when their birthdate was pulled in 4th or 5th or any early selection. What happened next to them? How many fled the country, how many immediately signed up so it would be on their record that they enlisted rather than be drafted.

#280. That was my birthdate. #280. All these years later I know my number.

So, what did I do? I dropped out of ROTC. It was just before I would be required to commit, no matter what, to join the military, regardless of my lottery number. I turned in my uniform, kept my shoes, since I owned those, and let my hair

grow. One by one, I saw the empty seats in classrooms. One by one, I heard stories over the next few years of people I knew that were never coming back. No one talked about the "injuries" only fatalities were mentioned on the news, and those were bad enough.

I went on with my life. I can't say that any of my friends were ever involved in calling returning soldiers bad names, which many talk about happening. I never did that. And I never knew anyone that did it. At the same time, it was rare that I saw someone in uniform who had returned from the war in Vietnam. I've always wondered just what they did when they made it back. Did they hang the uniform neatly in the closet, or did they burn it or throw it away? Did they look at the experience in a positive light that it was their choice to do their duty for their country, and were they proud that they had done that?

I do know there was relief across this country when the Vietnam War was over.

So, why should my story be part of any discussion about Veterans of the Vietnam War and their experiences? Because just like any story can't portray heroic achievements without the contrast of the villains, you can't tell an entire story without talking about how those on both the inside and outside have felt about things at the time, and any changes they have felt over the years.

(I was an altar boy, a lector, and worked within the confines of the inner Catholic Church. I know the private lives of Nuns, Brothers, and Priests. I know from what I speak about. Surely, I have seen both heroes and villains.) Have I met or been around any Vietnam Veterans? Sure. Many times. While many people have been heard more about homeless Vietnam Veterans. I've had neighbors nearby. And that is no surprise, since I live in a country setting, very much away from anyone else, where most people have built their own houses, usually with their own two hands. Most have few friends. Most keep to themselves, live off the land, and work for themselves.

In 1980, I bought my dairy barn to make into a house. Others followed, usually on at least 10-20 acres or more. The neighbor that lived behind me was a carpenter. He built his house out of nearby trees and other materials and built his workshop and made a decent living making furniture and custom cabinetry. One day, a teenage boy appeared, and he introduced me to his 'son that was just able to move here.' He was clearly "Amerasian." I spent some time with him, off and on, but was never close to the man. But he stepped up to his responsibilities as a father to that boy. That was clear to me. But he never once mentioned a word about 'That War.'

Another Vietnam Veteran also built his own home and helped me occasionally. People talk about a 'small world.' He went to high school with me, although he was "Track C," and I was "Track A-1." So, we really didn't know each other during high school that much. But that common element made a connection, and I ended up building a house on his adjacent property with him. We did talk a bit about Vietnam, but he had been more involved in building temporary bridges and fixing machinery, jeeps, and trucks, not really seeing significant action.

I have been around other Vietnam Veterans, the kind that wear a hat telling what outfit they were attached to, but that sort of sharing seems rare for Vietnam Veterans. It was from Veterans of WWII, and they share a lot and when I mention my father, they know much more about what he did than I will ever know or realize.

Have I been to the Vietnam Veterans Memorial? No, I haven't been able to do that. I haven't even considered going to the woods overlooking the memorial like so many have done. No, I haven't even been able to summon up the ability to even do that.

Is this some sort of "Survivor's Guilt" that I've felt all these years? Perhaps. My story is somewhere to the far edge past the stories of those that were drafted at the time but never actually sent to Vietnam. The story of Vietnam Vets includes those that stayed behind. Certainly, it includes those that received a telegram or visit from a somber member of the military about to give them devastating news. And yet, we rarely hear from those survivors of a War, only from the soldiers themselves.

Recently, I had a Vietnam Veteran that dropped an instrument by for me to clean and repair. When he came back to pick it up, I told him there would be no charge. That he had served for me, and this was the least I could do as a thank you. He had been trying to hand me money but after I was clear in my resolve and the reason, he put the money back in his pocket and shook my hand and said, "You're a good man."

There was nothing I could manage to say in return. He turned and left, happy that he could once again enjoy making music.

Steven Cramer is a highly sought after and acclaimed certified instrument repairman in Northern Virginia. Steve is also the founder of former professional theatre UPSTAT CROW.

53.

The Women

"Dealing with Misery…"
by Diane Carlson Evans

"Some of our medical staff dealt with the misery through alcohol, drugs, and sex. War time produces "geographic bachelors" who might have wives and children at home, but who had forgotten them for now. One of our nurses fell in love with a Navy pilot and the two talked of marrying when they returned to the states; both survived, but when she went to look him up in the U.S., she realized he'd given her a fake address. Later, she found out he had a wife and kids.

Some, not all, of the hospital pharmacies dispensed birth-control pills and condoms, something I didn't know at the time but later learned from a hooch mate, Edie.

"You living under a rock, Carlson?" she said.

"Hey, we can't even get tampons at the PX," I said, "because the GI's are buying them to clean their weapons."

I knew of nurses who'd gotten pregnant in Vietnam and had abortions performed by our doctors (abortion was legal in our military hospitals in Vietnam at the time) or flew to Japan for the procedure. I knew of nurses who fell in love with corpsmen or chopper pilots who helped get the wounded to us – only to learn his helicopter hit the side of a mountain or he had his head blown off from a grenade.

I wasn't interested in having a serious boyfriend in Vietnam. I remembered what Ann Cunningham had told me. But I had suitors – lots of male friends. Soldiers called us "round eyes;" we were a reminder of home. We were surrounded by tens of thousands of men, most of whom would've given anything to date a female nurse or American woman serving in Vietnam. We reminded them of home. And in a time when many were convalescing from painful wounds, we stood for comfort.

Frankly, female nurses in Vietnam embodied a complicated role. Beyond caring for a soldier's physical wounds, the unspoken assumption was that we were also to provide morale. But where was the line between morale and romance? And where was the line between sex and unwanted sex?

While we don't know the exact numbers, we know that many American women serving in Vietnam were sexually harassed, and some raped, but were afraid to report it to higher military authorities for fear of retribution. We were vulnerable and knew the Army Nurse Corps could not, or in some cases, would not, protect us. Women who did report these incidences were often transferred, lost promotions, or were marked as troublemakers. Our surviving Vietnam meant keeping secrets and watching our backs.

Some of us worried more about being raped than about being hit by enemy mortar rounds. We were young. And wartime provides a highly charged environment of testosterone and bravado. Men were miles away from home, had prying eyes, and with the numbers imbalance of males to females, we became prime targets.

Pilots – the older senior officers, in particular – could be a lot of fun. Many were my father's age. Most were good decent guys who simply wanted to have some female company over a steak dinner, a setup their air base offered every Friday night. Others were in the predator category; they frightened the hell out of me. I sensed I could trust the younger helicopter pilots who were more my age and often protective of us. Many of them flew Dustoffs - choppers that dove in quickly to snatch up the wounded. I admired them. They were fearless, flying hundreds of hours into enemy territory on terrifying rescue missions.

I was caring for a badly burned Dustoff pilot who had been recovering on my ward for more than two weeks. His record showed that day he was turning twenty.

"Can this be right?" I said to him. "You were nineteen, flying choppers?"

"Yes, Ma'am."

"How does this happen?"

"Simple. You lie about your age. No, really I graduated from high school when I was eighteen, went to Fort Wolters, Texas, for nine months of helicopter training, and here I am."

I was incredulous – a nineteen-year-old Dustoff pilot. He wanted me to go on R&R with him. He wanted me to be his girlfriend. It turned out, he wanted to marry me.

"I'm staying away from you guys," I said. "You'll just die on me."

"Hey, I haven't died."

"No, And let's keep it that way. Now take your meds and get some sleep."

When it came to drugs, Vietnam was like a vending machine that only took dimes and nickels. Pot, opium, hashish, and heroin – all were easily, and cheaply, obtained.

None, I found, would become my way of escape; I was afraid of them. I wasn't a goody-two-shoes and it wasn't my job to judge the choices of others; to each his or her own. But I hadn't been experimenting back in the States and I didn't want to take the risk in Vietnam. I understood how, amid the insanity of war, there is a tendency to look for comfort any way you can get it. I wasn't some sort of social outcast; I went to parties or to the officer's club. But, no, I cared too much about my job and I didn't want anything to rob me of the precious little sleep I was already getting.

So, I looked for other distractions. I wanted to learn about this place where I'd be spending a year. I worked at the orphanage. I'd commandeered a Jeep from a willing and smiling GI to take me for a ride off the hospital compound. The guys were careful; they knew we could get in trouble traveling around without orders. I accepted offers from pilots flying a variety of aircraft.

One pilot gave me a fascinating tour along the coast of the South China Sea. I looked down and saw the stark beauty; it all looked so peaceful, except for the bomb craters pocking the ground below. My biggest thrill was a ride in the U.S. Air Force's Jolly Green Giant, a search-and-rescue helicopter. Armed with two machine guns, it could lift twenty-five passengers or fifteen litters with casualties. The crew of four often flew under lethal operating conditions. They flew me over a junkyard.

"The only time I felt sick out there was going by the junked helicopters and planes," I wrote home in September. "Nothing but tangled, distorted heaps of metal. Really grotesque shapes and forms. Not so much the sadness of junked helicopters, but the lives which they cost."

I wrote lots of letters home, each addressed to "Mr. and Mrs. Newell Carlson & Family," Route 3, Buffalo, Minnesota. 'Sometimes with a zip code, sometimes not; they got there either way.

"Please send hand lotion, bath powder, candles, Clairol Hair So New Cream Rinse, fudge, and fruit cake," said a November 20, 1968, letter. "Have you heard yet about the Cardinal boy's death over here? Ronnie knows him. He's from Montrose. The bombing halt hasn't made any difference that I can see."

I sometimes wrote to my sisters and brothers, including Ward, who was only eleven. I drew pictures of what the Vietnamese children looked like and how they rode bicycles and carried water. "You'd love them," I told Ward.

At the 36th Evacuation Hospital, I made friends with roommates and colleagues, Lt. Mary Jane Haughney, Lt. Barbara Ward, Lt. Jean Phillips, Captain Manuel (Tony) Zuniga, my head nurse; the hard working surgeon Major Vincent DeAngelis, unhappily drafted out of his New York practice; and Specialists Ralph Broussard, Skip DeLong, and Cass Benavidez, three wonderful medics on Ward 6.

I spent a lot of my down time taping music from reel-to reel audio tape recorders. Music was priceless in Vietnam; it brought America up close and personal to us like nothing else could. I spent hours with The Kingston Trio, the Byrd's, Bob Dylan, Simon & Garfunkel, Peter, Paul and Mary, Joan Baez, The Beatles, and the like. Music spared me from insanity that year. I didn't mind the protest songs, and maybe they would actually help end the war,

It wasn't just American soldiers we cared for. For a month at the 36th Evac, I worked on a Vietnamese Ward, civilians who had been injured on the crossfires of war. A letter home reminded me: "Today we got three-day old baby admitted to the ward. Now we have them all the way up to age 84. I'm tired of colostomies, Foley catheters, and old men and women spitting on the floor. But I love the kids; they make working on the ward the worthwhile part. I debrided four burn patients today – takes several hours to do that." I remember emptying a colostomy bag from a sad old man; it was bulging with live and squirming Ascaris roundworms.

Sometimes along the line, a medic in Vung Tau gave me a peace symbol that he'd made out of hammered copper at a helicopter maintenance shop. It came on a leather shoelace. It was against regulations to wear any sort of jewelry, even earrings, while in uniform. But I tied it around my neck, tucked it inside my fatigues and vowed to wear it until I came home to the family farm. I was pro-soldier. But this was my private protest against the war.

Every day, six days a week, twelve to fourteen hours a day, I tended to the sick, the disfigured, the wounded, and the near dead as best I could. The little downtime we had just created boredom; it was easier to stay busy.

Most of us learned early on that to survive the accompanying misery and trauma of watching young men suffer and die was to detach ourselves emotionally. It wasn't a conscious decision. And it took time. But I learned to shut down my emotions, My skills were honed, and like a robot on an assembly line, I moved to the next patient and the next and the next.

Not that I ever lost compassion, but it was the only way for me to survive – and, really, for them to survive. I wished I'd had more time to listen and show that I cared more about a patient's psyche than simply hanging his IV or watching his ventilator. Each soldier had a story, a home: he was someone's son, someone's brother, husband, or boyfriend. But *someone* worth saving. And while careful to not let my emotions impinge on the task at hand, I wanted to do all I could to help that young soldier get back to his unit or back to what we coined "the world." But I couldn't help getting that young man home if I got too emotionally involved, even if at times it seemed impossible not to."

54.

Eddie Lee Evenson
by Diane Carlson Evans

November – December 1968

Ann Cunningham had warned me not to get close to any of the soldiers. At Vung Tau, I couldn't help it, though it wasn't in a romantic way. Specialist Four Eddie Lee Evenson was just one of those people who made the world a better place. He was admitted to my unit with injuries requiring a DPC (Delayed Primary Closure). I don't remember where the injuries were or what caused them. I remember *him*. He was from Thief River Falls, Minnesota, about two hundred miles north of my home in Buffalo Minnesota – so we had that in common. When you are eight thousand miles from home and find someone who lives a three-hour drive from you in the States, it forges an instant bond. We became fast friends, not in a romantic way; he was more like a fifth brother to me.

Eddie, at twenty-one, was the same age I was when I arrived in Vietnam. He was angular and strong, with a ready smile. And because he was considered ambulatory, he could move around. But because he was not ready to be released, he was happy to help us out.

No job was too small for Eddie Evenson. He cheerfully emptied bedpans, took blood to the lab, and helped ambulate patients using crutches.

There was no shortage of cynicism and bitterness in Vietnam; Eddie managed to rise above that. He reminded me of my brothers and the folks back in the Minnesota farm country, people who would return one of Dad's cows that had gotten loose or help him get hay in the barn before a storm rolled in. He was sweet and respectful, the kind of guy who lifted everyone's spirits and diluted their boredom. The medics and nurses loved him. So did I.

"Hey Lieutenant, let me do that," he'd say with his Minnesota accent. "What, you wanna do bedpans?" I'd reply with my Minnesota accent. "Well, guess it's better than pulling off those blood-sucking leeches from your buddy's private parts."

His laugh: he had a great laugh. Eddie actually *wanted* to do the "dirty work." He looked at it as some kind of privilege so nurses and medics would not have to do it. He saw us as having a higher calling. He realized we were busy and had little time to spend with each patient.

Eventually, he was ready to return to his unit. As his chopper warmed up beyond, he came to me to say goodbye.

"Promise me one thing," he said.

"Anything"

"Promise me you'll write."

"Of course, I'll write," I said. "We're Minnesotans. We keep our promises." And I did. Often.

My ward was quiet one night, and the supervising nurse on duty asked me to go sit with a patient in the ICU until – well, until he was gone.

He was a young black soldier wrapped nearly head to toe in white. I knew he was not likely to make it through the night; his wounds were just too severe.

"Ma'am," he said. "Please stay. I don't want to die. Don't leave me."

"I won't," I said. "I'm here with you."

And I was. At 7:30 p.m. the lights went out for the night. I stayed with him, holding a hand that got colder and colder. He died after midnight. I could not let go of his hand. A part of me was going with him and I could not let go. I was still breathing, but I was dying with him. I remember pulling the sheet over his face and I knew I would never ever forget him or that night at his side.

Often, a nurse would be the last person a soldier saw, touched, talked to, or smelled before he died. I knew he was dead, and his mother and father did not. I felt desperate to have those parents there instead of me. I asked God, why? Why allow this carnage? The soldier's loved ones would never know that he wasn't alone when he died. But if hearing is truly the last sense we lose, there's no doubt he heard during that one long night the love of a stranger telling him stories of life on a farm in Minnesota as he fell into peaceful, permanent sleep.

To counter the weight of such sadness, doctors, nurses, and medics often leaned on humor. In Vung Tau, I had treated a soldier who'd been bitten by a sea snake, which were common in the South China Sea. Soldiers on R&R in this seaside resort were at risk every time they stepped into the water.

"I'm from the Land of Ten Thousand Lakes," I told the medic who had brought in the soldier. "Never seen a sea snake. What do they look like?"

A few days later he showed up with one in a glass gallon jar and tried to hand it off to me. "Like this," he said.

Just before Thanksgiving, a storm slammed ashore. Surf rose to twelve feet. The beach was closed. Exciting. My spirits were high, in part because I'd received a certificate of achievement signed by the general himself, and Thanksgiving was done up right. We were treated to quite the feast: shrimp cocktail, roast turkey, cornbread dressing, turkey gravy, hot rolls, and butter – the works.

We each were given a written message from Gen. Creighton W. Abrams, commander of the U.S. Army. "We should never forget," it read in part, "that in Vietnam our actions are defending free men everywhere. We pray that peace will come to all in the world and that all of us can return to our loved ones in the not-too-distant future." By the end of 1968, "all of us" meant 540,000 American troops in Vietnam.

I was hoping he was right, though there was not much time to ponder the future. "The other evening, I got in twenty-one admissions all at the same time," I wrote home on November 24, 1968. "Was a little hectic. I am alone in the evenings except for a corpsman. Besides that, one of the patients came back to the ward loaded on pot (marijuana) and had to be carried in. I had the MPs there. He was soon air-evac'd out."

The United States' entanglement in the war was unnerving and complicated. For us women in the combat zone, the predatory behavior of some men in uniform could be as well, particularly those of higher rank.

Every day our unit received visitors: friends of casualties, platoon sergeants visiting their men, senior officers, generals pinning on Purple Hearts. One day a major with aviation wings on his uniform asked permission to visit a friend. A few days later, back for another visit, he came up to me.

"Would you like to go up in my plane and see the country?"

"Sure, that'd be fun!" if we broke the rules.

Ever since I had arrived in Vietnam, I'd loved flying in choppers and planes. Vietnam proved to be spectacularly beautiful and the only way I could see it was from the air. Nurses were forbidden to ride in convoys; travel was limited to specific orders. We were threatened with Article 15 punishment. But flying meant more than getting a breath of fresh air above the sickly smell of war; the perspective gave context to a geographic world that was otherwise hidden by the sloping walls of our Quonset hut. I loved the rush. Never mind that I'd be breaking the rules.

At any rate, he picked me up at my billet. He was in his late thirties, early forties, almost old enough to be my father. A major. But a forgetful major.

"Where's your flight suit?" I asked.

"Oh, I thought we'd go to the beach instead – after dinner downtown, of course."

"But I don't have a swimsuit or anything."

"That's OK, you won't need one."

Beginning with that change of plan, I never relaxed the entire evening. Not at dinner. Not on the ride to the beach, where the South China Sea lapped ashore. And certainly not when we got to the beach. He grabbed a bottle of wine and my arm, and – with an increasing sense of control – guided me away from the jeep. There was not a soul on the beach because we had walked past a Do Not Enter sign with concertina wire everywhere.

He sat us down on the sand and pulled out two wine glasses. Dusk was turning dark.

"I don't want a drink," I said.

"Fine."

He suddenly stood up and stripped naked, suggesting I join him. I looked away and knew I was in serious trouble.

"Maybe this'll help," he said flashing a book in my face with photos of people having sex. "I'll teach you to enjoy it. I'll be gentle."

I started to get up. He shoved me down and gave full attention to my jungle fatigues, which thankfully had lots of buttons. He started madly fumbling with them. When I pulled back, he lunged at me, tearing at my clothes.

"Please," I said, "just take me back."

He slammed me back on the sand and tried to muffle my mouth. I started kicking and twisted my head so I could talk. Officers didn't do this kind of stuff!

I thought of my roommate who saw me leave with this guy. I had told her his name. If he killed me and left me there, she'd know who done it.

"Stop!" I said, "Or you will never fly again! I will kill your career, your promotion, your family life back home."

He stopped. But what made him stop was not the sudden realization that he was taking something from me that didn't belong to him. No, it was the threat of something being taken away from him. Like a madman, he drove me back to my villa and all but tossed me out of the jeep, fuming because I'd rejected him.

I wouldn't tell anyone about the incident for thirty-eight years. But why had I said yes to him in the first place? Because I was still naïve and trusting. I hadn't been in - country long. This was a wake-up call.

Meanwhile, I was not going to let one bad night color my views of all military men. "I believe the American GI is the best patient in the world," I wrote in my diary. "They deserve the very best of everything – especially nursing care."

But there were also predators, sometimes unleashed on us by superiors. I had finished my shift and was leaving the unit at the 36th Evac when the senior nursing supervisor, a lieutenant colonel, called out to me.

"Lieutenant!"

"Yes Ma'am?"

"Lieutenant, I have a good friend coming in today, and I think you'd enjoy having dinner together," she said. Sounded interesting. I wondered who she was.

"He will pick you up at your villa at seven tonight."

I was incredulous. *He?* And it was all planned? Would I have dinner with him? Coercion from a superior? Yes. But I could trust her, right? He was her friend. So why, I wondered, wasn't she going out with him?

He was a colonel who, after dinner, started driving us toward the beach. The jeep hadn't even warmed up before I had him heading back to drop me off. I learned another lesson that night: the older nurses were not going to protect us; we had to watch our own backs.

On January 3, 1969, in the Mekong Delta in southern Vietnam, I was on a medevac flight to pick up patients from the 3rd Mobile Army Surgical Hospital. The VC frequently harassed the area with mortar-rocket fire, and we were getting in and out of there fast. As the chopper lowered onto the LZ (landing zone) near the emergency room, I saw sandbags stacked to the limit on all sides of the hospital. We prepared to transport a soldier with an amputation and get off the LZ and out of the way for several incoming ambulances. Suddenly, I heard a loud voice calling out to me from the open end of one of them, "Diane! Hey Carlson. Is that you?"

It was a Buffalo, Minnesota farm boy I knew - Charley Streiff, was wounded. We spoke quickly and went our separate ways. But it had been inexplicably comforting to see a familiar face and a reminder of home.

Speaking of which, I managed a phone call home over Christmas using MARS (Military Auxiliary Radio System), which required users to say "over" after each time they finished talking. I chose a day when I figured

Mom would be off work and Dad not working in the barn. They were thrilled to hear my voice and it felt good to make the connection, even if having to say "over" after each comment you made was awkward. It was my one and only call home from Vietnam that year.

I learned that after spending six months on an assignment we could request a transfer. It was January, and I had just finished a month on the burn unit at the 36th Evac. I wanted to go north, closer to where the fighting was. And I went to my chief nurse to say so.

"Ma'am, I'd like to request a transfer," I said.

"To where?"

"Pleiku."

There was a pause, as if she wasn't sure she'd heard me right.

"Are you sure, Lieutenant Carlson? That means going north. Hot fighting up there."

"Yes," I said. "Positive."

She nodded as to bless my choice.

Though Bob Hope had joked for the troops in Pleiku back in 1964, in the years since the site had become too dangerous for entertainers. It was jungle country, a few miles from the Cambodian border in the Central Highlands. I heard the 71st Evacuation Hospital was wrapped in concertina wire to keep out the NVA (North Vietnamese Army) and VC (Viet Cong) and that mortar attacks were common.

And there was a nearby fire base – an artillery battery set up to give fire support to surrounding units.

None of this deterred me. It was time for a change and a new experience in a different part of Vietnam. And the jungle would be a different world from the beaches and rice paddies I had lived around. I had no ties to the 36th and was ready to go.

My head nurse, Captain Manuel Zuniga, not only wrote me a letter of commendation for the job I'd done. I had no idea he thought I added to the morale of the unit; nobody got accolades when on duty, but he presented me with a petition from a bunch of people on staff and the ward full of patients insisting that I stay.

"The hardest part will be leaving all the people here I've made friends with," I wrote home. "Today, after two more weeks of working on my

Ward, was my last workday at the 36th Evac. Working with the "all Vietnamese" ward for a short time was a great experience for me. It brought me much closer to the Vietnamese people and to the realization that they are people with the same needs, wants, fears and feelings."

That day, several of the Vietnamese ladies and kids cried when I told them thru the interpreter that I was leaving. It touched a very sensitive part of me, and I couldn't help but feel sad yet so rewarded with the love and appreciation these people showed, too. I gave my friend Anthony a book with a message written in Vietnamese, "To my very good friend Anthony, I love you. I've fallen in love with the kids and it's very hard to leave their beautiful smiles and looks of love."

Before leaving for my new assignment, I packaged up some things to send home. "Please store for me," I wrote. I marked "DO NOT OPEN" - just leave closed and store."

My mother would respect my wishes – until that day in 1983 when she'd suggest it was time to unpack my stuff.

With permission - from her book, "Healing Wounds" *with Bob Welch.*

55.

"Goodbye, Vietnam"
by Diane Carlson Evans

July 1969

I remember my last patient in Vietnam like I remembered the moment President John F. Kennedy was assassinated. (Speech class, Buffalo High.) At Pleiku, the most critically ill patients were positioned directly across from the nurse's station so we could keep a close eye on them. They watched us as much as we watched them. I think they also knew they were chosen to be there because they were dying.

One of them was a very badly wounded GI with a tracheostomy; he was hooked up to a ventilator. He was restless and fearful and couldn't speak. For days, we had communicated with each other by jotting words on a notepad. The back and forth messaging eased his anxiety and provided the reassurance he needed to lessen his distress. My DEROS (Date Eligible for Return from Overseas) orders arrived.

"It's my time to leave Vietnam," I said to the soldier. "I'll miss you, but I have to say goodbye."

A look of panic locked on his face. His eyes darted left and right. He gestured for the notepad. "Don't leave me," he mouthed in words. He took the notepad and scrawled "Please don't go!!!"

He couldn't hold back the tears. I never cried in Vietnam, but at that moment I came close.

I hung yet another bottle of intravenous fluid, then touched his ashen face and looked into his sunken eyes. I stroked his soft, cold face. He scribbled something on his notepad. "Wish I could see my mom again," he wrote.

I nodded, kissed him on the cheek and then left. Though I can't remember his name, I will never forget him. I think he knew he wasn't going to make it – and I don't think he survived, although I've never been sure. But what else could I do? Nothing was ever neat and clean in Vietnam - goodbyes among them - because here's the thing: as much as I wanted to leave and needed to leave, I *didn't* want to leave. If that sounds like a contradiction, it's because Vietnam was one great contradiction.

I didn't want to leave that soldier. I didn't want to leave my unit, my hootchmates, my patients. I seriously had toyed with re-upping for another year. Another contradiction: just when we got good – really good – at our jobs, our tour was over, and we turned things over to the new people.

Barbie, my hootchmate, had lost a brother who was a helicopter pilot and had another brother on his way over to Vietnam. And yet she had re-upped for another year. I wasn't trying to "guilt" her, but I couldn't help but ask. "How can you do that to your parents?"

In her mind, she had rationalized staying. In my mind, I had rationalized leaving, perhaps because I still remembered my father crying when I left and still remembered all of the letters my mother and Nola wrote to me once I'd gone. They deserved to have me come home. I'd written my folks weeks ago that my ETA in Minneapolis would be about Augst 9th, 1969. Emotionally, this was more about them than about me. But, physically, it was all about me.

I was exhausted. I was sick, having had a low-grade fever for the last week. And I was losing weight. I was 5'5" tall and always thin, rarely over 110 pounds. But now I was flirting with double figures. Copter pilots offered me their hand when we loaded in beneath the rotors. "Hell, girl, take it or you'll blow away," one said.

I hastily stuffed my clothes and mementoes given to me by patients - poetry, brigade and division patches, a rabbit's foot, a Green Beret, letters, dog tags, a VC flag, a Montagnard bronze bracelet, and more – into my footlocker. I said goodbye to my ward nurses, medics, hootchmates, and docs.

As I approached the helipad, with my duffle bag in hand, I encountered more than a dozen desperate and wailing Montagnard women with about as many kids lining up and vying to get on the same chopper. Something terrible must have happened in their village. The pilots and crew hopped out and shooed them away. And as the helicopter lifted off, I looked down at the red whirling dust and saw young mothers scatter into oblivion. The apocalypse was behind me. Or was it?

Leaving railed against every nursing instinct I'd ever had. I had no sense of relief for having survived for 351 days in Vietnam. I had never run away from anything in my life, and this felt a little like I was. More U.S. soldiers died in Vietnam in the two calendar years I was there – 1968 and 1969 – that at any other time during the war.

I felt no sense of having neatly tied the knot of an adventurous two years of my military life. And I had no picture of what exactly I would be doing with my new life in the states. In a letter home, I'd asked my Mom to inquire about working at the Buffalo hospital. So, I must have assumed my future would include being a nurse. But even that image was diffused and uninspiring, like trying to peer out one of the farmhouse's frosty windows and seeing only the faintest of images ahead.

I arrived in Japan, feverish and fatigued. I checked into a Naval Bachelor Officers Quarters in Tokyo, staying ten days while waiting for the fever to break. An elegant, well-coifed woman noticed me sitting alone in the officer's mess. I know she saw me as forlorn; she couldn't have known how unfamiliar it was for me to be sitting at a table covered in white linen with silverware and fresh flowers in a vase.

She introduced herself as the wife of the captain of an aircraft carrier that was arriving soon. It was my first true conversation with someone outside the military in a year. She was lovely, poised, and relaxed – and yet interested in me, where I had been and where I was going - not that I had much of a clue about either. We talked late into the evening. She insisted on buying me dinner. In my transition home, beyond the two GIs who stood up for me in an airport, she would be the only one who seemed to really care about *me* as a returning Vietnam veteran.

I'd been warned not to wear my uniform home - that such attire would only bait the soldier-haters in the airports. But *not to* seemed like surrendering to the idea that we should be ashamed, that war couldn't be separated from the warrior. For my last leg to San Francisco, I threw on the uniform and, for the first time, wore my peace symbol – on the outside.

I thought briefly of home. The farm. Mom, Dad, My brothers. My sister. "Please don't plan anything for me when I get home," I'd written the previous month. "The only thing I want is for everything to be the same as when I left."

As the jet winged its way home, I sensed a numbness, a listlessness, an indifference in me that did not trigger the usual nurse's response of seeing what's wrong and fixing it. Instead, as the thrum of the engines lulled me to sleep, my last thought was: *If this plane were to crash right here in the middle of the Pacific ocean, I honestly wouldn't care.*

At Travis Air Force Base, near San Francisco, I was initially surprised that when I got off the plane, nobody spit on me, verbally unloaded on me, or gave me a look of disdain. Then I remembered: *You're still in the military bubble.*

It was time for my discharge physical. I understood why I'd been feeling so poorly over the past few weeks.

"Ma'am, it appears you have a spot on your lung," said a military doctor after taking x-rays. "We're going to send you to Madigan Army Hospital, up in Tacoma, Washington, for another opinion.

At Madigan, I was told to have it looked at every six months No mention was made of tuberculosis, which I'd later be diagnosed with, but not compensated for – even though I'd treated Vietnamese patients with it,

With that, I was handed my DD-214 discharge papers. The U.S. Army Nurse Corps and I were officially parting ways.

"And where do I pick up my tickets for Minneapolis?" I asked.

"Oh, you're on your own for that," the corporal said. "Seriously?"

I was not trying to be smarmy, but news that the U.S. Army wouldn't get me back home seemed like the ultimate insult.

"Even though I live in Minnesota, you're really not paying me to get back there?"

"Sorry. Protocol."

Protocol? It was like forking over $3,500 for a new Mustang and finding the dealer was charging you for the bag of popcorn you ate in the showroom. I'd paid a huge price to give to my country and my country couldn't pay a small price to get me back where I had started this journey?

"You're out of the Army now, Ma'am," he said. "Rules are rules." I shook my head and left. As far as last words go, my country could have done better. I'd have preferred "thank you for your service- and here's your prepaid ticket home." It didn't need to be first class; I'd been flying in open-door choppers that sounded, and felt, as if you were in a giant belt sander. But, yes, a "thanks" would have been nice.

That was the first shoe that dropped. The other followed at the Minneapolis-St. Paul International Airport when I arrived at the baggage carousel and was belittled by one of handful of protestors when getting my duffel bag. I was out of the Army, but I was still wearing the uniform. Two uniformed enlisted men stood by me as we waited for our bags. As I moved to pull my duffel bag off the conveyor belt, one of them said, "I'll get that for you, Lieutenant!"

"Let her carry her own damn bags," a long hair protestor sneered. "She's in a man's army."

With a single punch, the GI bloodied the guy's nose.

"You know," I said, 'we didn't start the war. We're over there defending people like you."

I found it interesting – no, disturbing – that nobody in the crowd said or did anything to support us. Bystanders - they had just stood and watched. It was a metaphor that I would experience often in the years to come.

I would hear of other degrading welcomes for military personnel returning from Vietnam: civilians spitting, throwing eggs, shouting, swearing, and protesting with in-your-face antics aimed at us. "Go back to 'Nam, Army pigs!" read some signs. "Baby Killers Not Welcome." One of our 71st Evac nurses, Lynda Van Devanter, tried to hail a cab, "Fuck you, army bitch," the driver said and sped off.

So, you leave as a defender of the free world and return as an enemy. I was stunned at how quickly people could race to conclusions at the simple sight of a uniform – or, in particular, a woman in uniform. That kid who'd hassled me didn't know me. He didn't know our medical team saved the lives of hundreds of South Vietnamese and Montagnard children. He didn't know that I was probably more anti-war than he was – because I'd actually seen the war in living color instead of only on TV and knew it to be mainly the color of blood. And those of us who wore the uniform basically had pledged to shed ours, so protestors like that kid could enjoy the splendors of freedom. All around, our nation was drowning in anti-war violence.

Did many of us in the military like how our leaders were lying to us and putting more soldiers in harm's way, sacrificing thousands of lives so the brass might somehow save face? No way. But I wanted to say to that kid: Before you paint all of us as crazy-eyed baby killers, at least find out who we really are. You might be surprised.

Mom and Dad were late picking me up, for which I was thankful. They missed the fiasco. It would have crushed Dad; he hated the war, too, but couldn't understand the animosity toward the veterans. He was part of the World War II generation where men and women came home from duty with honor for their service and their victory.

Dad grabbed by duffel bag and we got in their 1966 Rambler Ambassador to take me home. I can't remember a single thing we said in the car.

56.

My Military Journey
by Connie Chance

Women have served in the U.S. military for over two hundred years. In 1969, soon after graduating from high school, I entered the U.S. Navy. Upon completion of boot camp and Yeoman's school, my first duty assignment was in communications at Naval Air Station, Corpus Christi, Texas. I quickly learned that in "this man's Navy," a woman had to stand tall and overachieve to be considered equal. I was more than ready to confront and win in this area.

During my duties in communications, Corpus Christi was hit by Hurricane Celia. It was the most devastating hurricane in years. As I sat at my desk with one of only a few telephones operational in the area, the phone rang. It was the Red Cross...looking for ME! My parents had been watching the hurricane on TV and were more than a little concerned. My young mind told me that "I knew I was ok – so they must know too." I hadn't even considered calling them. We connected within minutes of my hanging up with Red Cross.

After a few months of working in communications, a LCDR requested that I be transferred to his office. I then moved to Aviation Safety in the OPS (Operations) hangar. I had a steady flow of paperwork and delved into it with a sense of pride. I love aviation! A Cobra helicopter sat outside of our office for use by my boss. As part of his duties, he would have to go on Search and Rescue (SAR) missions. Most of these missions were aligned with young student pilots landing on Padre Island to flirt with the girls on the beach.

The most tragic incident report I had was of a Marine pilot that experienced a malfunction in an F-4 Phantom. He was too low for the canopy to open. He ejected through the canopy, split his helmet in two, and was pronounced dead at the scene. Later on in life, I discovered that my boss, now a commander (CDR), had been awarded the Navy Cross for his role in the Vietnam War. He flew Apache/Cobra helicopters to rescue personnel on the ground.

I completed my Active tour of duty in 1972. I enlisted in the Naval Reserves soon afterwards. Two key points: I belonged to the NIRA (Naval Internal Relations Activity), which was journalism-based. We were assigned to put together a press kit for the opening of the new Pensacola Naval Air Museum. We spent two weeks gathering information and pictures of proposed additions to the museum. This was a decade before computers and graphic designing tools. I designed and drew the folder cover for the presentations that I typed up. I still have a copy of that! I have enclosed a picture of our team. The second key point was being assigned to the U.S. Navy Spacecraft Recovery Force Atlantic in Norfolk, Virginia. This was in July 1975, for the Apollo-Soyuz Test Project. I was assigned to work for the Vice Admiral in charge of the project there. Although the module was to splash down in the Pacific, we were assigned to be on standby in case of a misdirection of the module into the Atlantic Ocean.

One assignment I was given was to clean out a filing cabinet of old papers and pictures. I found a large envelope in the bottom of the drawer that had 8x10 glossies of astronauts, moon landings, negatives of moon landings, positives of moon landings, and even an artist's conception of what the Space Shuttle would look like. This was before the actual Space Shuttle was built and I at once thought "There is NO WAY I can throw these things away!" I went into the Admiral's office and asked him to please reconsider destroying this envelope of history. He said, "I agree. But I don't want them in this building. They have served their purpose. If you want them, please take them." I still have them!

After nine years in the Navy, I joined the Air Force Reserves. My duties were basically the same, but the cultural shift was confusing. Such a difference in many areas. Take for instance the E-6 exam. I had neglected to take it while still in the Navy, so I thought "how much different could this be?" To my amazement, the test, just as easily, could have been written in a foreign language. Wow. It would have been a miracle if I had passed that test; however, due to unforeseen occurrences, before knowing

the turnout, I took an early discharge,

During my time there, I was assigned to work for the base commander. The caveat of this was having the Colonel ask if I would like to see what it's like flying over North Carolina airways, refueling a B-52. I went, of course. I was given permission to lie in the boom of the aircraft during the refueling. I will forever be in awe of those Airmen that control the boom. The accuracy and patience it takes to connect the two aircraft is breathtaking.

My experiences during my time in service (1969 – 1981) are a blend of wonderful and the wish-I-could-forget memories. Although I requested a transfer to Vietnam, I was told that the only females were WAVES. I genuinely had hoped to go, do my part, and hopefully help wherever I could. Would I do this all again? ABSOLUTELY! Especially knowing what I know now...I would change a few things. My fellow brothers (Veterans) always talk about having 'boots on the ground.' Even the VA holds those individuals highest. For the women in uniform during that Era, we had our own war. A war that continues. I realize we have never had

bullets, or shrapnel removed from our bodies, or lost limbs, but scars are still within us. We have fought a war. Only now has it been recognized – and I hope one day, there will be no more wars – for all of us.

(Left) Connie's father.

Connie Chance enlisted in the Navy in 1969, at the age of 18, after her graduation from high school. She served nine years in the Navy as a Yeoman and then transferred to the Air Force Reserves. Connie is a life member of the American Legion and Disabled American Veterans. She has also been involved with the U.S. Navy Sea Cadet program.

57.

Nobody had Ever Welcomed Me Home
by Karen Offutt

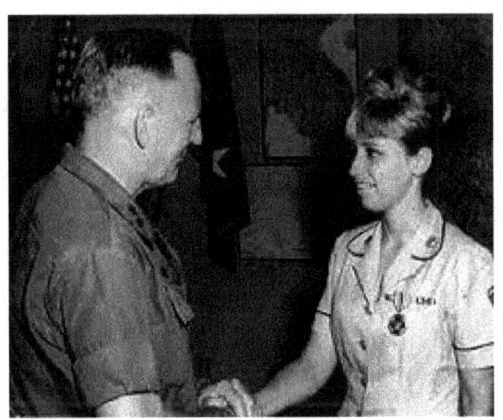

In the late 1960s, I was a teenager and considered myself very patriotic. I got chills whenever I heard "The Star-Spangled Banner." At 18, I dropped out of nursing school and enlisted in the Army and was deployed to Vietnam.

I told my daughter Kristin that I felt proud to have the uniform on.

As an executive stenographer, I had Top Secret 'eyes only' clearance. Many times, they would call me in the middle of the night to come in — if we were going to do an airstrike on a certain village.

I also experienced degrading treatment as a woman in the Army. I had to look like a cutie, with my hair and my lipstick done properly, and serve tea. Whatever needed to be done I did it. Including having to pose as a "Bunker Bunny."

I had to do what I was told, or you didn't last long in the service. As a woman, I also didn't get the same recognition that a man would get for helping save lives. One day, I smelled smoke in the hotel room where I lived. I saw the hamlet next door was on fire. I just ran down and started grabbing people and dragging them out. The hamlet chief wanted me to have some kind of award and they put me in for the Soldier's Medal. But they said, 'We don't really give those to women and so we're going to give you a certificate of appreciation for heroic action.' And so that's what they did, and I thanked them, and I went back to work."

I never talked about being in the service when my children were growing up. Their father didn't allow me to talk about Vietnam. So, I didn't talk about for 16 years until I left him. Later, slides that were tucked away in the house were found. I remember just sitting there crying. I think it was when you must put something away and lock it inside of you for so long and you're not allowed to speak of it, I just felt lost.

My daughter, Kristin, asked me if there's anything that's helped me through the challenging times. I told her I think talking to veterans.

In 1996 I went to the Moving Wall, the traveling half-size replica of the Vietnam Veterans Memorial. I remember standing there, staring at those names because I knew some of those guys on the wall. This man came up and put his arm around me and he said, 'Welcome home, sister.' And I just started bawling because nobody had ever welcomed me home."

I needed to find a way to honor and memorialize my brothers and sisters who gave their all in Vietnam. I finally authored this poem to which is dedicated to them:

"Memories"

As I looked at him, his eyes returned the stare
His skin was black, mine white, though we didn't care.
Instant brothers, as from one mother's womb,
Now lying together in our earthen tomb.

He held my hand as he gasped for breath,
Our blood mingled as we fought against death.
We had met as youngsters only months before
And now lay dying, old men, from this war.

57. Nobody had Ever Welcomed Me Home

We talked quietly in our muddy hole.
We shared those moments and bore our souls.
He told of a wife and a baby due. He spoke of his little boy, now only two.

He was afraid of dying, of leaving them alone.
He started to cry, and in pain, then, to moan.
It seemed insane that moments before,
We both had been healthy - had life by the door.

I had been walking just a few feet ahead
Hadn't noticed the mine planted in the field's green bed.
He lunged ahead, tried to push me away
The mine had exploded; our world turned to gray.

His legs were torn off, as though they didn't exist
His lips had been touched by Death's final kiss.
He gave up his life without any regret
To save me, his brother, he had only just met.

We held each other as the choppers grew near.
We held onto life, so precious and dear.
Both of us knew, they'd arrive too late,
Death was waiting, holding open its gate.

The tears ceased flowing from his eyes of brown.
He pulled me closer, lifting his head from the ground.
"I'm dying, my brother," he whispered low,
"Tell them at home, so that they will know

That I died for my country, our freedom to save
For others to live, my life gladly I gave.
Don't let them forget us or the blood that we shed,
For to die without cause, when you die, you're just dead."

"Make them remember what their freedom costs.
Help them to know it can be easily lost.
Don't let them forget me or the other Vets
For we gave our all and paid a large debt."

He let out a sigh, as I gave him my vow,
Then he lowered his head, as though in a bow.

A smile appeared upon his face
And I knew he was now in a better place.

I'll never forget him - what he gave up for me
And for you, my brother because you see,
He died for us all and we cannot forget
He died bravely - a Vietnam Vet.

Karen Offutt served as an Army executive stenographer in Vietnam from 1969/1970. She worked for the generals at MACV in Saigon, after first being stationed in Long Binh. Her story is in dozens of books and two documentaries. Due to her exposure to Agent Orange, her children were all born with cancer, grand mal epilepsy, bone abnormalities, ADHD. Her Grandchildren have Juvenile Diabetes, Hashimoto's, and ADHD. Her medical problems are too many to list. Karen was the 10th woman in history to receive the Soldier's Medal for heroic action. She never considered herself a hero, but this was because of a huge fire in a hamlet in Vietnam where she assisted.

58.

A Vietnamese Refugee's Story
by Brittanie Ngo

Forgive how emotional I will become when I convey these thoughts – as I wish every one of you knew the extent unto which each of you are ingrained in my thoughts and a part of my very being.

I do not know how I became a recipient of the winning lottery ticket to become a citizen of this great nation -- but I can duly say that the veterans and family members each played a part in it.

I am a Vietnamese refugee, having escaped during the fall of Saigon.

Today and always, I do not forget the sacrifices that were made by U.S. and Vietnamese soldiers and the compassion of Americans who enabled the escape and livelihood of so many refugees.

I could tell you the turbulent story of the dangers we faced and the sacrifices that led to our escape here. But here, I will share with you the abridged version of my family's journey:

I came into this world in a hospital -- not surrounded by the comfort of a bassinet, but rather the sound of persistent shelling.

With the help of a CIA agent, my family was given the opportunity to flee the country by plane shortly before the airports were bombed to prevent escape.

As to not alert would-be spies, we were snuck into the airport in clandestine fashion in specially marked vans.

There, we sat in a large hangar awaiting direction, not knowing if at any moment we would be captured and turned over to the North Vietnamese. Assuredly my father would have been killed or placed in a Communist "re-education camp" due to his time fighting alongside the Americans.

Every moment was one of fear and trepidation, surrounded by chaos. Eventually my family boarded the buses, and were immediately instructed that once the doors opened, to run with every ounce of strength towards a C-130 rolling forward on the runway.

Hundreds of refugees sprinted frantically: Men and women shielding babies and children. The wind from the jets was so powerful, pushing back with such force, that many could barely stand. We were flanked by U.S. soldiers who were there to protect us to the best of their ability.

As the cargo doors closed, there stood the last semblance that we would ever see of our once free nation.

There were no seats in this gutted cargo plane with a normal payload of about 100 troops -- now filled triple to capacity. Wall to wall were those seated on the floor, or standing, such as my father who held me on one leg for the duration of the flight.

There was no air conditioning. It was sweltering hot at low altitudes which then plummeted into freezing temperatures at 30,000 feet. As I was only six weeks old, my father was uncertain if I was dead or alive. We were flown to Clark Air Base, then to Wake Island, and eventually to Camp Pendleton, California.

Here, young Marines were tasked with leveling fields of grass to set up refugee camps. Some of us would be housed in tents, others in corrugated steel structures known as Quonset huts. These Marines provided supplies, serving food to thousands of the displaced, doing so with dedication and compassion. This, despite rampant communication and cultural barriers amidst the backdrop of one of the most controversial wars in history.

My mother remembers that many Vietnamese had never seen an apple before, and they could not be more thankful for such exotic and delectable fruit.

It is so important to me that society is reminded to honor our military brothers and sisters, American and ARVN, accounted for and missing, past, and present. As long as I breathe, I never want their sacrifices to be forgotten.

Dearest Veterans, family members, and supporters, because of your sacrifices -- this American dream and many hundreds and thousands of others have been realized. As Ronald Reagan once said, "Freedom is never more than one generation away from extinction... It must be fought for and defended by each generation." I am here today because each of you drives my life's purpose. I will do everything in my power to preserve the freedoms of this great nation -- for you, your children, your grandchildren, and generations to come – and this was made possible by the lives you have led.

I have authored a poem that I hope in some way enables you to grasp the extent of gratitude that should be bestowed upon you today and always:

"How do you pay tribute to the men and women whose impact on our lives has been so very clear?

How does a speech or a poem ever truly honor the legacy of those who chose the military as a career?

Is it altruism? Is it bravery? What drives you to lead such a life of honor?

To face danger and adversity, to have sacrificed yourself for the freedoms of another.

You've seen the unfathomable, you've endured as no one should.

Monuments and regimes have crumbled, but your spirit and loyalty have withstood.

For those who were embraced by a unified country full of ticker tape parades,

To those who suffered at the hands of an ungrateful nation, only to be betrayed.

We can't begin to understand your experiences, we dare not have such hubris.

We are simply grateful to have your presence today and mourn for those who are no longer with us.

As the national anthem begins, it takes all my willpower to remain standing.

And not to collapse -- and kiss the ground of this nation I am so grateful to be in.

We owe you our gratitude and herald the freedoms for which you have arduously fought and won.

And this room gathers, to ensure that never again, will your sacrifices ever be forgotten."

It is my desire to spend the rest of my days thanking and appreciating our military and veterans, and to my beloved Vietnam Veterans, to have you hear the stories of American successes that have resulted from your sacrifices that should have been told repeatedly for the past 5 decades. I stand here quite certain that mine is just simply one of thousands that need to be told. Whether one is a NATURAL BORN CITIZEN or a refugee – we MUST honor and remember your sacrifices.

There is not a day that goes by that you are not in my thoughts. I agonize over the youth that you will never recapture, the comrades you have lost, and the things that you cannot unsee. When the memories rear their heads, when the sleepless nights haunt you, when you question the meaning of it all, know I am with you always:

- I remembered you in elementary school when I belted out "America the Beautiful" with all the love and pride I could muster despite my slight accent.
- I remembered you when I was blessed enough to attend one of the top universities in the nation, UC Irvine, determined thereafter to open my own non-profit to pay it forward in honor of all those that gave in my time of need.
- I remembered you when I worked at the nation's top Fortune companies, Ingram Micro, Microsoft, and the Walt Disney Company - all of which enabled me to use their community outreach programs to honor our veterans.
- I remember the family members of our veterans – who struggled and sacrificed in your absence, OR whose pain and loss are etched in memorials throughout this country.
- And TODAY I live my truth in the culmination of this American life – serving as a Specialist in the California State Guard Army Component Command as well as a civilian in the United States Air Force 412th Communications Squadron at Edwards Air Force Base.

I know my life's purpose is fulfilled if even one individual in this room understands that **your life and your sacrifices were NEVER in vain.**

As seen on the Honor Flight Southland shirts, Will Rogers once said, "We can't all be heroes because somebody has to sit on the curb and clap as they go by."

Brittanie Ngo.

Thus, as long as I live -- I will do so. I will clap. I will herald your sacrifices. I will espouse my gratitude to anyone that will listen. I will continue to voice my undying love of this nation and ceaselessly pay it forward because you have enabled this life of freedom. Due to your compassion and bravery, myself and so many others whose stories you've heard today continue to live and pursue the American dream. I can't express enough how much it means to me to be here with you and the memories these selfless volunteers at Honor Flight Southland have enabled for all. I love you Luci Miller, Sandi and Craig Van Doren and I am grateful to you for allowing me to share my gratitude – marking yet another milestone in this American life.

This vignette is taken from a Vietnam Veteran's Honor Flight Speech given by Brittanie Ngo. Brittanie is a Vietnamese refugee who, along with her family escaped during the fall of Saigon.

59.

POW/MIA/KIA

The Longest Enlisted POW

by Captain Bill Robinson, United States Air Force (Ret)

While serving as a crew chief aboard a U.S. Air Force rescue helicopter, Airman First Class William A. "Bill" Robinson was shot down and captured in Ha Tinh province, North Vietnam. Robinson endured 2,703 days in multiple North Vietnamese prison camps, including the Hanoi Hilton, the Briarpatch and various compounds a Cu Loc known by inmates as the Zoo. Robinson was the longest serving enlisted POW during the Vietnam War.

The small cotton-mill town of Roanoke Rapids, North Carolina has been our family home since 1920. After high school, I applied for the apprentice program as a welder at Newport News Shipyard and Dry Dock company. If accepted, it offered me an alternative, a type of deferment to military service. While in limbo, I decided to talk to family, friends, and recruiters about joining the service. I examined the Marine Corps and Navy before deciding on the Air Force. Upon turning 18 years of age, I joined the Air Force with the intention of making it a career.

We sometimes fondly say that we classify ourselves as one of the longest rescues in military history. On 20 September 1965, I, and my fellow crewmen of the Air Force Search & Rescue team, call sign Dutchy 41, left Nakhon Phanom Royal Thai Air Force Base, Thailand, on a rescue mission to recover Air Force pilot Captain Willis E. Forby, whose F-105D Thunderchief had been shot down in Ha Tinh Province in North Vietnam, near the Laotian border.

F-105 Thunderchief.

I was among the first three dozen captives in North Vietnam and saw the development of the North Vietnamese prison network. I spent time at the Hanoi Hilton, but as the number of prisoners increased and the prison system expanded, I was moved to Briarpatch, described by some as the most primitive of the camps because of lack of electricity and running water as well as the prevalence of malnutrition among the prisoners. Later I was held at a prison camp called the Zoo, where I spent most of my seven and a half years of captivity and endured the full range of North Vietnam's torture program. I survived without benefit of anesthesia, an emergency appendectomy at the four-year mark of my captivity. The officers held in other cells and camps with me recognized what they said to be my exemplary conduct and took the unusual step of awarding me and two other enlisted prisoners battlefield promotions to second lieutenant. While there, the three of us completed an officer training program, taught by our fellow POWs.

Throughout my captivity, my family lived through their own nightmare. They received my letters on an intermittent basis, which offered very little information about my treatment or the conditions of our cells or the camps. Several photos of me appeared during my imprisonment in major media outlets, at sporadic intervals, beginning with a dramatic depiction of my capture and a disturbing snapshot published in *Life* magazine. These provided some assurance that I was still alive.

After my release from North Vietnam in 1973, my fellow crewmember Arthur Neil Black and I became the first two enlisted men to receive the Air Force Cross, a combat award that ranks only second to the Medal of Honor. I was also awarded the Silver Star, Legion of Merit, Bronze Star, the POW Medal, and Two Purple Hearts. In 1986, the Air Force inducted me into the Enlisted Heritage Hall.

My homecoming was not idyllic. I had disappointments in my military life and my personal life. Tension, old wounds, and new injuries led to a twenty-year estrangement between me and my nuclear family. I remarried in 1994, after my first wife died, which marked a new beginning personally and with respect to my time as a POW. I repaired the rift with my family with the help of my new wife Ora Mae and I became more involved with POW organizations.

In May 1995, Ora Mae and I traveled to Vietnam and met with some of my former captors. This trip formed the basis for a Japan Broadcasting Corporation documentary. Since the mid-1990s I have been in demand as a speaker. I refuse to charge speaking fees but tend to speak to school groups and enlisted personnel and at informal Veterans' reunions.

My story offers an opportunity to examine the POW experience in North Vietnam from the perspective of an enlisted man. I have distinction to say that I was the longest held enlisted Prisoner of War in American History.

By permission of Bill Robinson, Captain, USAF(Ret) taken from discussions with Bill Robinson and from his biography "The Longest Rescue" *by Glenn Robins.*

60.

Triumph over Captors

by Capt. Bill Robinson, United States Air Force (Ret)

On Sept. 20, 1965, I was an Airman 1st Class and part of a helicopter team trying to rescue a downed pilot in North Vietnam. Enemy ground fire nailed our helicopter. After crash landing, our four-man crew and pilot were captured. The Vietnamese would not release me for 7-1/2 years, making me the longest-held enlisted man in U.S. military history.

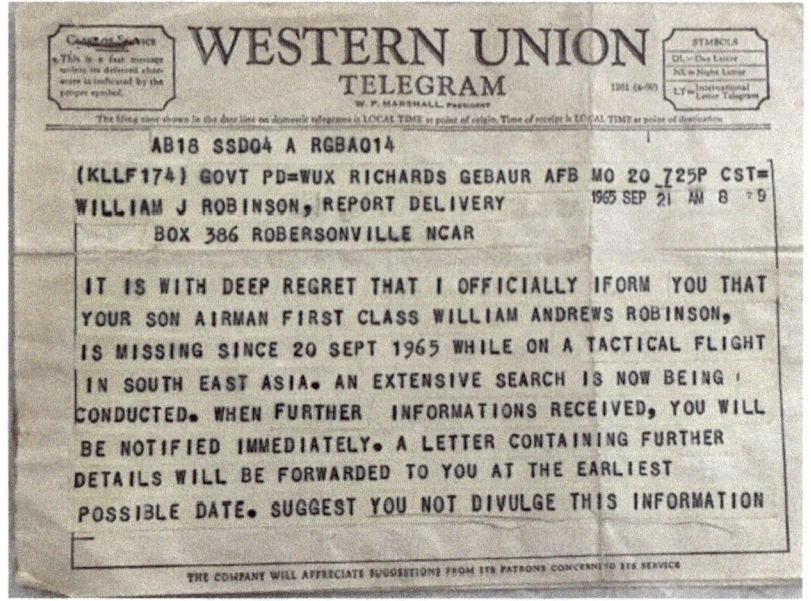

Telegram to Capt Robinson's parents.

When you are being tortured, you concentrate on the moment and getting through that, and not worrying about what happens next. The key to my survival mentally and physically for me was being brought up by my mom in a Christian home. I always remembered that she told me I would never be given a burden greater than I could bear. But I had to do a lot of tall praying for 2,703 days.

My mother, Lillian, had trouble making ends meet because my father, William, was with the Army overseas, on the road selling something, or with a girlfriend, and rarely sent money home. Lillian died when I was fifteen, and I moved in with my grandparents. Three years later, I joined the Air Force and did basic training in San Antonio, Texas, then stayed on to learn how to repair helicopters.

Off To Asia

Assigned to a B-52 bomber wing in Altus, Okla., I was with a group that flew parts and personnel to 12 Atlas nuclear missile sites. In 1963, my unit ferried negotiators between North and South Korea. In April 1965, I went to Bangkok, Thailand, to provide support for a helicopter rescue group. President Lyndon Johnson had ordered Operation Rolling Thunder over North Vietnam that February, and it would continue for four years, the longest bombing campaign in U.S. history. Crews of planes shot down were being captured by North Vietnamese.

Trying to prevent that from happening were rescue teams in the modified Kaman HH-43B Huskie, a chopper with heavy armor and firepower that could travel 110 miles on one trip. I flew on two rescue missions as the crew chief or flight engineer. For this May mission, eight years later, I would receive the Silver Star Medal.

HH-43B Huskie.

In Sept. 20, our crew consisted of Capt. Thomas Curtis, the pilot; 1st Lt. Duane Martin, the co-pilot; and Airman 3rd Class Arthur Black, the pararescue medic. We flew as the low bird assigned to pick up Capt. Willis Forby; the high bird hovered to scout and provide covering fire. Escorting all of us were A1-E Skyraider fighters. Arriving at the site at 3,700 feet, our chopper fell into communist cross hairs, with harrowing results after our crash landing. The local militia took all five men prisoner.

A-1E Skyraider.

I was just 22 years old. I arrived Oct. 1 in Hanoi. During the war, fifteen prison camps operated in the region, most of them filthy, with rats, mosquitoes, cockroaches, and ants crawling over the prisoner's plates of rice. Soup was often boiled grass. Occasionally came a hairy piece of pork fat or a vegetable that had been fertilized with human feces. Sometimes the Americans went weeks without being allowed to bathe. Temperatures were often blistering or freezing, as we had inadequate clothing and blankets. Disease was rampant.

At first, the enemy used torture to try to extract confessions of war crimes. Pointing to the trials of Nazi and Japanese leaders after World War II, North Vietnam wanted to justify executions. After an international backlash, the torture backed down but the North Vietnamese tried to use confessions for propaganda purposes and to gain information about our military operations.

The code of conduct for the U.S. military urged noncompliance, which POW leaders saw was not realistic. Our officers told us to resist until we were going to suffer permanent bodily harm and then to try our best to avoid divulging anything that was of importance. We would joke about it, like when I came back after a beating and told my cell mate, "You should have seen what they did to him."

A sense of humor helped us survive. I developed my three-day motto: Yesterday was the day that I was captured, today is today, and tomorrow is the day that I go home.

The communists used a variety of techniques to force the POWs to talk, making the Americans:

• Sit bent over for days in caves that were only four feet high and half-filled with cold water.

• Run through trenches blindfolded and with hands tied behind their backs, which resulted in hitting their heads against obstacles.

• Kneel for extended periods of time with an iron bar between their kneecaps and on the concrete floor; it made their knees bleed and swell up.

• Sit — in a darkened room, a single beam of light shining in their faces — on a cinder block that rose eight inches high, with their hands behind their backs, putting all the weight on their tailbones.

Surviving

Every early captive in the North has said that the two keys to survival and resistance were the chain of command and the development of ways to communicate with other prisoners. Early on, we were often in separate cells and developed a code to tap messages. We found that we could talk through brick-and-mortar walls by pressing a tin cup against the wall, we used sign language and scratched messages on the bottoms of plates and cups.

Occasionally, we were allowed to write to our families and receive replies, in compliance with international rules of war. I found that helping others gave me a sense of purpose. I repaired leaky faucets, rolled cigarettes, or built mousetraps. In 1969, officers decided that I should be one of three to receive a battlefield commission, raising me to second lieutenant on completion of a six-month oral course when guards were not around.

With the Paris Peace Accords in January 1973, the North Vietnamese released the names of 577 prisoners of war. I was in the first group to be freed on Feb. 12, arriving at Clark Air Base in the Philippines for good meals, medical checkups, debriefings, updates on world events since captivity and phone calls to families.

(Left) Captain Bill Robinson – coming home.

Proud Comeback: Although our Vietnamese captors had tried to strip American prisoners of our dignity and self-worth, most of us had remained faithful to our oaths of enlistment and the values expressed in the Code of Conduct. By donning our military uniforms, medals, and ribbons (after being freed), we reclaimed one personal signifier of our loyal service to the U.S. military and to our nation.

After I arrived for the emotional homecoming in Roanoke Rapids, NC. I could barely sleep for several days. My sister, Jackie, was astounded that I was not bitter about my experience. I kept a positive attitude and optimistic outlook.

The next two decades were full of troubles. I abandoned my dream of becoming a pilot and settled for supervising aircraft maintenance.

My 1975 marriage to Sue Gill was miserable. She forced me to retire in 1984 after 23 years of service with the rank of captain. After her death in 1993, I married Ora Mae Creel and adopted her daughter as well as Sue's. Ora Mae went with me to Vietnam for a documentary about my experiences, in 1995, and we plan to visit what was South Vietnam for the first time in December. We became active in setting up the National Prisoner of War Museum at the former Confederate prison in Andersonville, Ga. I have a plaque on the wall in my study which says that there are two people who died for you; One was Jesus Christ for your sins, the other was the American soldier for your freedom.

In World War II, there was 100% mobilization, where everyone on the home front was involved. During the Korean War, it was 50%. By Vietnam, it was 10%. Now 1% are still willing to give their all. For me, every day is a good day when I am not in handcuffs and leg irons.

61.

Colonel Donald Cook, USMC, Medal of Honor
by J. Christopher Cook

My name is Chris Cook, I along with my sisters Karen and Victoria and brother Tom are the children of the late Colonel Donald G. and Laurette Giroux Cook. My father was posthumously awarded the Medal of Honor for heroism in Vietnam while held prisoner from December 1964 to December 1967.

Shortly after my father and mother married in 1956 in Burlington, Vermont, my dad left for Officer's Candidate School at Quantico, Virginia and was commissioned a Second Lieutenant on April 1, 1957. He received his promotion to First Lieutenant on October 1, 1958, while stationed at Camp Pendleton, California. In 1960, he attended Army Language School in Monterey, California, studying Chinese. Dad was then assigned to Camp H.M. Smith, Hawaii in 1961 and promoted to Captain on March 1st, 1962.

In 1964 the family returned to Vermont when dad was transferred to Okinawa. In December 1964 he was reassigned to the Communications Company, Headquarters Battalion, 3rd Marine Division. That same day, he and eight other Marines were issued orders to continue to Saigon Republic of Vietnam, and report to the Senior Marine Advisor.

On December 31st, Dad volunteered to conduct a search and recovery mission for a downed American helicopter and set off with the 4th Vietnamese Marines. Ambushed on their arrival at the crash site, dad rallied the Vietnamese Marines who went with him, tended to the wounded and was trying to drag others to safety when he was wounded in the leg and captured. He was taken to a POW camp in the jungles of South Vietnam near the Cambodian border, where he quickly established himself as the senior American (even though he was not) and provided guidance and strength to his fellow prisoners.

Dad's actions were in direct defiance of his captors who attempted to remove all semblance of military rank and structure among POWs. He expressed to the Viet Cong that he was senior and therefore spokesman for the POWs, fully aware his actions would lead to harsh treatment. He was subjected to physical abuse and isolation, but he resisted all efforts to break his will and was used as a "Bad Example" by his guards. Surviving on limited rations, he tried to maintain his health in his 10-foot square cage. He could be seen exercising and running in place for hours. Once, while assigned to a work detail with a Viet Cong guard, he stepped up the pace to embarrass his captors. Eventually, the jungle prison took its toll on dad's health and he and others found themselves in a weakened state.

It was this weakened state that caused him to contract malaria shortly before moving to a new camp. He was so weak that he staggered when he walked, could not traverse log bridges, and lost his night vision due to vitamin deficiency. Still, he refused to allow anyone else to carry his pack or otherwise put a strain on themselves to help him. By the time they reached the new camp, even the camp commander complimented dad on his courage. He regained some of his strength, he took on the bulk of the other's workloads so they may have time to recover. His knowledge of first aid prompted him to nurse the severely sick and was instrumental in saving the lives of several POWs who were convulsing with severe malaria attacks. Even though he was on half-rations, Dad shared his food with the weaker POWs, even giving up his allowance of penicillin.

Because he was isolated, he devised a drop-off point for communications, instructing his fellow prisoners to continue resistance and offering the means to do so. Repeatedly, he refused to negotiate for his own release, knowing full well it would mean imprisonment for the rest of the war. After a failed escape attempt, a gun was held to his head and Dad calmly recited the gun's nomenclature, showing no fear. Knowing that in his deteriorated condition he would not survive a long imprisonment, he continued to offer food and medication to his fellow POWs.

Dad was last seen on a jungle trail by another prisoner, Douglas Ramsey, in November 1967. When Ramsey was released in 1973, he was told Dad had died from malaria on December 8th, 1967, while still in captivity, and was buried in the jungle by his fellow POWs.

No remains were ever returned to us by the Vietnamese government. On February 26, 1980, our father, Colonel Donald G. Cook was declared dead under the Missing Persons Act of 1942. On May 15, 1980, a memorial stone was placed in Arlington National Cemetery, and the flag from the empty grave was presented to our mother, Laurette. The following day our father was posthumously awarded the Medal of Honor. December 4, 1998, *USS Donald Cook* (DDG 75) was commissioned, with the ship's motto, "Faith Without Fear," epitomizing our father's courage and faith in God and country.

Joseph Christopher Cook is the oldest of four children of Medal of Honor recipient Colonel Donald G. Cook. Chris agreed to share his family's story of their father when asked by playwright, Harry Kantrovich, who was the commissioning Command Master Chief of USS Donald Cook (DDG-75).

62.

The First
A-7 Pilot Prisoner of War

by Captain James Hickerson, United States Navy (Ret)

As a Lieutenant, I attended Naval Test Pilot School at Naval Air Station Patuxent River, Maryland. During this time, I became the 5th Naval Aviator to fly the A-7 Corsair II and took part in the early testing of the aircraft. I joined VA-147, the first A-7 squadron, at Naval Air Station Lemoore, California, in June 1967, and deployed aboard the aircraft carrier *USS Ranger* (CVA-61) in October 1967 as a Lieutenant Commander and part of Carrier Air Wing 2. In early December 1967, the *USS Ranger* arrived in the Gulf of Tonkin bringing the all-new A7A Corsair to combat.

I was a section leader in a flight of several aircraft from VA-147 on December 22, 1967. We were about 10 miles south of Haiphong when my aircraft was hit by surface-to-air missile (SAM) and I was forced to eject over North Vietnam. I was taken as a Prisoner of War, becoming the first A-7 pilot to be captured.

Approximately one out of six Americans shot down in the Iron Triangle (Haiphong, Hanoi, Thanh Hoa) region of North Vietnam who were known to be alive on the ground were recovered by search and rescue units. At best, a pilot could expect an extended stay in the Hanoi prison system. On the other end of the spectrum, stories circulated about pilots who were literally clubbed and beaten to death in villages.

(Left) A-7 Corsair II.

After my release, I was briefly hospitalized to recover from my injuries at the Naval Hospital in Oakland, California and then regained flying status serving as Commander VA-12 at Naval Air Station Cecil Field, Florida aboard *USS Independence* (CV-62) from February 1975 to February 1976 and other follow-on tours before retiring from the Navy November 1, 1986.

I might be considered one of the luckier ones. Although my next five years (1,909 days) were spent in the torture and deprivation of the North Vietnamese prisoner of war facilities, I survived to come home in Operation Homecoming in 1973.

(Left) James Hickerson – 2023.

Captain James Hickerson, USN(Ret) was born in Lenoir, North Carolina on 14 February 1934. He attended high school and college in Atlanta, Georgia, graduating from Georgia Tech in 1956 with a Bachelor of Civil Engineering Degree and his commission as an Ensign in the United States Navy.

63.

Missing in Action

An MIA Daughter's Story
by Pam Cain

I am not the only person who remembers a date like it was yesterday. Many of us recall where we were or what we were doing when shocking news events break: JFK being shot, September 11th, 2001, and the Challenger explosion are some that are vivid in our hearts and memories. For my family and me, another date is etched in our lives forever: February 15, 1966, the day my dad, Col Oscar Mauterer, USAF, was shot down over Laos during the Vietnam War and listed as Missing In Action (MIA). It was a time of political and social unrest in our country and little did we know it would be the beginning of a 57+ year journey of growth and maturity, anger and frustration, sadness, and longing. The journey continues.

This is a story of dedication to bringing Dad home and fighting for the fullest possible accounting of all our unreturned Vietnam veterans. It is a story of finding hope and being surrounded by many: motorcyclists (ok, bikers!), veterans, men, and women of all ages, who care, inspire and are pushing for the same answers we family members are. For along the way, I, the older of two children, became involved with the National League of POW/MIA Families, The Ride Home, Run for the Wall (RFTW) and Rolling Thunder. My life has been blessed by those who never knew Dad but who have taken on the POW/MIA issue and have enveloped me in their passion to bring him and others home. Though this story is about Dad and how our lives changed, it is a story that includes the organizations above, veterans' organizations and numerous individuals whose support and efforts are simply extraordinary! Many never received their own "Welcome Home"! I salute them as I share my story.

Much has been said about those who face holidays and other special times with an empty chair at the table. If you have experienced the loss of a child, someone abducted, those killed in battle or in accidents or from disease, you know about that empty chair. I must admit that for me, at least, it does not get any easier as the years pass. For years we bought greeting cards for Dad, celebrated his birthday with his favorite lemon meringue pie and candles, commemorated his shoot-down date, even had a memorial service for him when MIAs were reclassified as "KIA-body not recovered" or "KIA-presumptive finding of death" by the Carter administration. He has a marker in Arlington National Cemetery. His name is on the Vietnam Memorial. The sense of loss and not knowing is pervasive. And it does not end.

I was fortunate to know Dad, experience childhood outings with him, learn from him and try to live up to his expectations. Even when away from home, he was a parent who held us accountable, who wanted us to accept responsibility and take leadership roles. He was a cigar-smoking, rangy golfer whose passion for flying and his country led him to a career in the Air Force. He volunteered to go to Vietnam because, as he said, he was trained to serve and had taken an oath to protect the U.S. – and our freedom. His sense of humor, determination, intellect, and integrity were always noted by those he met and knew. He made friends easily, was a

63. Missing in Action
An MIA Daughter's Story

great teacher (including to South Vietnamese student pilots), had a soft heart for animals, and had a zest for life and living that was reflected in everything he did. Born and raised in NJ, Dad loved watching and playing sports, from football to swimming to bowling. He and Mom enjoyed entertaining, playing bridge, hunting (or at least shooting!) and they prioritized time with their children.

When he was shot down, at the end of a mission from Thailand into Laos, his A-1E Skyraider was on fire. He radioed that he was bailing out and his flight lead watched his parachute deploy and then descend to the ground. After three days, search and rescue efforts were stopped due to heavy ground fire and there was no sign of Dad. He never entered the prison system. He remained missing. At home just outside Washington, DC, my mother, brother, and I suddenly found ourselves isolated and "different" from others. We waited. We cried.

We were told not to discuss what happened or where it happened. We received reports that correlated to his case but could never be verified. We received hostile phone calls – some from callers who condemned Dad for being a killer and getting what he deserved. It was a tough time to be a teen and realize how many hated not only the war but those who fought in it. My mother was nothing short of a heroine! She was a rock, while enduring the heartbreak of losing a husband and not knowing what happened to him. Mom hunkered down and raised her children, sheltering us from the destructive and hateful situation around us. She also followed what Dad had told her to do should something happen to him: listen to what the government told her and have faith.

Years later, when her confidence in our government's efforts to find Dad dissolved, Mom joined me at National League of POW/MIA Families annual meetings. There, our sense of isolation was replaced with support from other family members who understood. We compared data and networked. We learned to be active in our case, to demand the fullest possible accounting, to push for answers and to plead for our nation to honor its commitment to bring home those who fought for their country. The years of complacency were over! It was time to demand results. It was also a time to anguish again, because so much time had passed and along with it, lost opportunities to find our missing, Dad included.

For years, Dad was considered a "last known alive" case since he was known to have made it to the ground. He has been investigated by Joint POW/MIA Accounting Command (JPAC), and first-hand witnesses produced a photo of him in 2010. These same witnesses led a team to an alleged burial site and that site was excavated in 2014. While results were not positive, the U.S. government assures me that they will not stop trying to resolve his case. They will return. They will continue the search. And I will continue pressing them to do so! I will also urge our government to fund Defense POW/MIA Accounting Agency (DPAA), the new agency charged with accounting for our POWs and MIAs, work closely with family organizations and go wherever I can make a difference.

For the past several years, I have spoken on the issue, traveled domestically and to S.E. Asia and met some incredible people. I also found I enjoyed riding on the back of a Harley! Traveling to Americus, GA, years ago, I was shocked to learn that one of the events during The Ride Home was a service to honor MIAs. A large poster of Dad's photo was hanging in front, along with others, whose families I knew. People cared! We weren't alone! As family members, our numbers are small. But a growing number of organizations who focus on our nation's obligation to bring our men and women home would have an impact. We could be heard. The POW/MIA issue could reach a level of prominence again. With the public and families demanding funding, accountability, and answers, we could bring more home, resolve more cases.

Since then, The Ride Home has given even more attention to MIAs in its programs. As an MIA daughter, my life has been enriched by relationships made in GA and during Run for the Wall in May of each year. Riding across the country from Texas to Washington DC. (RFTW travels from CA to DC and I have been able to go "all the way" a couple of times and join the pack enroute for several other years). It gives me the privilege of joining other patriots and concerned citizens, to say thank you to veterans and to share events that I treasure with people whom I consider family. All sustain me as does the attention focused on POWs and MIAs during Rolling Thunder's Freedom Ride in DC, now hosted by each state. I was fortunate to ride during many annual Rides.

63. Missing in Action
An MIA Daughter's Story

My life was forever changed on February 15, 1966. Though I have had a wonderful career, became a wife, mother and grandmother of a family that has grown, seen other losses and had much happiness and prosperity along the way, Dad is always at the forefront. My promise is to do all I can to bring him home. I can't do it alone and hope you may find something in this story that causes you to react – and take positive steps: write Congress, fly the POW/MIA flag, tell others that we still have unreturned veterans waiting to come home, support organizations like Mission: POW-MIA so we can continue the work needed. And finally, remember and honor those who are still missing. Each has a story. Each has a family. Each should be returned to his home.

Dedicated with love to my mother, Evie, who passed away in March 4, 2015.

Pam Cain.

Pam Cain became active in the POW/MIA issue in the early 1980s, when she finally realized that her Dad, Air Force Colonel Oscar Mauterer, MIA LAOS, 2/15/1966 was not coming home until and unless she became vocal, knowledgeable about the issue and did everything she could to get answers. Pam, the wife of a retired Navy aviator, served on the Board of Directors of the National League of POW/MIA families, traveled to Southeast Asia as a member of a family delegation, is a member of the U.S. Air Force Survivor Advocacy Council, Navy League of Jacksonville, FL Board of Directors, Rolling Thunder FL Chapter 4, and is the current Vice President of Mission: POW-MIA. Pam also rides Run For the Wall every May in honor of her father and all those still unaccounted for. In Pam's words: "This is not a journey I would seek out for myself, but my Dad and every other MIA is worth it."

64.

My Journey Home
by Cindy Stonebraker Reed

On October 28th, 1968, my father left Udorn Airfield in Thailand, flying the RF-4C, on a solo night recon mission over North Vietnam, and he never returned. This year will mark 55 years that my father has been Missing -in- Action.

Growing up, his "Missing-in-Action" designation was something we didn't talk about. We didn't talk about it at home, and we certainly didn't talk about it in Public. After my father went missing, my mom moved us from Shaw Airforce Base in South Carolina to a small little hippie town in Northern California. I grew up in a town with NO military connection. None of the kids I went to school with had dads away at war. Half our town didn't even know we were at war, and the other half was totally against it. I grew up feeling abandoned, like nobody cared and that my father had been forgotten.

During the next 40 years, I had several things happen that I can only describe as a God thing. When I was young, I met a man at a monument dedication in Indiana that I had attended with my grandmother. (I spent several weeks every year on the farm with my Grandparents) After the ceremony, I was walking, and had stopped at a display table. The man sitting at the table asked me who I was representing. I told him I was there for my father. He asked his name. I said "Kenneth Stonebraker" When I said that, he held his arm out, and on his arm was a POW/MIA bracelet that had my dad's name on it. At that point, neither one of us could speak. His wife reached into her purse and pulled out a photo of their wedding. She said it was on her wedding day that she realized that the bracelet was non-negotiable. She had asked him not to wear it, begged him not to wear it, and threatened him not to wear it. But you could clearly see it on his arm in his wedding picture. I asked how it was that he ended up wearing my dad's name. He said 20 years before, he had been at a rally, and they had thousands of these bracelets laying on tables. He picked this one up and thought what an unusual name. He put it back down and kept looking but he kept going back to that one. Then 20 years later, he got to meet the daughter.

A few years after that, I flew to South Carolina to visit with a friend from school.

RF-4C.

64. My Journey Home

My plane had issues and we were diverted to Georgia. While we were waiting in the airport, I noticed a tall man in an Air Force uniform standing against the wall across the walkway from me. After about an hour, I walked up and asked him if he was from Shaw Air Force Base. He crossed his arms, looked down at me and said yes, then asked why I would ask him that. I was very quiet and shy at that point and got flustered. I told him my dad had been stationed there. We ended up talking and sat next to each other on the plane. As we were getting ready to take off, he asked what my dad's name was. I told him "Stonebraker" He turned white, and said "Kenneth Stonebraker?" Then I turned white. He was the air traffic controller that had given my father permission to take off… on the mission he didn't return from. It was his first day on the job there, and this was the first plane he released. He said he has been haunted by that his whole life. He almost quit that day. He asked if I would visit him on base while I was in town. As it turned out, he was the base commander. He sent a car for me and spent the day giving me a tour of Shaw Air Force base. He took me into a classroom where there were framed aerial photos all around the room. He said my dad had taken those, and they were still using them to teach from. He said my dad had a reputation of doing great work.

As I had mentioned, my mom did a great job at keeping my brother and me in touch with my dad's family. Every summer, mom would put us on a plane, and we would spend several weeks with my grandparents on the farm in Indiana. When we would get there, grandma always had a blue suitcase sitting at the end of the couch. That was the first place I would go every year. In that suitcase were the things that came back from Thailand after dad went missing. We had nothing at our house that belonged to my dad, so this was the only time I had the opportunity to talk or be around anything that was my dad's. In it was his name plate for his desk, some papers, and his bible. I would sit for hours with that bible. It was in a black zipper leather case. I would open it to the first page, where his name was written in blue. I would run my fingers across that name, knowing that he had written it. It was the closest I could get to him. In his bible were little pieces of envelope, which he used as bookmarks. I would sit and turn to each page he had marked and read the passages he had underlined. It was like he was talking to me. My grandmother passed away 12 years ago.

When I went to the funeral, I asked my aunt what had happened to dad's bible. She said she didn't know anything about it. I told her it was in the blue suitcase that she kept in the attic. The next morning, she showed up with it in her hand. It was in the suitcase, which was in the corner of the garage in the pile of stuff goodwill was picking up that afternoon. If I had not asked about it, it would have been gone. I don't have much that belonged to my dad, but I know I have the thing that was the most important to him. He was teaching bible studies in Thailand. He said it wasn't just the soldiers that were being saved, it was the villagers. His plan was to get out of the Air Force in December and go to seminary. He wanted to go back in as a Chaplain, because he saw a mission field, he would not otherwise have access to.

Since this was an issue we never spoke of, I never shared those stories with anyone. Let's fast forward to just 9 years ago. I was driving from Kentucky to Tennessee. I stopped at the Rest Stop to pick up a map.... all I wanted was a map. When I pulled off, there were seven Rolling Thunder Members hoisting the POW/MIA flag. There wasn't anyone else there, just seven men reverently hoisting the flag. I sat and watched. When they were done, for the very first time, I walked up to them and told them that my dad was still missing in Vietnam. They embraced me, which was scary at a rest stop with a bunch of bikers. They told me that I was the reason they did what they did. It was me and families like me, that they kept this mission going, and that my Dad had not been forgotten. I can honestly say that stopping at the Rest Stop forever changed my life.

A few months after my meeting with Rolling Thunder at the rest stop, I received a call from them. I was sitting in the parking lot of my son's school waiting for him to get dismissed. I was invites to attend an event called The Ride Home, in Americas Georgia. This was an event where they invited former POW's and families of those Missing-in-Action for a weekend where they do nothing but honor you. I remember saying "So let me get this right…you want me to take off with a bunch of bikers and go to Georgia?" That made no sense to me. But I had a "gut" feeling that I needed to go. I talked with friends and family and could not get one person to tell me that this was a good idea. Not being able to find anyone to go with me, I got in the car by myself and headed to Georgia. Three times I turned around, as nothing about this trip made any sense to me. It was completely outside my box to do anything like this.

Once I arrived in Georgia, I met seven other MIA children. I met seven other people just like me. For the very first time in my life, I felt like I belonged someplace. For four days we shared stories of our dads and what it was like growing up with the unknown of what happened to them. I didn't have much to share about my dad, as I knew very little, but the connection with the other "Sons and Daughters" changed my life.

Because of my trip to Georgia, I attended my first National League of POW/MIA Families Annual Meeting in DC. This allowed me to meet even more MIA Families. It also gave me the opportunity to sit across the table with the Department of Defense POW/MIA Accounting Agency (DPAA) who were actively working on my case. For 45 years, I didn't know anyone was still working on this. I also found out that I could get all my dad's military records and that he was eligible to have a Memorial Marker at Arlington National Cemetery. On the way home from that trip, I filled out the paperwork, and three months later, a marker was installed at Arlington, in Memorial Section K. This marker was placed just days before my dad's birthday on December 25th, Christmas.

After returning from my first trip to DC, I was helping my mother in her attic. I found the reel-to-reel tapes my mom and dad sent back and forth. Of course, I had nothing to play them on. I found a man in Nashville, TN who could put them on CD for me. Once I received them, I was able to hear my father's voice for the first time in 45 years. Out of the five tapes I found, only 1 had my dad's voice on it. Mom would get the tapes, listen to them, turn them over and record over them. The tape with my dad's voice was mailed on the way to the mission he didn't come home from. These tapes had been in my mom's attic for 45 years, and they were so brittle that they were disintegrating as they were going through the machine. The man went inch by inch to get the voices off. On this one tape, there is six minutes of my dad just talking to me. When I hear his voice, he doesn't sound like an officer in the Air Force who had been shot the night before and spent all day redoing his flight plan to go on the same mission that night. You hear a daddy talking to his little girl.

Cindy Reed and her Father.

I had the opportunity to meet three men that served with my dad. That was an incredible day. After driving all night to get to Ft. Walton Beach, we sat around the table for close to six hours. We laughed and cried, and they were so generous with sharing stories. I had a thousand questions. I didn't want to just know about the plane, the food, and the missions. I wanted to know the stupid things. I wanted to know all the things I never got to know. What was my dad's favorite color, what was his first car, did he like math, what kind of music did he listen to? They couldn't answer all the questions, but they were able to answer some.

After several hours of talking with them, I started to wonder if they really knew him. Was I just wanting this connection so bad that I was falling for everything they were telling me? As we were walking into a banquet, one of the men leaned over and asked, "How did you like your Dollhouse?" I stopped. My birthday was ten days before my dad went missing, and that year my dad sent me a Dollhouse from Thailand. I asked him how he knew about my Dollhouse, and he told me he was with my dad when he got it, and that my dad was extremely meticulous about which one I got. He said shopping for my Dollhouse was the one moment of normalcy in a world of chaos. All my life, I felt like this issue had only affected me. It hadn't, it had affected all those who ever served with him.

Cindy Reed with a photograph of her Dad.

Nine years ago, I was a chicken farmer in Kentucky, and I knew nothing about my father. My entire life changed by stopping at a rest stop to get a map. I've had the blessing of being able to take the loss of my father and to help assist connecting families across the country, to make sure no one ever feels all alone, that nobody cares, and that their Loved Ones will never be forgotten. Being able to relate to others like you can change your life.

Cindy Stonebraker Reed is the daughter of Missing in Action Lt. Col Kenneth Stonebraker. Cindy currently serves on the Board of Directors of Mission: POW-MIA. She also been on the Board of Directors for the National League of POW/MIA Families; participated in the 2019 Delegation trip to Vietnam, Cambodia, Laos, and Thailand; served as the Assistant Director of Programs for the Woody Williams Foundation, overseeing the building of Gold Star Families Memorial Monuments in all 50 states, and is a founding member of a Gold Star Families Services Coalition. She has worked with the Army's Survivor Outreach Services and the Air Force Families Forever Advisory Council to support Gold Star

Families; a member of Sons and Daughters in Touch, an organization to connect children who lost loved ones during the Vietnam War; a Gary Sinise Foundation Snowball Express volunteer and has participated in several Tragedy Assistance Program for Survivors (TAPS) events across the country. Cindy initiated Kentucky Senate Bill #122, to allow Children of fallen Service Members, access to the Gold Star License Plate for their vehicle in the State of Kentucky, and in April of 2018, she received the first Gold Star Daughter license plate in the state of Kentucky.

65.

Finding Answers
by Colleen Shine

(Left) LtCol. Anthony Shine, USAF – 1971.

I was eight years old in 1972 when my father, Lt. Colonel Anthony Shine, an Air Force fighter pilot, was listed as Missing in Action during the Vietnam War. For the next 24 years, I waited for answers. Was my father still out there and trying to get home, or had he died when his plane went down? Was he being held as a prisoner of war? After he was listed MIA, my family received 14 different reports about my father: some had pictures of remains reputed to be his, and some were live sightings. These reports continued into the mid-1990s, and the family faced each lead while trying to track down the truth.

Uncertainty is the crux of the POW/MIA issue. When my dad's younger brother, an Army first lieutenant, fresh from West Point, was killed in action in Vietnam in 1970, his wife knew at that point she was a widow. She had a truth to face and move forward from. It was hard for everyone in our family, but it was finality, and something you could face and begin to build your life from ... there's a peace of heart and mind that comes with knowing the fate of a loved one.

I made a trip to Vietnam in 1995 that would answer many of my questions. While traveling with a guide to check out a site, I saw the wreckage of my father's plane, along with a helmet with his name scribed inside. My finds led to the eventual discovery of my father's remains.

I did not have that, so after I had found evidence of my father that investigators missed, I took to Capitol Hill, calling for higher government accountability in finding POW/MIA service members, and to remind officials of the promise to leave no man behind. That promise, made to U.S. military men and women, is one the Defense POW/MIA Accounting Agency (DPAA) holds in high regard. It is an agency created by the Department of Defense in January 2015, which combined the former Defense Prisoner of War Missing Personnel Office, the Joint POW/MIA Accounting Command, and the Life Sciences Equipment Laboratory into one organization to "more effectively increase the number of missing service personnel accounted for from past conflicts and ensure timely and accurate information is communicated to their families."

Many different organizations and personnel within DPAA engage in the effort to bring missing Veterans home to their families. Denise To, a supervisory forensic anthropologist, performs the recovery analysis and identification of human skeletal remains at the Central Identification Laboratory in Hawaii.

The environment in Vietnam is full of variety. It can be cold, but often, it is hot and humid. Also, unlike a common misperception, the country isn't just composed of small villages scattered in the jungle; the economy is quickly expanding into cities with large high-rise hotels and bustling enterprise. However, most of the DPAA's work isn't done near a nice, comfortable air-conditioned hotel.

"The easier sites to process have already been done, so the only ones left now are the ones that are extremely difficult because of logistics and topography," To said, describing digging under a thick triple canopy or on the side of a remote mountain. "It's very physical labor. It's back-breaking, and it's done a lot of times in direct sunlight in austere environments, on a 60-degree side of the slope where you are harnessed in like a Billy Goat wearing repelling equipment, and (you're) trying to do science at the same time."

The sites in Vietnam are excavated in the same way a thousand-year-old royal tomb is excavated. Heavy equipment and shovels may be used because we are expediting the process and are also trying to answer different questions.

Over time, nature tends to reclaim the burial or crash sites, and it's further expedited by Vietnam's highly acidic soil, which can erode remains entirely. By the time the pieces of aircraft, gear, and bone fragments make their way into the labs for analysis, they can be difficult to identify.

At the Central Identification Laboratory, forensic anthropologists do what they can to glean answers from the bones found on site. They primarily use mitochondrial DNA to help identify individual service members. They also use other lines of evidence, such as historical data, clavicular data, dental records, material evidence and archeological data.

"Imagine you are putting a puzzle together," To said. "It's three dimensions, someone has taken half the pieces away, someone's put new pieces that don't even belong in the puzzle, and you don't have the box top to see what the puzzle is going to look like, and you're blindfolded with one hand tied behind your back. That's how the puzzle is for us … When cases get solved, and we're able to identify individuals, it's because we have been able to put enough pieces together to make a positive identification."

The work that goes into bringing a missing service member home and definitively identifying them is tremendous, but it's all worth it.

After the Paris Peace Accords were signed in 1973, 591 POWs who had been captured during the war in Vietnam, Laos, and Cambodia were returned, according to the DPAA; however, the number of veterans who were still unaccounted for quadrupled that count. It wasn't until over a decade had passed that the U.S. was able to successfully perform the first humanitarian mission to bring any of the remaining lost service members home from Vietnam.

In 1985, after many persistent requests, a U.S. team was granted access into Vietnam to recover a B-52 Stratofortress crew. That aircraft had crashed 10 miles outside of Hanoi during the war. Once the team got to the crash site, the recovery team realized that houses had been built over the area. The team purchased the homes so they could be deconstructed, and excavation could begin. The effort kept the crew in Vietnam over the Thanksgiving holiday, but their work paid off sooner than they had expected. After 22 feet of dirt had been removed, they recovered one engine, one landing gear, and also began to find some remains.

The process has come a long way since then – it is now a team effort between the U.S. and Vietnam. Over the past 30 plus years, relations have improved between the two countries, and it all began with the POW/MIA issue.

In search of any information that can drive a recovery effort forward, researchers investigate leads from many sources. In addition to speaking with witnesses, they scan through Vietnamese books, newspapers, documents, and previous interviews. Though the incidents in question happened 40 to 60 years ago, the group continuously searches for any new clue that will provide them with answers.

DPAA's mission is to provide the fullest possible accounting of missing U.S. personnel to their families and the nation. They try to find every single unaccounted service member from previous conflicts, but, unfortunately, they may not always be able to bring them home.

As time passes, the DPAA investigators become increasingly familiar with each unresolved case. They reread all steps taken for recovery and try to plan a way forward. The researchers get to know more about the person they are looking for and often also know the service members' families.

I continue to stay involved in the mission to bring home missing or lost service members. There was no road map or path for my mom and the wives or parents of young men who were missing back in the 1960's and '70s. Now there is.

I am thrilled to see the overhauling of the POW/MIA issue to make it more of an integrated and efficient process for families and our missing. I would hope that anyone in an active-duty uniform knows that should they be left behind or kept behind following a war, there would be a responsible effort to account for them. I feel great passion and gratitude for that."

65. Finding Answers

At Arlington National Cemetery in October 1996, my family presided over a memorial service for my father. I now know that my father, Tony Shine died when his plane went down in December 1972. My father's case is no longer open – he is home.

My hope for the many families that I know who still have loved ones missing in action is that they will know that our government made an honest effort to account for them; that any answers that are available will have been tracked down, found and revealed to them, with a wish that "if the answer is that their loved one was killed in action in Vietnam decades ago, they will be able to bring him home and have an honorable burial on American soil and know that they have kept the fight and the faith for him."

Colleen Shine.

Colleen Shine has served as a member of the Board of Directors of the National League of POW/MIA Families, Sons and Daughters in Touch and Gold Star Children, and closely supports the work of the Vietnam Veterans Memorial Fund and Tragedy Assistance Program for Survivors. In addition, Ms. Shine is the family liaison for the USAF top gun fighter pilot award presented annually in her father's name.

66.

Killed in Action

The Long Goodbye
by Michael Archer

    Michael Archer was born and raised in Oakland, California and served as a U.S. Marine in South Vietnam, which notably included the 77-day siege of Khe Sanh. Mike is an award-winning author of numerous books, including "THE LONG GOODBYE," which this story encompasses

    July 6, 1968, the day the untenable American combat base at Khe Sanh was finally abandoned, twenty-year-old Lance Corporal Thomas P. Mahoney III, the most well-liked, confident, and optimistic member of his company, inexplicably walked away from his unit's defensive position and was shot by North Vietnamese soldiers hiding nearby. His fellow Marines fought tenaciously to recover his body, resisting a direct order from their regimental commander to permanently vacate the position until darkness fell—only then ruefully leaving their friend behind.

(Left) Thomas P. Mahoney III.

    Tom and I had been close high school friends in Berkeley, California amid the growing civil unrest and protests American involvement in Vietnam. Despite this, we joined the Marines in 1967 to evaluate ourselves in what we would quickly learn to be a romanticized notion of combat heroics. I arrived at Khe Sanh first, enduring three months of siege, constant enemy shelling, and regular ground attacks against our positions. When our decimated regiment was ordered out, Tom Mahoney's battalion took our place.

A few weeks before Tom's perplexing walk into oblivion on Hill 881, U.S. political and military leaders realized what a costly mistake they had made in ordering us to defend that remote combat base, where thousands had already suffered and died, for no good purpose, and now began the process of secretly abandoning the place. Tom's bitterness and frustration grew as his unit fought several vicious battles, all the while knowing they were merely stalling for this calculated retreat

I survived the war and returned home to face Tom's family (his father and namesake had died during the Korean War) and disdain from our former schoolmates for having fought in Vietnam. Tom's mother showed me a letter that he received just days before his death. It that had been among his personal effects sent to her from Vietnam. It was from his girlfriend, the daughter of a wealthy industrialist who was profiting handsomely from the war. She was breaking up with Tom in the harshest terms; the letter was filled with antiwar epithets like "baby killer." I immediately recognized that in his already disconsolate frame of mind, this letter may have helped trigger his end.

Tom's family never recovered from his loss, broken apart and plagued by emotional issues, worsened by alcohol abuse. It was only years later that I would learn the real tragedies of Khe Sanh did not happen on that infamous battleground, but inside the families of those involved—the place where all wars eventually have their endings.

The time I learned the heartbreaking news of Tom's death in Vietnam I began searching for information about the circumstances. I was left incredulous, which eventually propelled me on a decades-long quest to find out what had happened and find redemption from my guilt and remorse at having survived that terrible place instead of him. Along the way, I would make a series of often implausible connections, steering me back to Vietnam and Khe Sanh.

By 2010, I had found a dozen survivors from Tom's platoon. After the war, most had worked through the difficult transition and become successful in a variety of professional fields. Some, however, were too psychologically scarred to readapt, and struggled with drugs, alcohol, and mental health issues. Yet, the two things they all had in common were a clear personal recollection of the day Tom died, and incessant remorse and guilt at not having brought him back.

Tom's closest friend in Vietnam, Allen Williams, became a successful stage, film, and television actor upon his return to civilian life. Allen contacted me after being diagnosed with early onset of Alzheimer's and he needed to talk about Tom. I soon understood the tragic complexity of his situation: unburdening himself might help mitigate his decades of guilt at surviving his friend and thus the depression that worsened his medical condition. Allen also knew that Alzheimer's would soon steal his memory and he didn't "want to lose Tommy again." We were both weeping at the end of our first conversation.

After diplomatic relations with Vietnam warmed in the 1990s, a great deal of information became available to the U.S. government about those missing in action. Despite all this, I was frustrated with the poor methodology being employed by the U.S. Joint POW/MIA Accountability Command (JPAC) in their efforts to find Tom's remains. My research from military reports had provided the precise map coordinates of where Tom was last seen, yet JPAC ignored my pleas and continued to look for Tom's remains a half mile from where he fell.

Many of his platoon mates had been told in the weeks following his death that a Marine reconnaissance team had secretly returned and retrieved the body. As such, they were shocked when I told them that his remains had never made it home—adding further mystery to his disappearance. The JPAC located a former reconnaissance Marine who claimed to have accidentally come across and buried Tom's body one night a few weeks after his death. He was brought to Hill 881 twice to find the site, but an excavation in August 2014 found the grave to be empty. This would not be the only time that hope for a conclusion to our search ended in disappointment. It was after this 2014 dig that JPAC sought my help in pinpointing the correct location.

A few years earlier, in 2006, Robert "Doc" Topmiller, a friend of mine during the 1968 siege, contacted me after 35 years. Now a university professor and one of the country's leading authorities on the history and culture of Vietnam, Doc traveled extensively throughout that country. Also frustrated by JPAC's "inexcusable" and ineffective efforts, Doc suggested we do things the "Vietnamese way," which included meeting with a psychic, or "soul caller." Though skeptical, I agreed, returning with Doc to Vietnam in 2007.

Doc suffered from severe PTSD from the daily horror he'd experienced as a 19-year-old corpsman trying to save the lives of young Marines mangled from the constant artillery fire at Khe Sanh. In 2008, several months after we returned from Vietnam, Doc died from a self-inflicted gunshot wound - yet another casualty of that war so long ago.

Because of Doc's contacts in Vietnam, I had become friends with several former adversaries from the Khe Sanh battlefield. I also received help from newly translated Vietnamese military histories, including one having an astonishingly graphic description of the look on Tom's face at the moment he was gunned down.

As the *History of the 246th Regiment* graphically describes:

At 1400 on the following day [July 6, 1968], we saw one American walking outside the entrance to the outpost. His face was red, and his eyes were blue like a mean animal. He was looking toward Mr. Luong's team. The sounds of AK weapons roared immediately, and the American fell. Mr. Luong and Mr. [Tran Ngoc] Long jumped out of their positions and dragged the American's body down. They placed the body in front of them to create an ambush for the other Americans coming out of their bunkers.

The report listed three others present in the squad, including Nguyen Tien Thanh who I eventually found in a village near Hanoi. In getting to know Thanh, I was astonished to learn he had been a practicing Catholic during the war, discriminated against for promotion by his unit's Marxist political officers, and derided by many of his fellow soldiers. To prove his loyalty, Thanh volunteered for the most dangerous assignments, including one in July 1968 that took him to the last trail Tom walked.

In June 2016, JPAC escorted Tom Mahoney's former platoon commander, Frank Ahearn, and his former squad leader, Tom Northrop, back to Hill 881 South to find where they had last seen him. The two men were confident about the location they found, but, as of May 2023, there has been no action taken to excavate.

My search for Tom's physical remains continues, and, as the toll of shattered lives fades into the past, what remains is the revelation that despite the cruelty of war, many who had suffered through that developed a profound appreciation of human dignity and compassion and carried with them an unremitting sense of loyalty to a missing young Marine who had briefly touched their lives.

While on the Hill where Tom died, I left a plaque that I had made. It's inscription:

In Memory of
Thomas Patrick Mahoney III
Lance Corporal
United States Marine Corps
Age 20
Killed in action at this spot on July 6, 1968
They shall not grow old, we that are left grow old; age shall not weary them, nor the years condemn. At the going down of the sun and in the morning we will remember them
Dedicated this 20th Day of December 2007
By your family, friends, and the loyal men of
Company B, First Battalion, First Marine Regiment
who so valiantly struggled to bring you home.

67.

The Wall

by Diane Carlson Evans

November 1982

The boots, I remember the jungle boots!

A cool breeze swept across the National Mall as I joined a growing crowd. The throng gently pushed me along the path, people unaccustomed to such gatherings but loosely tied in purpose. Though cocooned in this pack of people, I felt a quiet solitude as I neared the names etched in granite on the Vietnam Veterans Memorial that was being dedicated this day.

Flags and field jackets, Combat boots and boonie hats. "You were at Chu Chi?" you'd hear someone ask. "Damn, just missed ya. Arrived in sixty-seven. Tunnel rat. Glad you made it home buddy. Too many didn't."

Now, as I approached the Wall, and fifty-eight thousand names of the dead carved in its black granite, any revelry or pride I'd momentarily felt had morphed into numbness. The noise had given way to a deep quietness within me. It was news of the names on the Wall that had summoned me to this place, but I still feared the memorial's power and meaning.

A kind of gravity pulled me along the path, down a slope, toward the names. But I kept my head down. I looked at the man's boots in front of me, and other people's shoes. It gave me a good excuse to avoid eye contact.

I stopped when realizing the granite plates of 1968 – 1970 loomed before me. Was I ready for this? To look up at the names etched on this wall. Since August 1969, when I'd returned home, I'd look up, instinctively, every time a helicopter flew overhead. But otherwise, in the aftermath of Vietnam, it was safer to keep your head down in moments the war might be discussed. Safer, when meeting someone, to say I'd been a nurse in Washington or Texas instead of Vung Tau and Pleiku. Safer to not make eye contact, not reveal more than I'd want to. Safer to rationalize that the soldiers who came to my dreams on stretchers, especially a kid named Eddie, would go away on their own. Safer to keep busy, losing my life in the comings and goings of my husband and children. Safer to scrub the kitchen floor every night, finish folding the clothes at midnight, and get up early to make the peanut-butter-and jelly sandwiches for lunch that day.

The result? I'd never shed a tear over my time in Vietnam. I had no tears. They didn't solve problems; they only made them worse. Tears would be a copout, proving the experience had affected me, which was easier to not believe. As the years rolled by, hunkered down in survival mode, I'd try my best to forget Vietnam. It was less painful to live in the present if you could pretend you had no past. I sought to convince myself that I was meant to keep my head down, over there (and to convince my husband that he should never bring it up).

So, yes, even though I came to the Wall as if on a pre-ordained mission, now that I was here, I kept my head down. I was here, but in some ways didn't want to be, as if to do so was violating my unwritten self-promise to not look back. I looked at the tennis shoes, penny loafers, flats, sandals, and hundreds of jungle boots of the people around me.

Right in front of the Wall, the shoes stopped moving. Some shoes turned toward other shoes and I knew the people in those shoes were embracing. I heard muffled sobs, reminding me of my patients – my guys – who'd tried so hard to stifle their pain. I heard gasps from men startled when seeing a name on the Wall they recognized. I heard outright sobbing. I was terrified I might do the same and break down. Uncontrollable sobbing. I was terrified. No one would ever see me do that. Ever!

I had a fleeting thought that I'd been wrong not to invite my husband, Mike. We had met in 1970 at Brooke Army Medical Center in San Antonio, Texas where he had just finished his internship and was doing a general surgery residency, so he was no stranger to military life. Maybe, to protect me, to protect him, I'd always kept him at arm's length from my war, thinking he could never understand what I understood because he had never been there. Now, I felt a loneliness which suggested I was wrong. I suddenly missed him.

I followed the shuffling of boots. Had I once started an IV on the guy in the boots to my left? Had I cleaned the sucking chest wounds of the guy in the boots to my right? Had any of them been my patients, guys whose names I never knew but had never really left me? As opposed, of course to the guys who took their last breath in front of me – the reminders of war that came in the night, jolting me out of sleep as if I were still in my Pleiku hootch? The Wall knew 57,939. I needed to see, up close, two specifically, one a soldier I had cared for at the 36th Evacuation Hospital in Vung Tau, one a nurse whose death haunted me in the night.

Instead of my boots, I'd brought only one thing with me from Vietnam to the Wall: my boonie hat, with patches from the 44th Medical Brigade and the 71st Evacuation Hospital. I hadn't thrown that into my Vietnam footlocker that I hadn't seen for years and I wasn't sure it still existed.

The crowd around me thinned a bit. I was in the front row, standing before the names. I pushed back the boonie and against all instinct, looked up. Oh My God – So Many, Names. Names. – The death. So much death.

The names stretched left and right, like a blood-stained horizon, seemingly forever. The Wall took my breath away, the names as thick as late-night stars over the Minnesota farm of my childhood. *Who of you died on my watch? I'm so sorry we couldn't save you. I'm so sorry for your heartbroken families. We tried. We all tried. WHY?*

Then, while the emotion temporarily ebbed, I had a revelation: the memorial itself, created amid much controversy, was powerful. It was perfect.

The two names I now began looking for were those of Eddie Lee Evenson, Panel 28W, Line 17, and Sharon Lane, Panel 23W, Line 112. I looked again at the locations I'd scrawled on a piece of paper, then back at the panel where I thought they'd be. First Eddie's. I threaded my way through the thick crowd until I came to Panel 28W. My gaze climbed up the panel. There he was. Blonde hair, youthful face, lean body. Smiling. Innocent. He had been one of mine. I touched his body – dressed his wounds and removed his stitches. And now, I was touching him again.

The emotion jolted me out of my trance. I reached to touch his name, but as I did so, a hand lightly tapped my shoulder. I turned. It belonged to a thirty-something man wearing a faded field jacket. His eyes riveted to me as if he knew me – or thought he did.

"Ma'am, were you a nurse in Vietnam?"

It startled me. It wasn't a question I'd ever been asked. With a touch of hesitation, I nodded yes.

He gulped. He looked as if gathering his thoughts, or rehearsing, or both. He looked nervous.

"I've waited fourteen years, "he said, voice quivering, "to say this ... to a nurse ... but I never came across one. Until now." He paused. I felt a twinge of uncertainty as his eyes pooled with tears. He took a deep breath and exhaled; then said two words I'd never heard since getting off the plane at Travis Air Force Base in California. "Thank you,"

I nodded, feeling anxious. Unused to being in this position. Unsure of his emotional expression.

"I can never thank you nurses enough. I love you. Thank you for being there for us. You're all we had."

He buried me in a smoldering hug that felt like no other I'd been given. Just as I never wrote down a patient's name and remembered only one name from that long list of my patients in Vietnam, I did not get his. He was as nameless to me as all the others. But like the others, he was "mine" in that moment. I don't ever remember being hugged in Vietnam by a patient. And now, a desperate, wounded warrior was unabashedly hugging me with gratitude. The ice was melting. Yes, along with doctors and medics, some nurse had helped save this man's life, and, because of it, he was looking at names on the Wall instead of *being a name* on the Wall. I felt his genuine warmth and desire to simply say thanks. He needed me to accept it. I heard those words "thank you" - I never realized how much I needed to hear them.

It was called healing, an act, I would learn, far more powerful than we might imagine. And one that had everything to do with so many of us feeling we were, after all these years, still far from home.

The soldier nodded and moved along; I just stood there, transfixed, feeling blessed, full, and empty, all at the same time. A new feeling emerged. *I belonged!* I actually belonged here, to these people. To this place. This place was also my place. If he belonged here, so did I. If Eddie belonged here, so did I.

Gathering myself, I reached again for Eddie's name and slid my finger left to right. I wondered if I'd been the first to touch his name. If he lived, he would've been thirty-four. To me, he was still twenty-one, the age he was when he first came in by stretcher. Injuries among the wounded were a blur to me. I don't remember his specific injury except that he had a DPC, delayed primary closure for his wound. We administered pain meds, irrigated, and dressed the wound, and loaded him with antibiotics, and he started to heal. But there was never certainty in Vietnam. A soldier who got better was often told to get his boots back on, grab his rifle. Such was the case with Eddie.

I took a deep breath and moved toward Panel 23W, Line 112. I was shaken, but amid the crowd of others, was hardly alone in struggling to keep my composure. I had not known 1st LT. Sharon Ann Lane, but we nurses felt we did know her, bound by a common cause. Lane, twenty-five, of Canton, Ohio, was one of eight female nurses whose names were on the Wall. She was killed in Chu Lai on June 8, 1969 – two months before I'd left Vietnam for home. As my fingers swept across her name, something inside me shattered like broken glass. For the first time since

Vietnam, I cried. Years of contained tears flowed for Sharon, for Eddie, and for the soldier I'd just met who embraced me. I cried for the men I'd been privileged to save and for the countless others I had not.

Try as I might, I could no longer hold back thirteen years of tears. I'd been terrified of crying – afraid that once I started, I wouldn't stop. But now it felt liberating. They weren't simply tears of loss. They were tears of anger, injustice, futility. They were tears of the betrayals by our presidents, their cabinets, and others who had no clue what fear looked like in the eyes of a nineteen-year-old kid whose entrails were half in, and half out. For the first time since leaving Vietnam, I felt no shame whatsoever.

I didn't lose the war, nor did the men who fought it. The high command lost the war. And after it was over, they didn't stand up for us. Veterans had to build their own memorial – with their own initiative, time, and money. Congress had to pass a bill so we could have this memorial; all they had to do was lift a pen to their fingers. But almost three million men and women who served in Vietnam lifted things far heavier – and carried those things every day, long after the war was over.

On November 13, 1982, I left the Wall drained and weary. In those magical and mysterious moments, touching the names of Eddie Evenson and Sharon Lane, and being hugged by a stranger, I had, for the first time, given myself permission to *feel*. And nothing felt so good and bad at the same time. In the years and decades to come, I would return to this place many times, but for reasons beyond honoring Eddie and Sharon. I would return because on that day, I understood for the first time, the power that honor plays in the process of healing.

And with this I would like to end with a touch of humor from both American and Vietnamese soldiers:

From the American side -- I had the opportunity to take part in an Honor Flight in 2017. I asked a 101-year-old WWII vet I, Bernard James, if he could share a piece of wisdom with our youth, what would it be?

He said, "The first 100 years are the hardest."

I can't stop laughing to this day, what humor, and wit through so much adversity!

So, when I think about how difficult this life has been, I also think about how grateful I am to be here in the most perfect of imperfect nations.

From the Vietnamese side, there was my father, who was trying to learn the nuances of the English language. He would accidentally use the terms "potluck" and "jackpot" interchangeably.

To all our warfighters past and present:

Because of you: Life, liberty, and the pursuit of happiness is not simply a catch phrase -- it is my reality.

Because of you, I have truly hit **"THE POTLUCK."**

For future speeches: Of the many regrets that life brings, mine will be that I have but one life to give for my country -- and this was made possible by you.

Diane Carlson Evans is a former Captain in the Army Nurse Corps who served in the combat zone of Vietnam. She is the founder of the Vietnam Women's Memorial Foundation, Inc. She served as president and CEO of the foundation's board of directors headquartered in Washington, DC for thirty years. Today she advocates for veterans and speaks nationally about the contribution of women during wartime.

by Diane Carlson Evans with Bob Welch

400   Voices from Vietnam
Interviews, Letters, Vignettes, and Reflections, 1964-1982

www.ingramcontent.com/pod-product-compliance
Lightning Source LLC
Chambersburg PA
CBHW060449170426
43199CB00011B/1138